W9-AVC-812

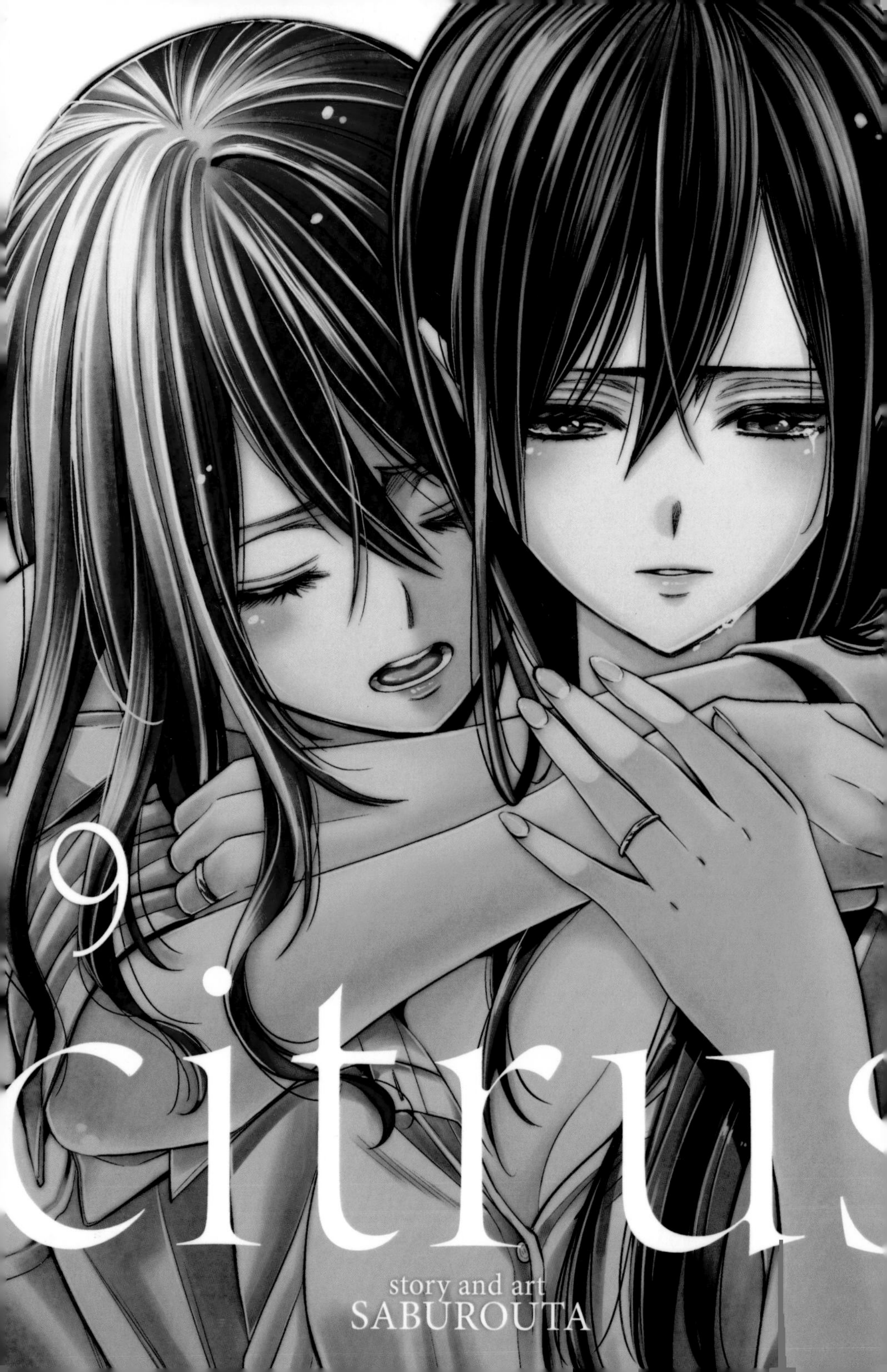
9
citrus
story and art
SABUROUTA

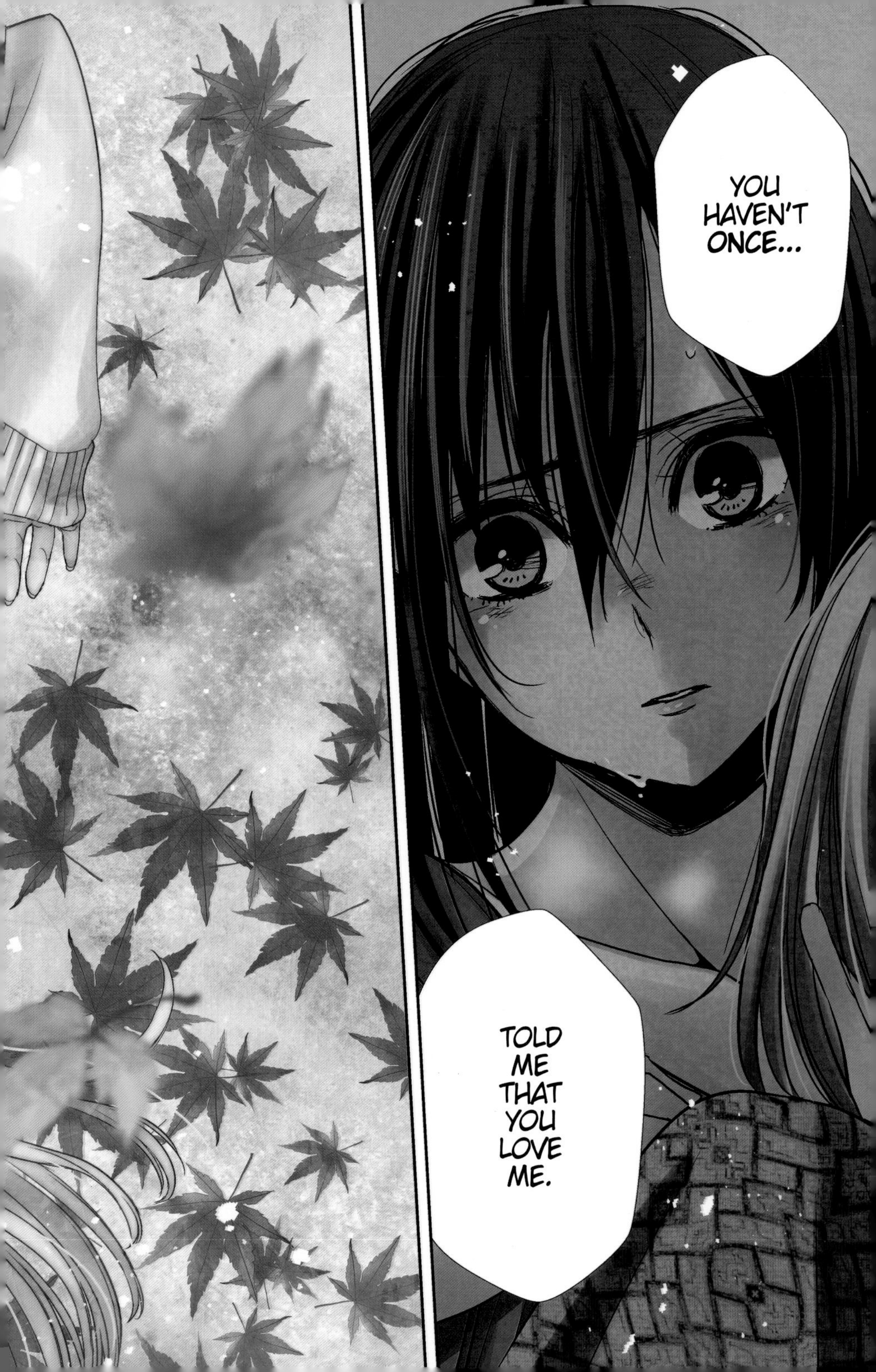
YOU HAVEN'T ONCE...
TOLD ME THAT YOU LOVE ME.

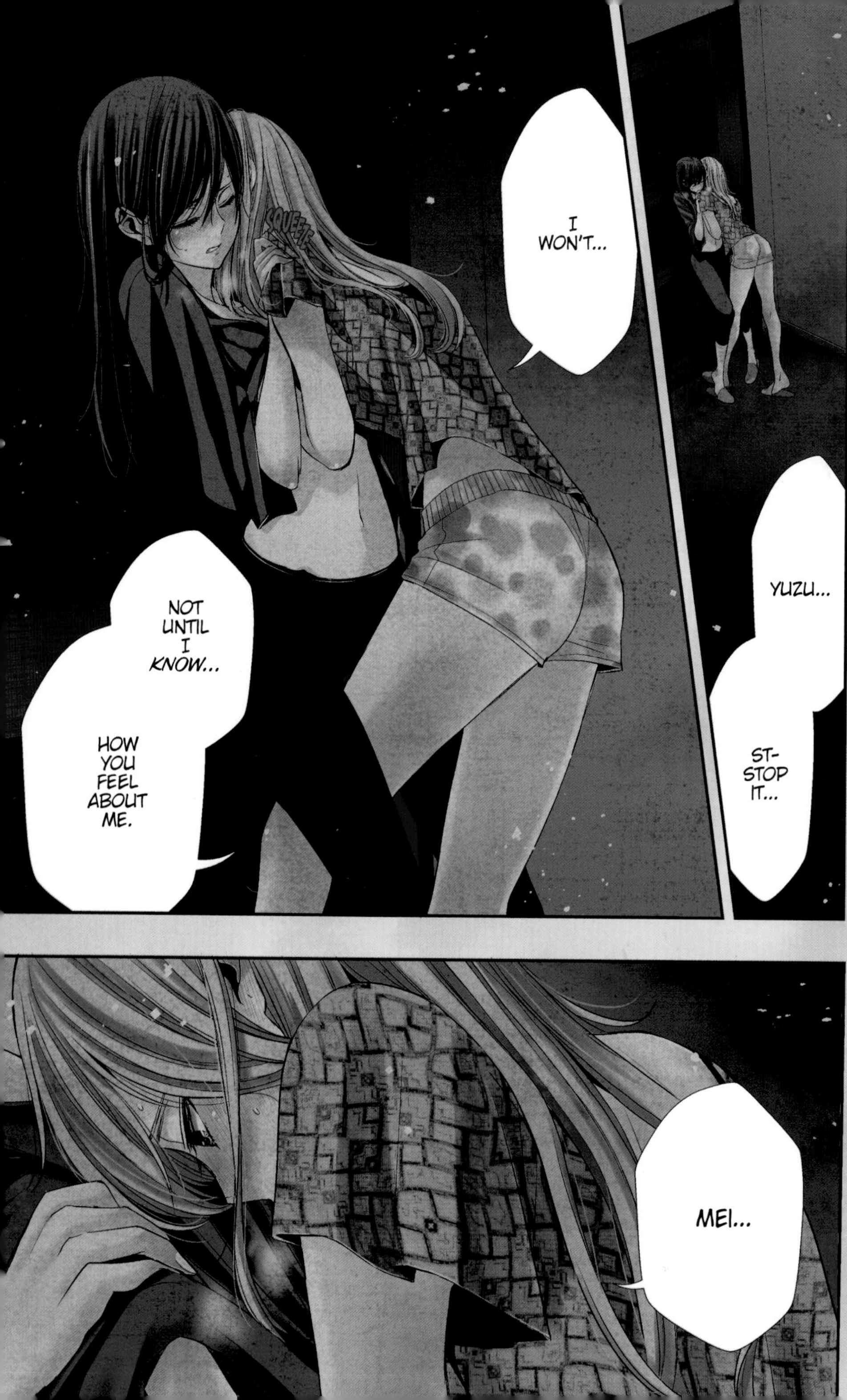
YUZU...
ST-STOP IT...
I WON'T...
SQUEEZE
NOT UNTIL I KNOW...
HOW YOU FEEL ABOUT ME.
MEI...

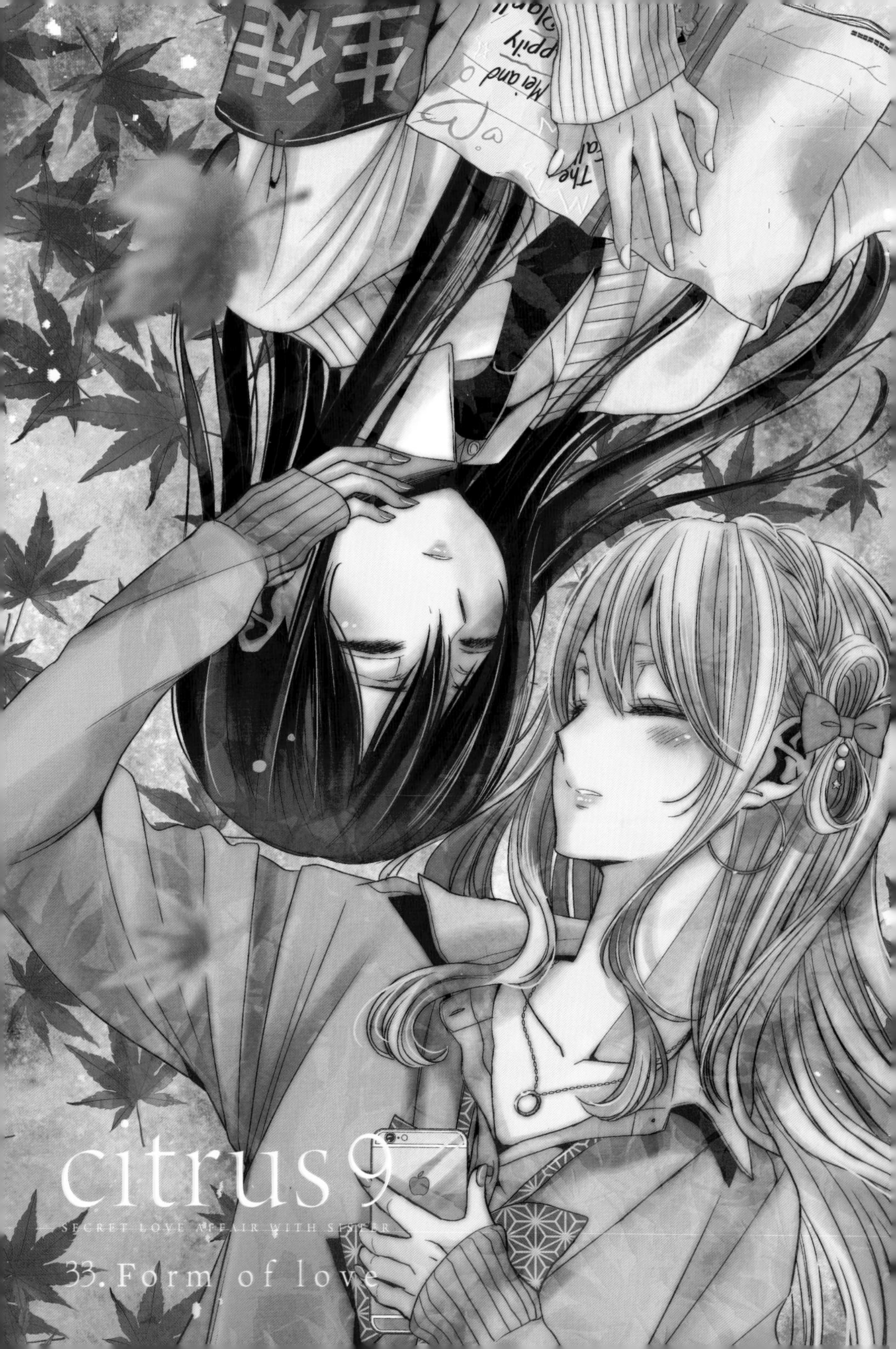
citrus 9
SECRET LOVE AFFAIR WITH SISTER
33. Form of love

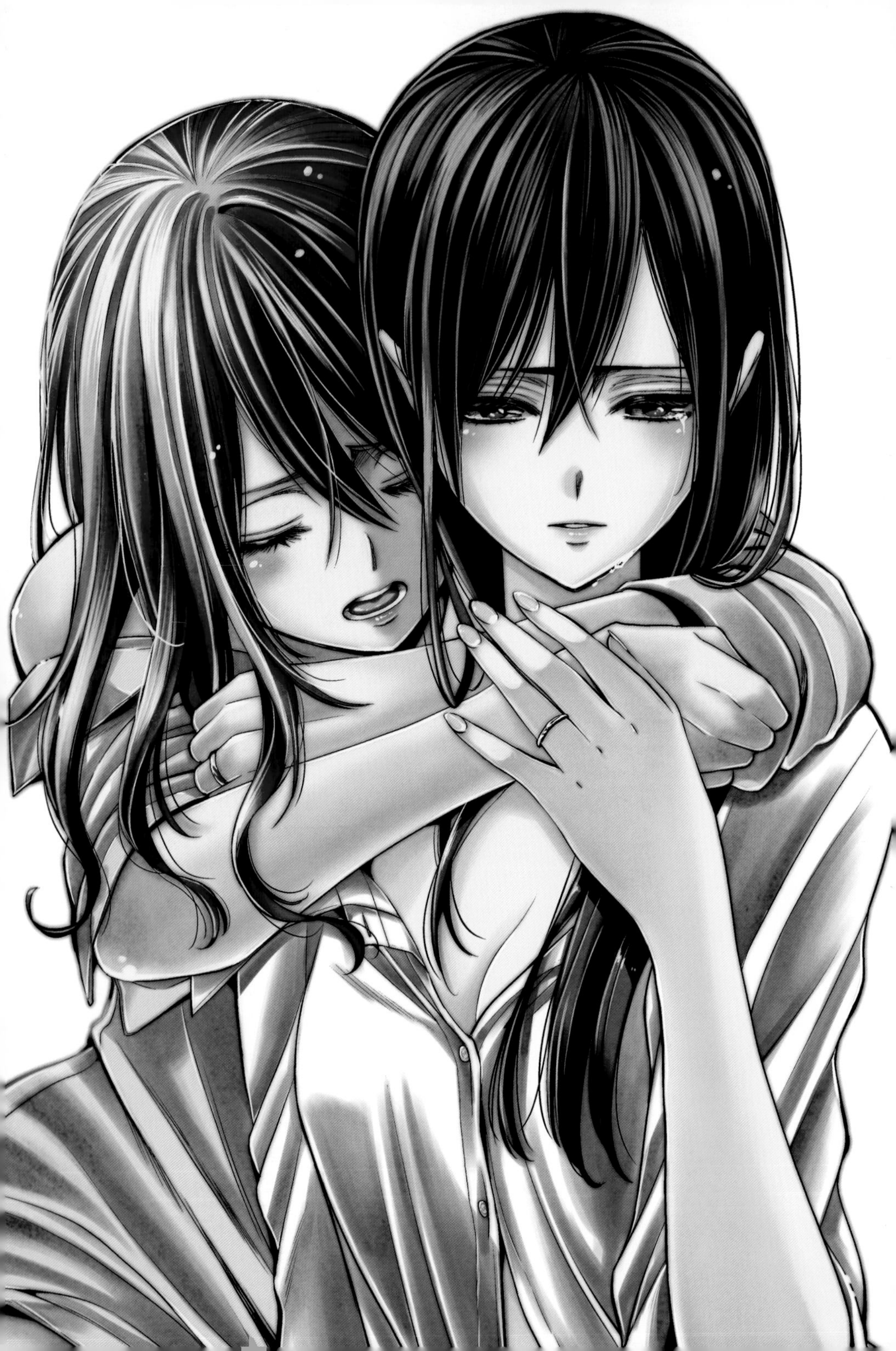

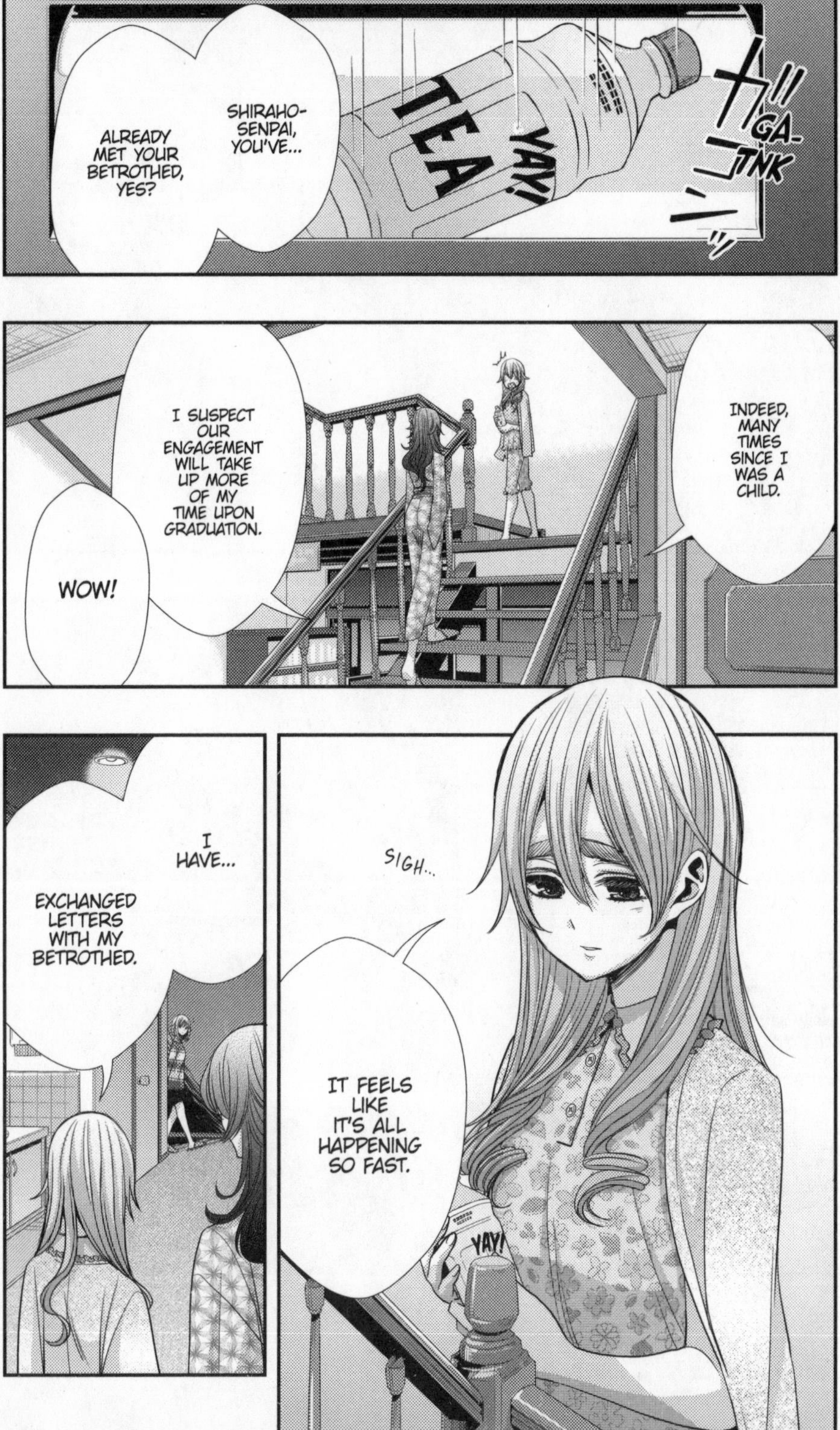
GA-TNK
TEA
YAY!
SHIRAHO-SENPAI, YOU'VE...
ALREADY MET YOUR BETROTHED, YES?
INDEED, MANY TIMES SINCE I WAS A CHILD.
I SUSPECT OUR ENGAGEMENT WILL TAKE UP MORE OF MY TIME UPON GRADUATION.
WOW!
SIGH...
IT FEELS LIKE IT'S ALL HAPPENING SO FAST.
YAY!
I HAVE...
EXCHANGED LETTERS WITH MY BETROTHED.

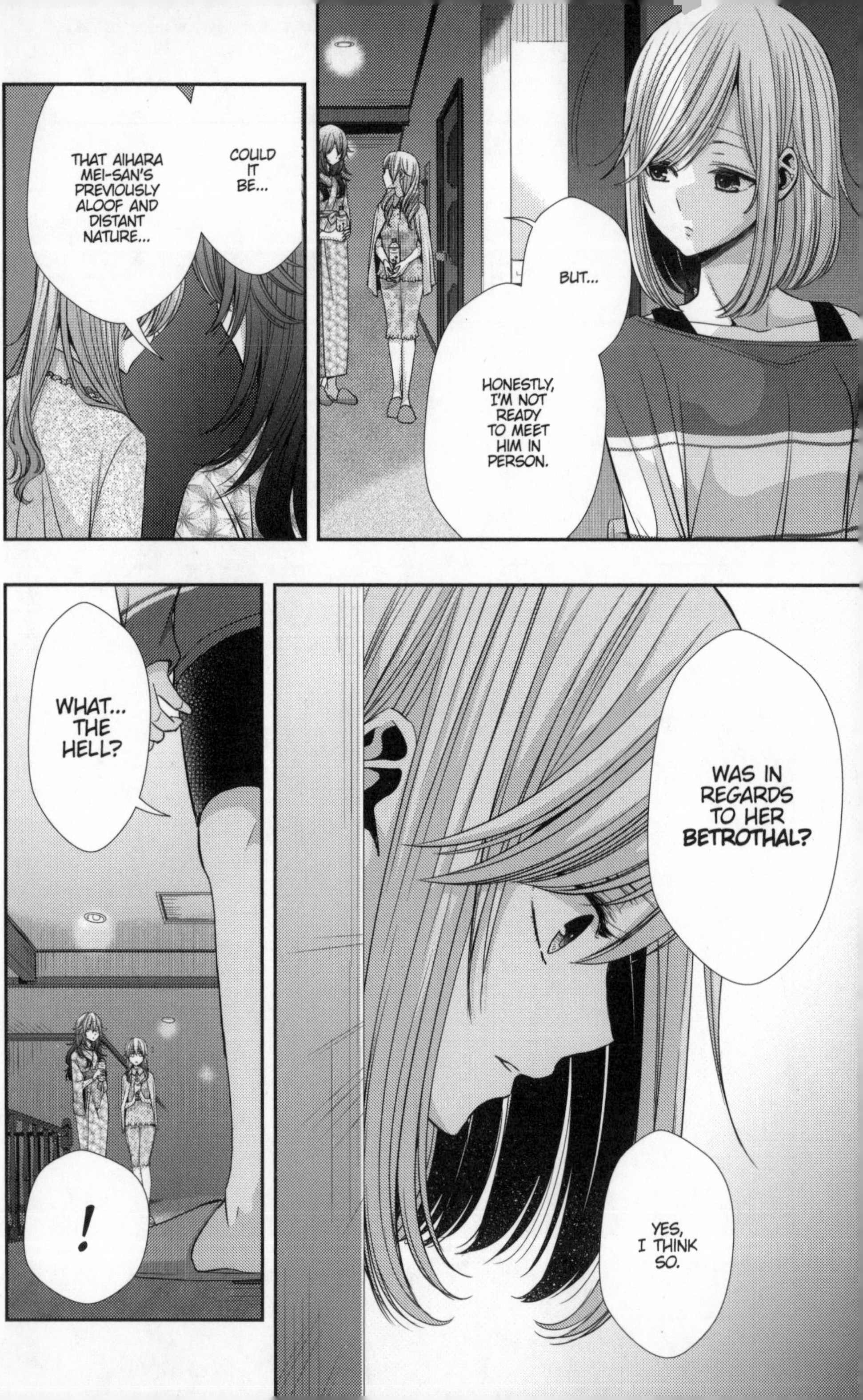
BUT...
HONESTLY, I'M NOT READY TO MEET HIM IN PERSON.
COULD IT BE...
THAT AIHARA MEI-SAN'S PREVIOUSLY ALOOF AND DISTANT NATURE...
WAS IN REGARDS TO HER BETROTHAL?
YES, I THINK SO.
WHAT... THE HELL?
!

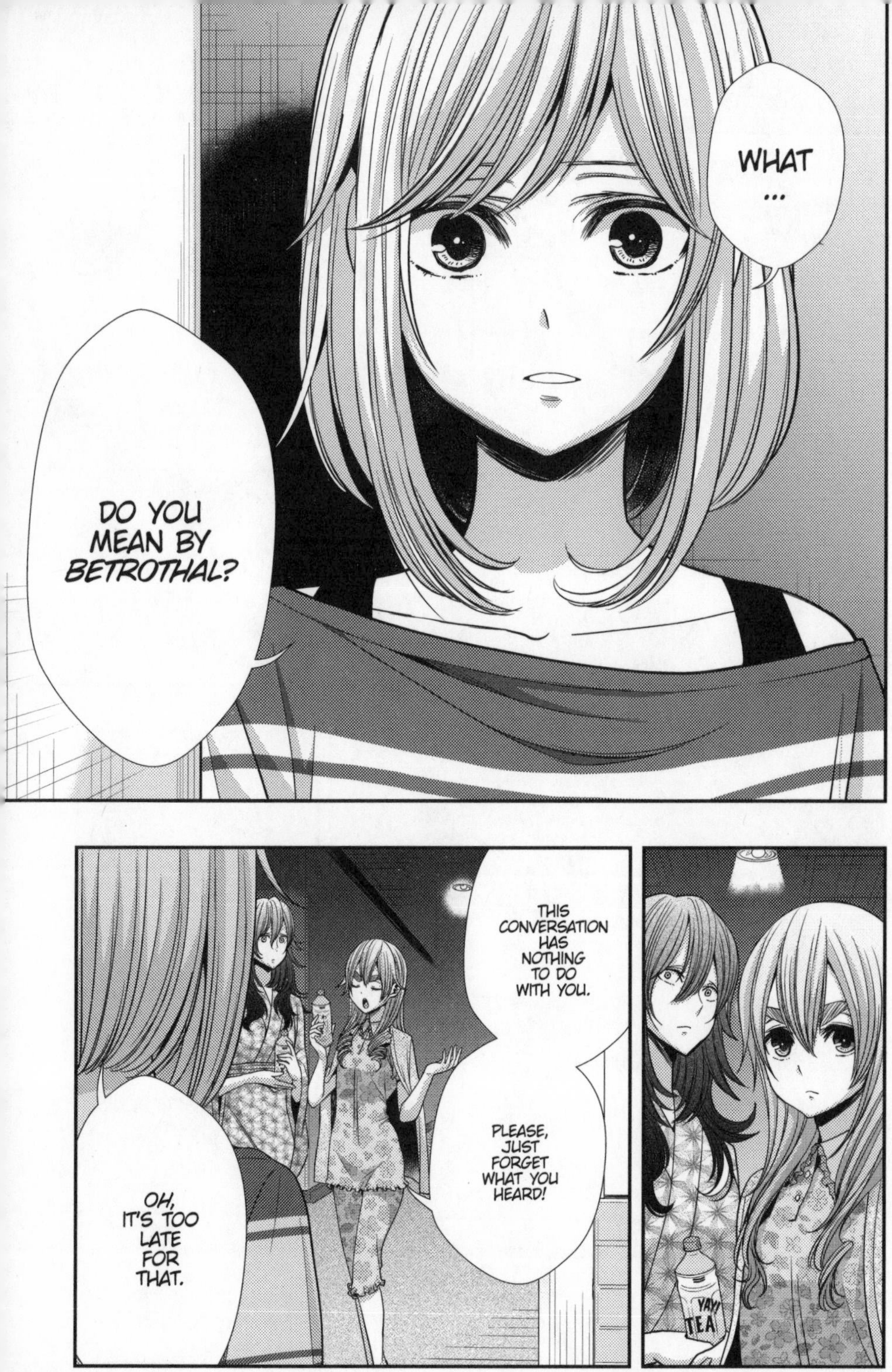
WHAT ...
DO YOU MEAN BY BETROTHAL?
YAY! TEA
THIS CONVERSATION HAS NOTHING TO DO WITH YOU.
PLEASE, JUST FORGET WHAT YOU HEARD!
OH, IT'S TOO LATE FOR THAT.

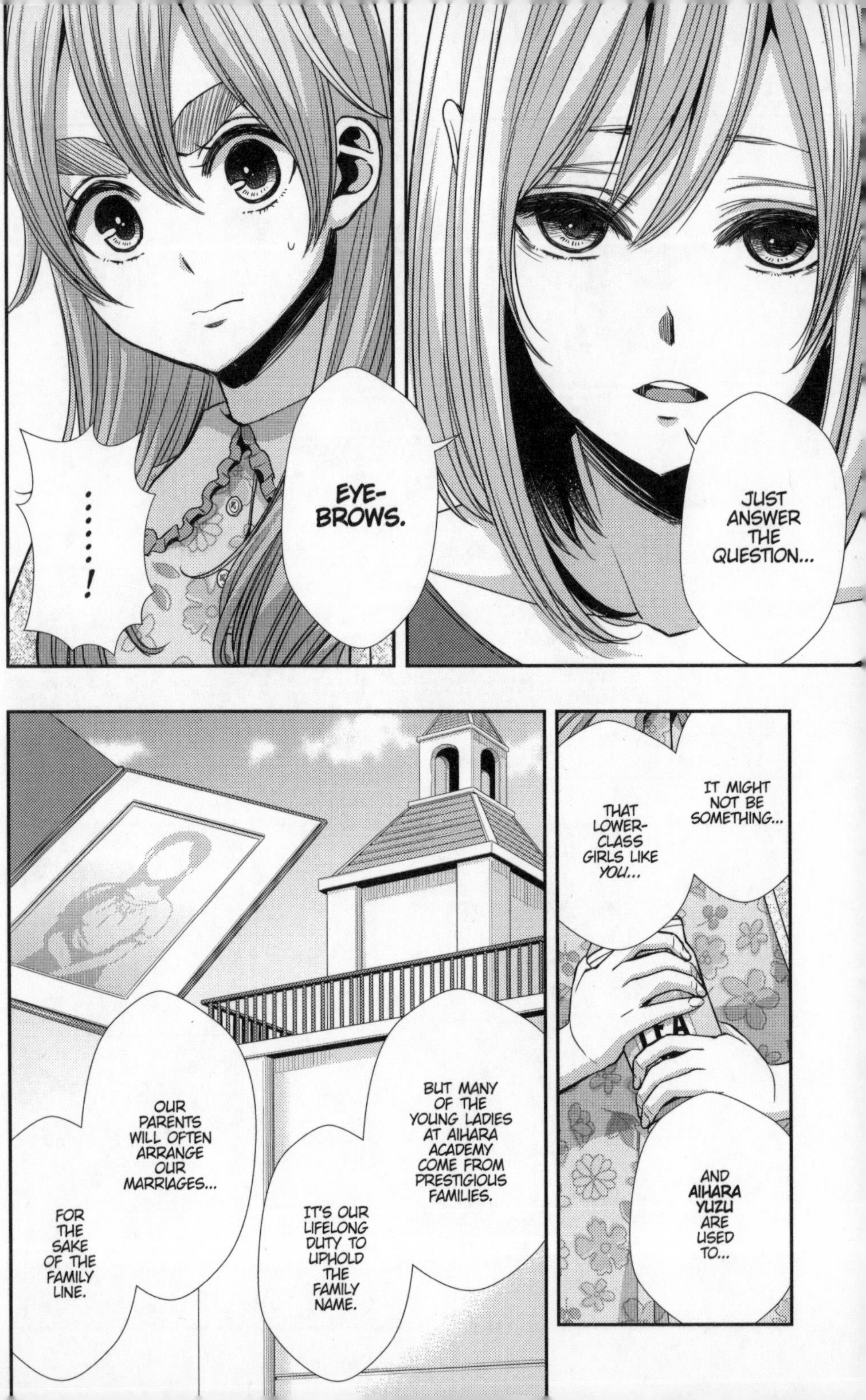
JUST ANSWER THE QUESTION...
EYE-BROWS.
......!
IT MIGHT NOT BE SOMETHING...
THAT LOWER-CLASS GIRLS LIKE *YOU*...
AND AIHARA YUZU ARE USED TO...
BUT MANY OF THE YOUNG LADIES AT AIHARA ACADEMY COME FROM PRESTIGIOUS FAMILIES.
OUR PARENTS WILL OFTEN ARRANGE OUR MARRIAGES...
IT'S OUR LIFELONG DUTY TO UPHOLD THE FAMILY NAME.
FOR THE SAKE OF THE FAMILY LINE.

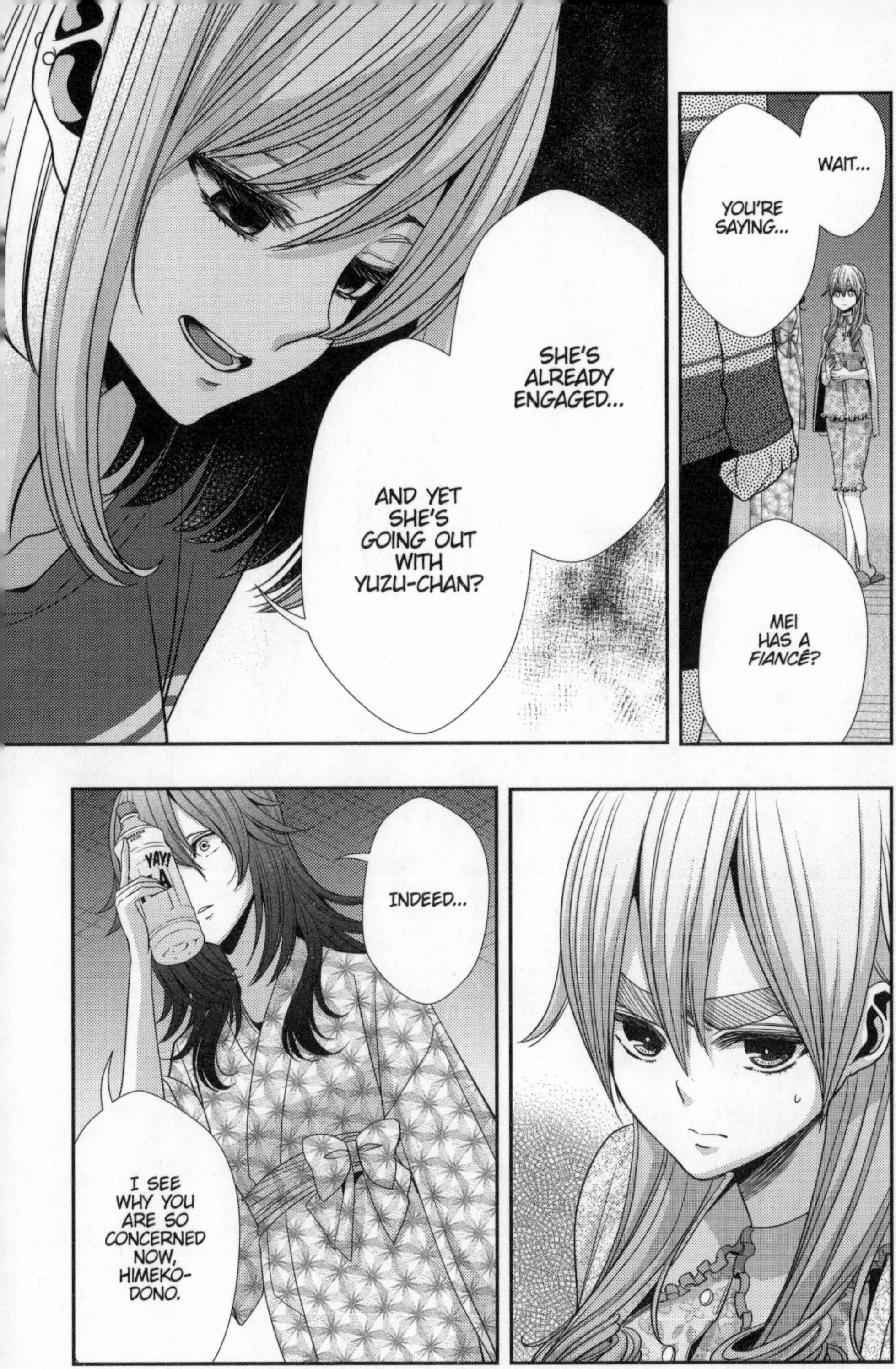
WAIT...
YOU'RE SAYING...
MEI HAS A FIANCÉ?
SHE'S ALREADY ENGAGED...
AND YET SHE'S GOING OUT WITH YUZU-CHAN?
YAY!
INDEED...
I SEE WHY YOU ARE SO CONCERNED NOW, HIMEKO-DONO.

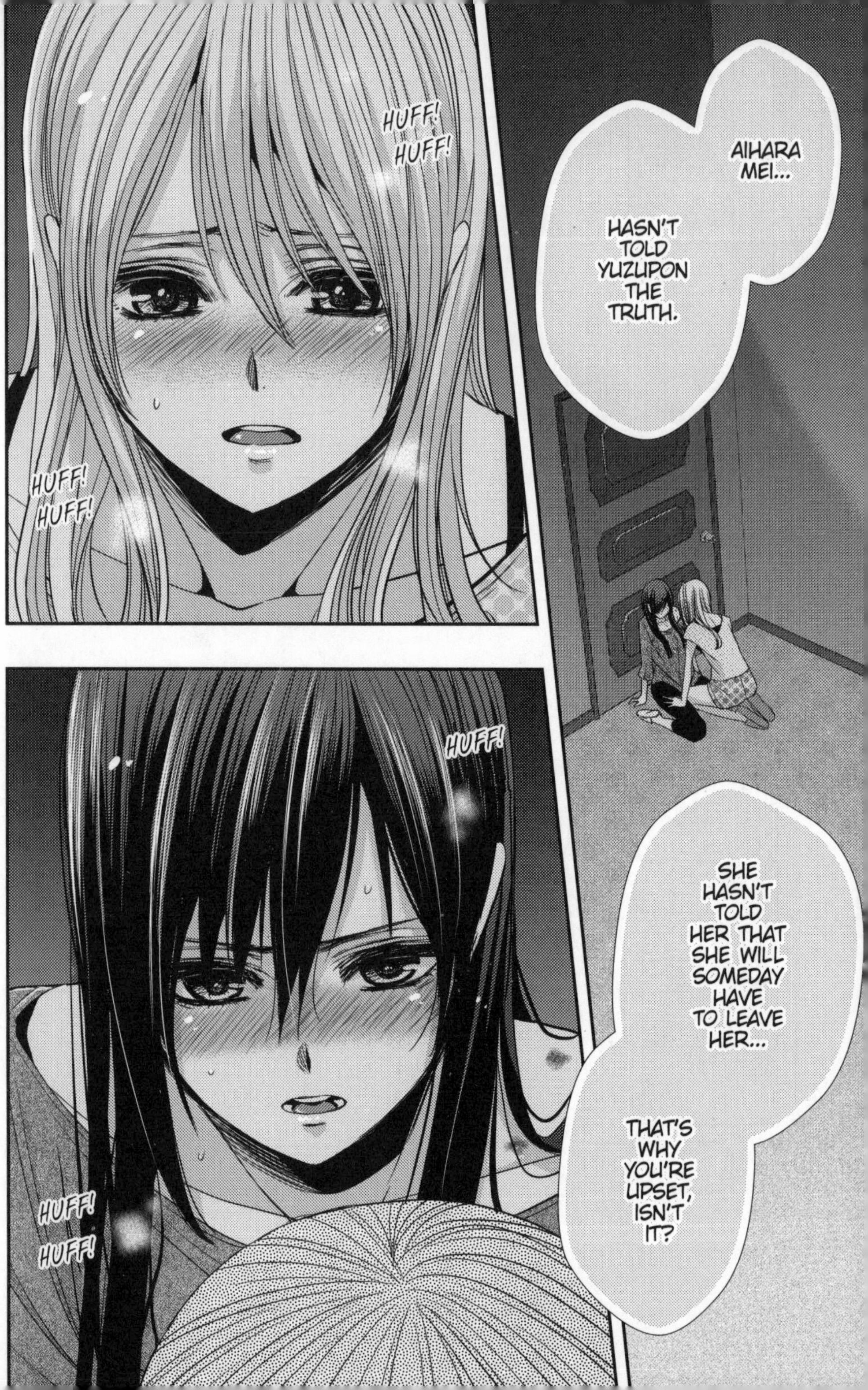
AIHARA MEI...
HASN'T TOLD YUZUPON THE TRUTH.
SHE HASN'T TOLD HER THAT SHE WILL SOMEDAY HAVE TO LEAVE HER...
THAT'S WHY YOU'RE UPSET, ISN'T IT?
HUFF! HUFF!
HUFF! HUFF!
HUFF!
HUFF! HUFF!

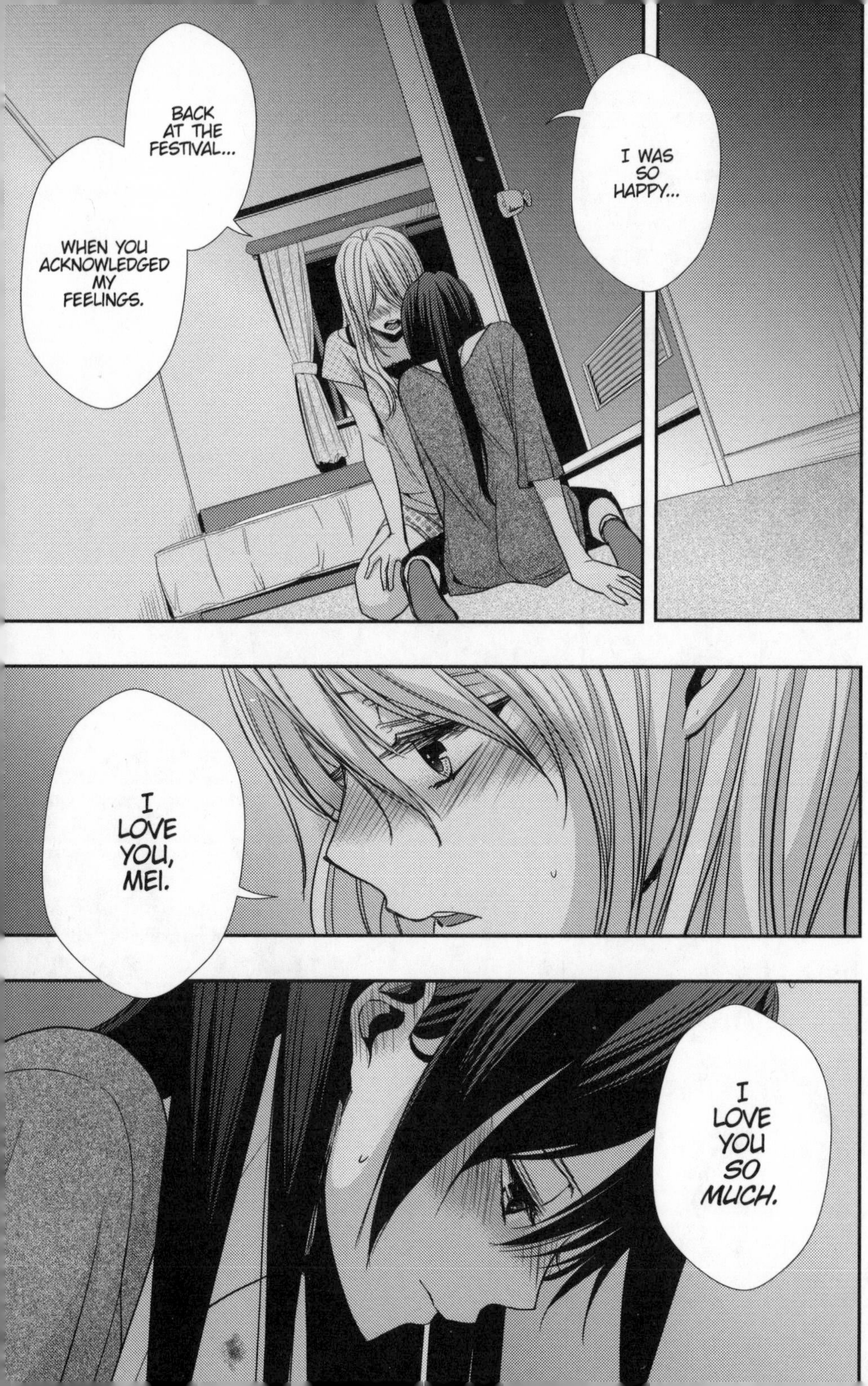
I WAS SO HAPPY...
BACK AT THE FESTIVAL...
WHEN YOU ACKNOWLEDGED MY FEELINGS.
I LOVE YOU, MEI.
I LOVE YOU SO MUCH.

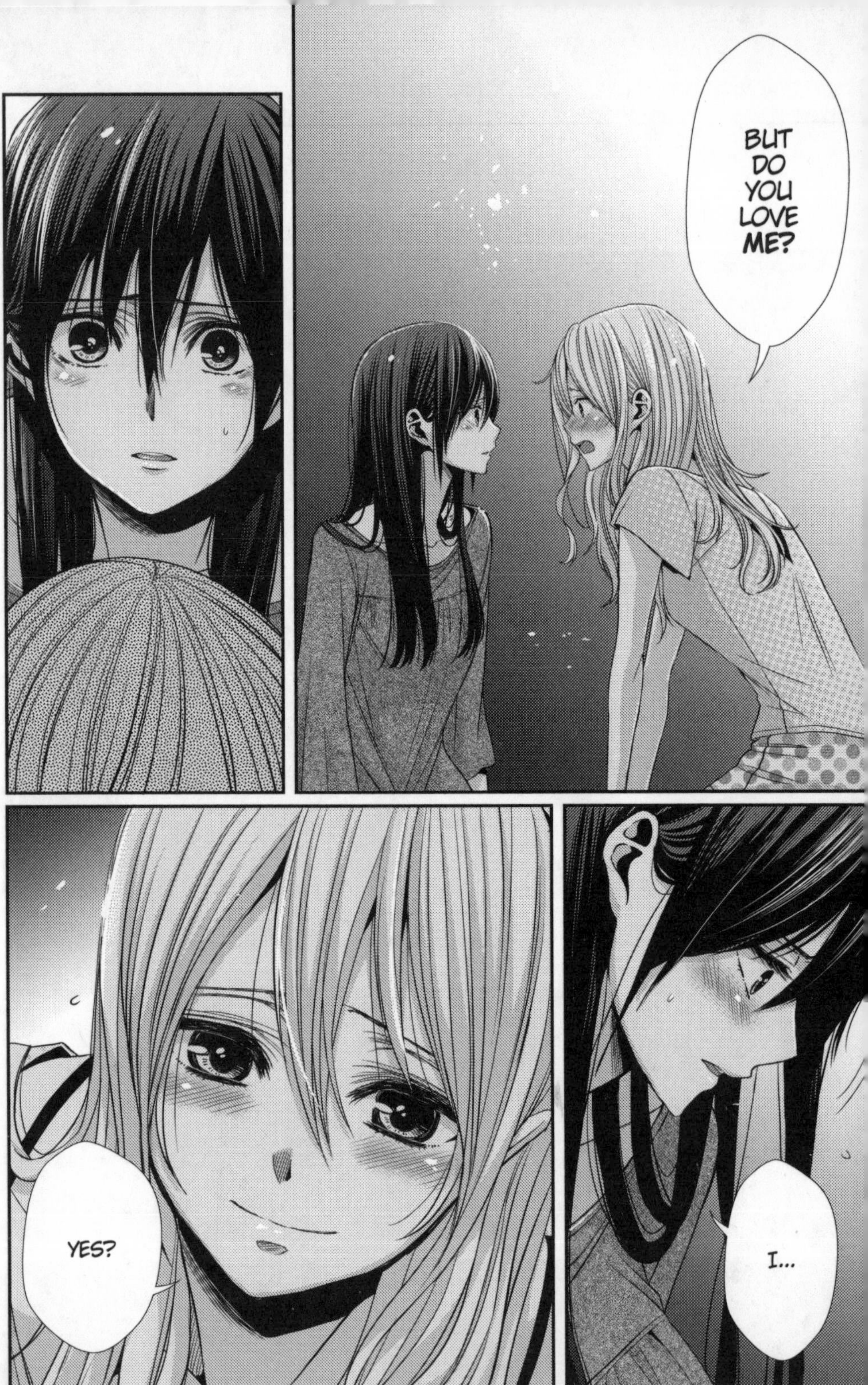
BUT DO YOU LOVE ME?
I...
YES?

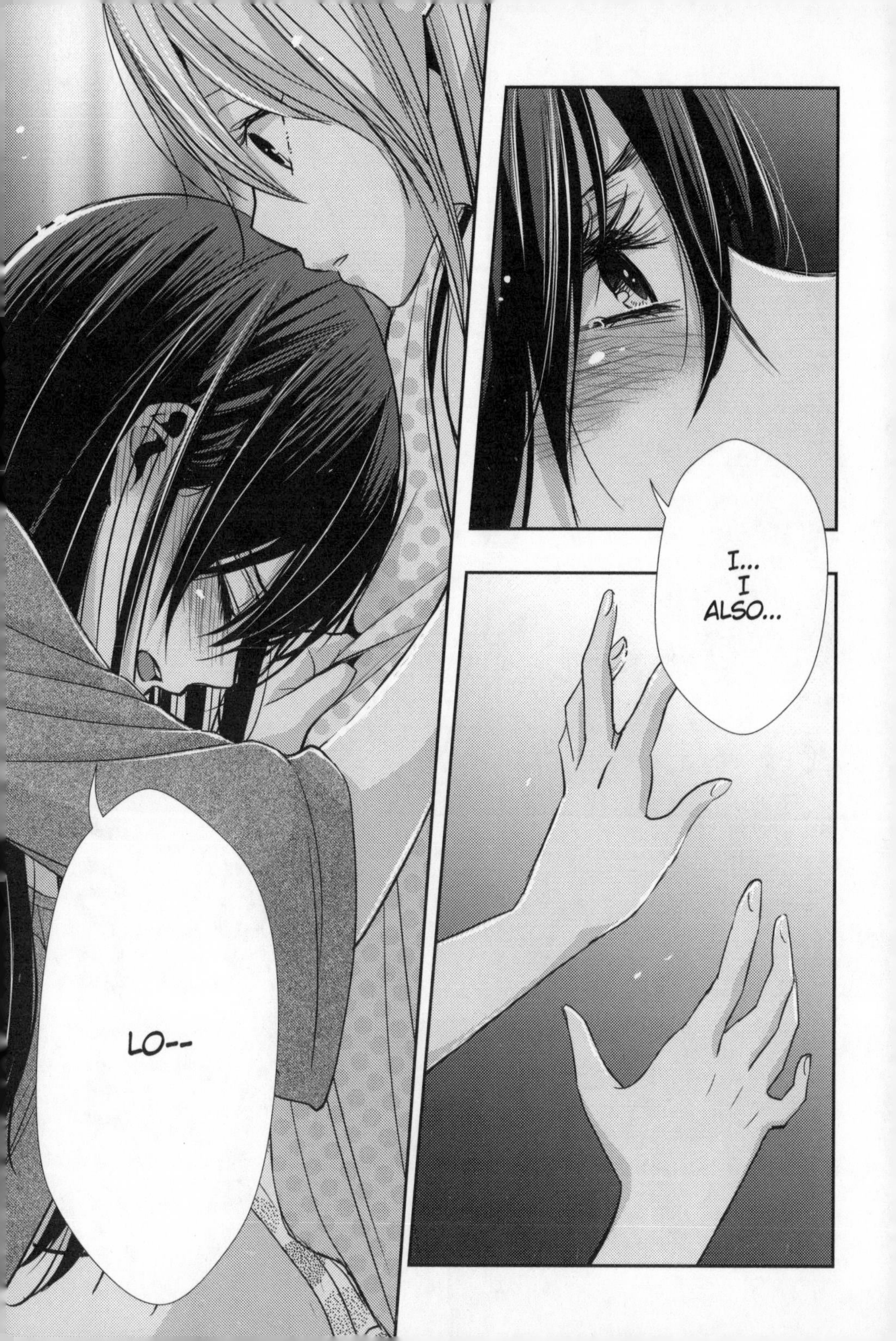
I... I ALSO...
LO--

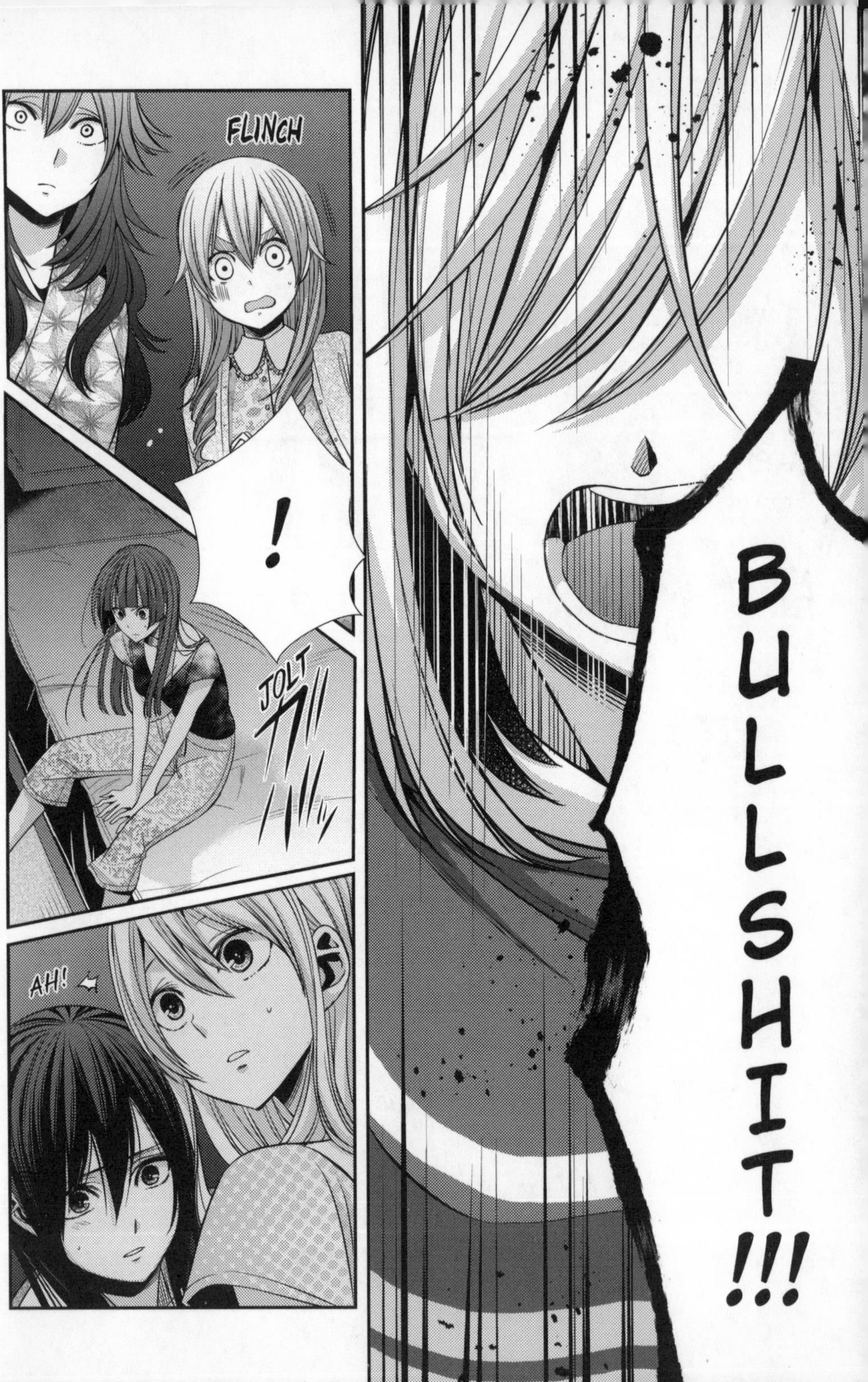
BULLSHIT!!!
FLINCH
!
JOLT
AH!

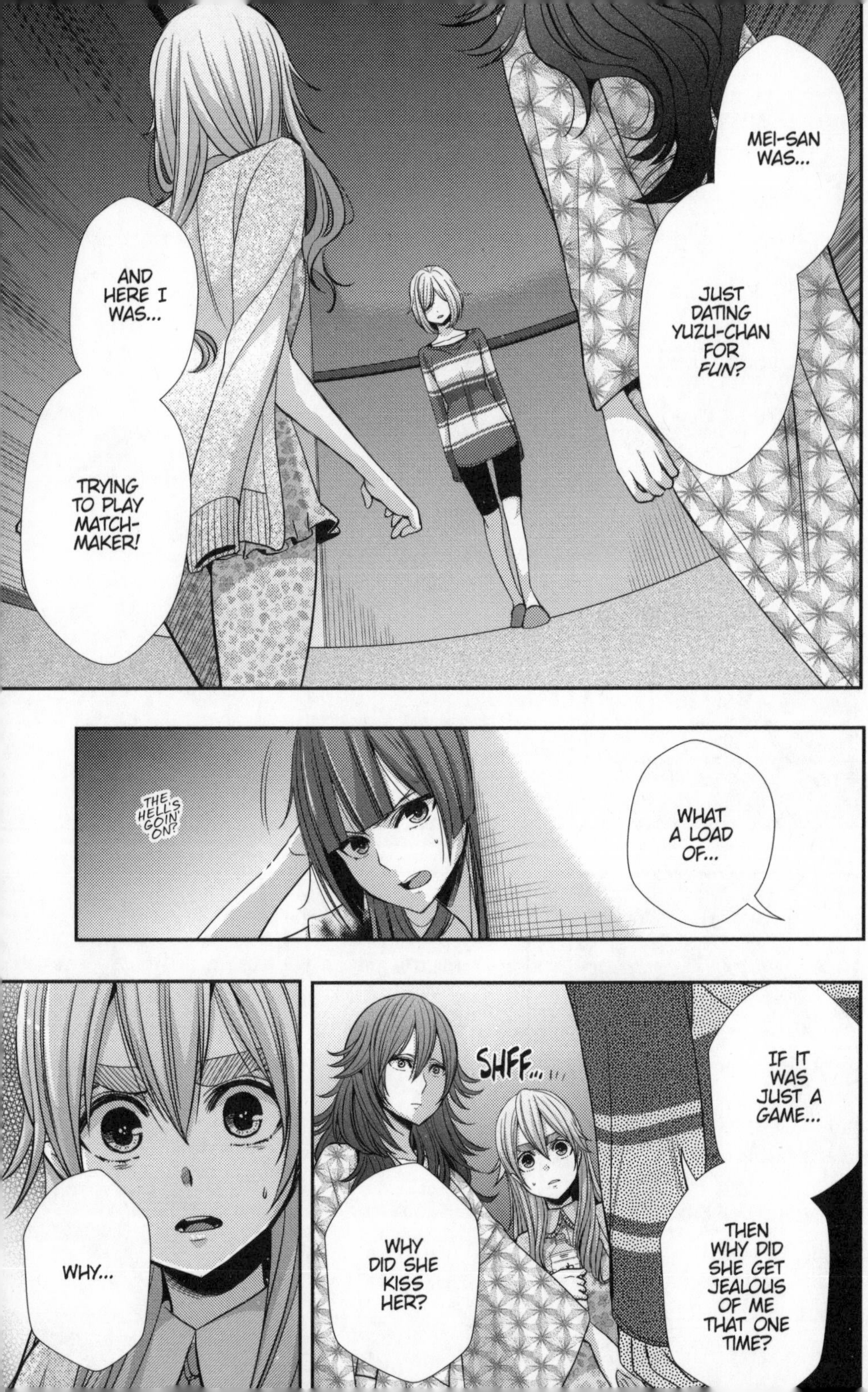
MEI-SAN WAS...
JUST DATING YUZU-CHAN FOR FUN?
AND HERE I WAS...
TRYING TO PLAY MATCH-MAKER!
WHAT A LOAD OF...
THE HELL'S GOIN' ON?
IF IT WAS JUST A GAME...
THEN WHY DID SHE GET JEALOUS OF ME THAT ONE TIME?
SHFF...
WHY DID SHE KISS HER?
WHY...

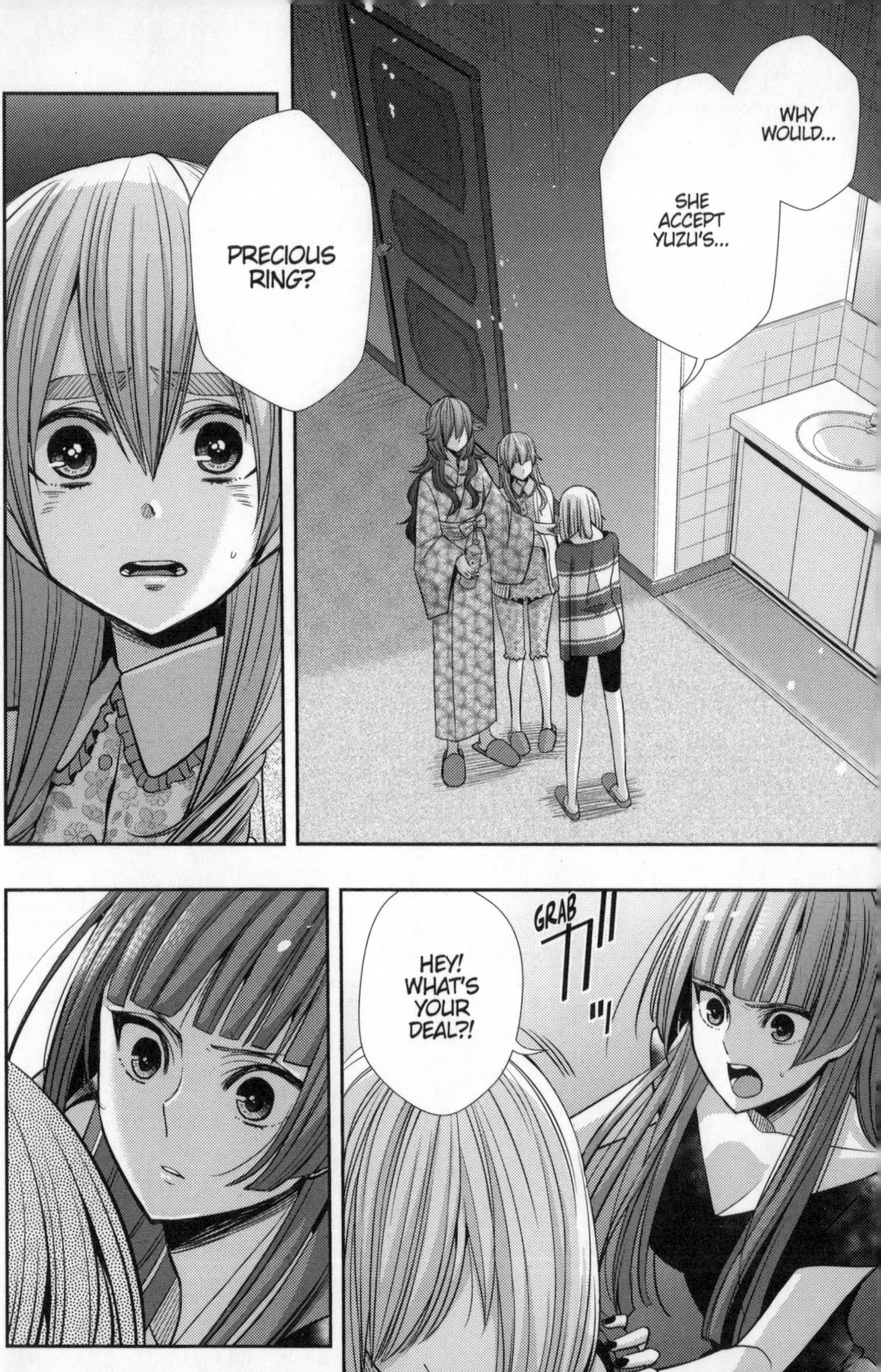
WHY WOULD...
SHE ACCEPT YUZU'S...
PRECIOUS RING?
GRAB
HEY! WHAT'S YOUR DEAL?!

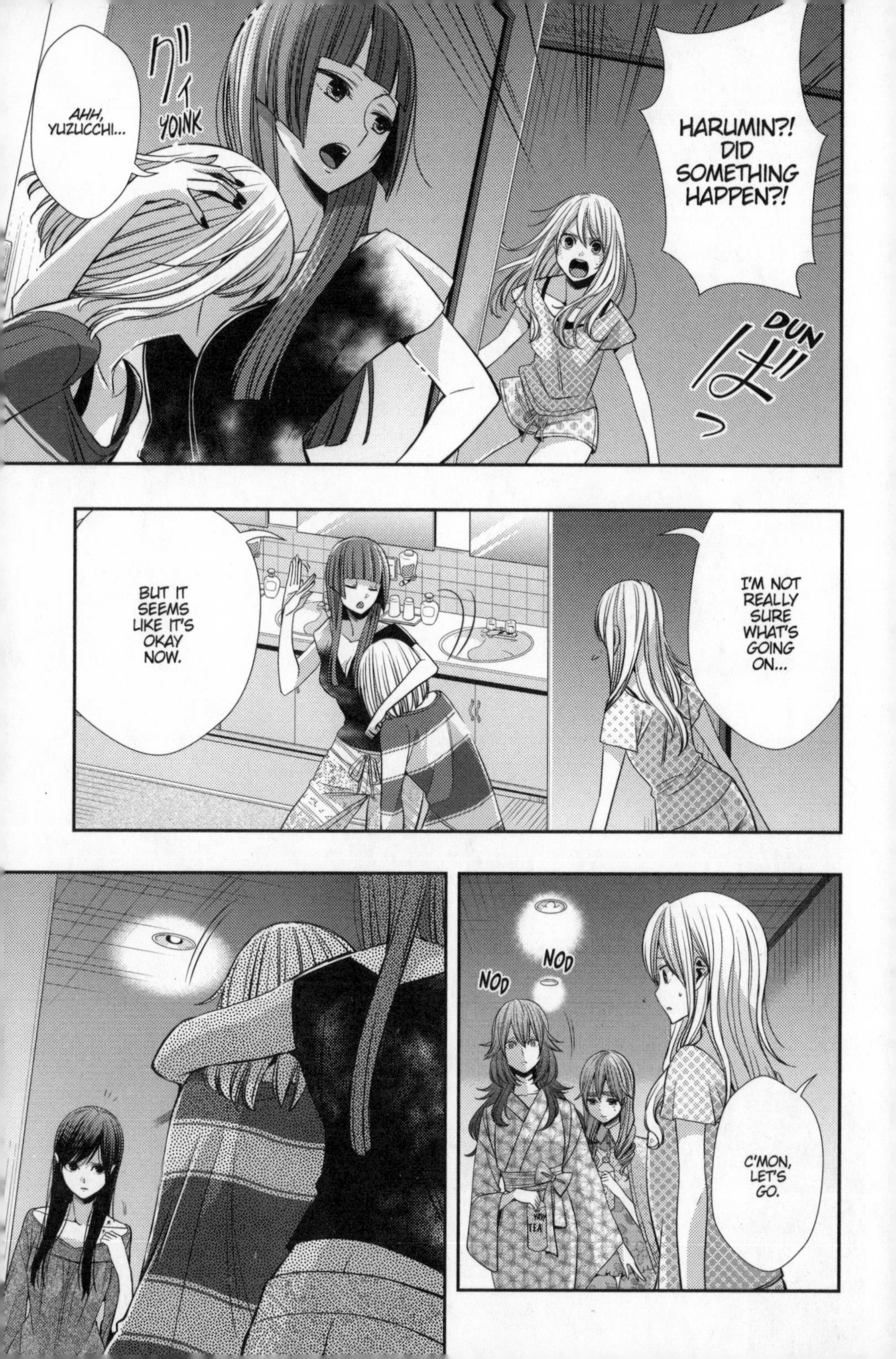
HARUMIN?! DID SOMETHING HAPPEN?!
YOINK
AHH, YUZUCCHI...
DUN
I'M NOT REALLY SURE WHAT'S GOING ON...
BUT IT SEEMS LIKE IT'S OKAY NOW.
NOD
NOD
C'MON, LET'S GO.

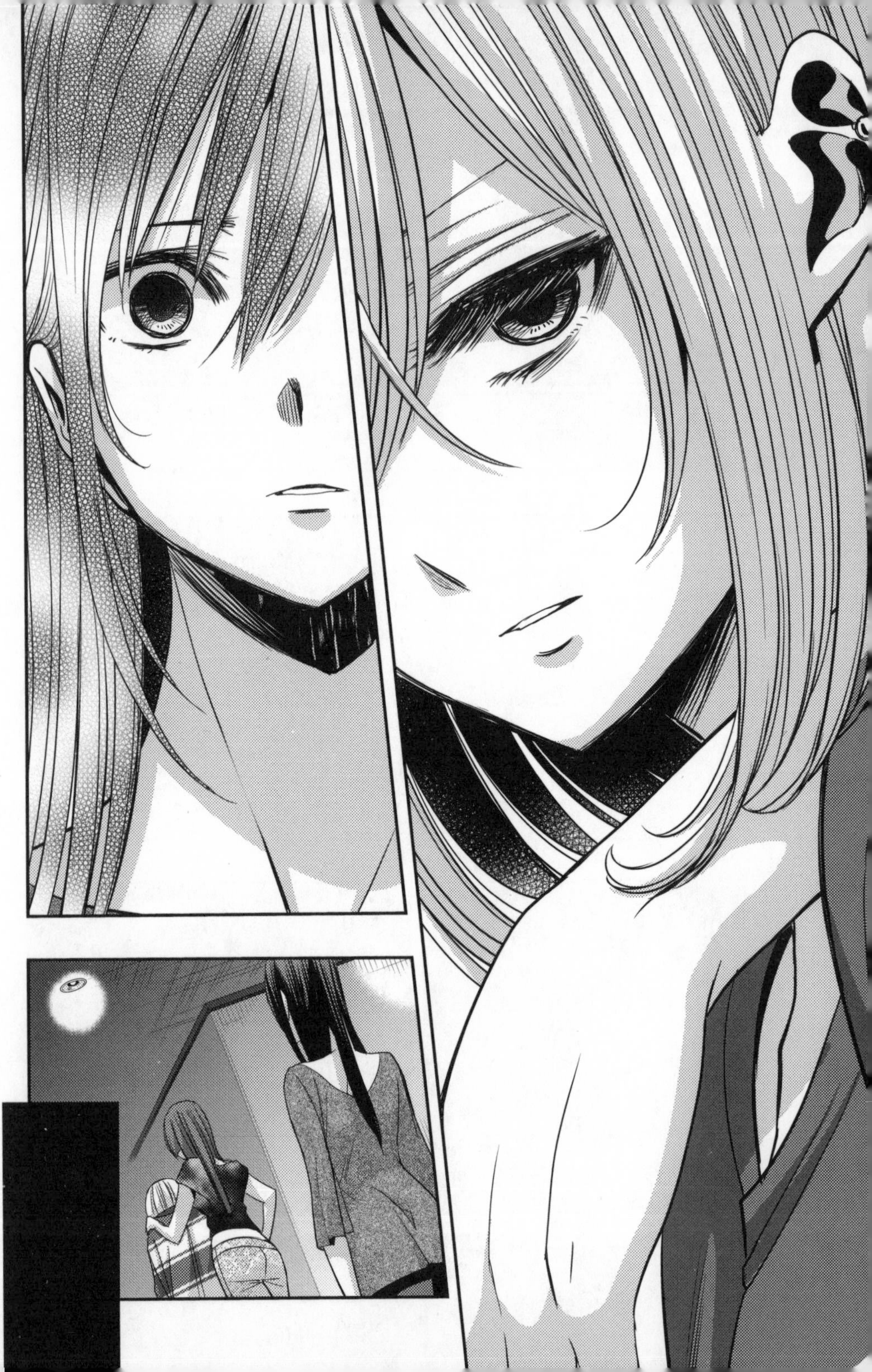

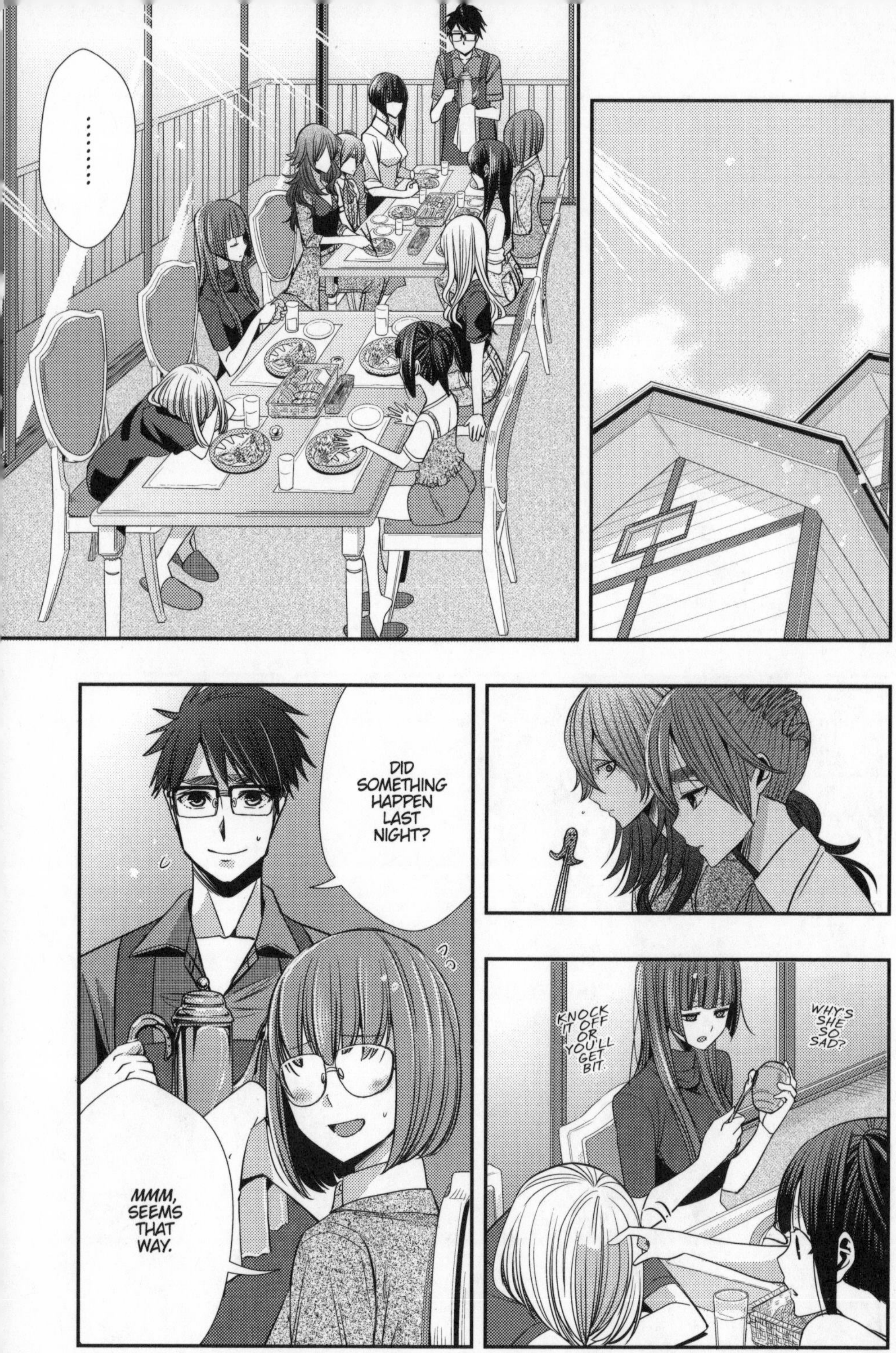
......
WHY'S SHE SO SAD?
KNOCK IT OFF OR YOU'LL GET BIT.
DID SOMETHING HAPPEN LAST NIGHT?
MMM, SEEMS THAT WAY.

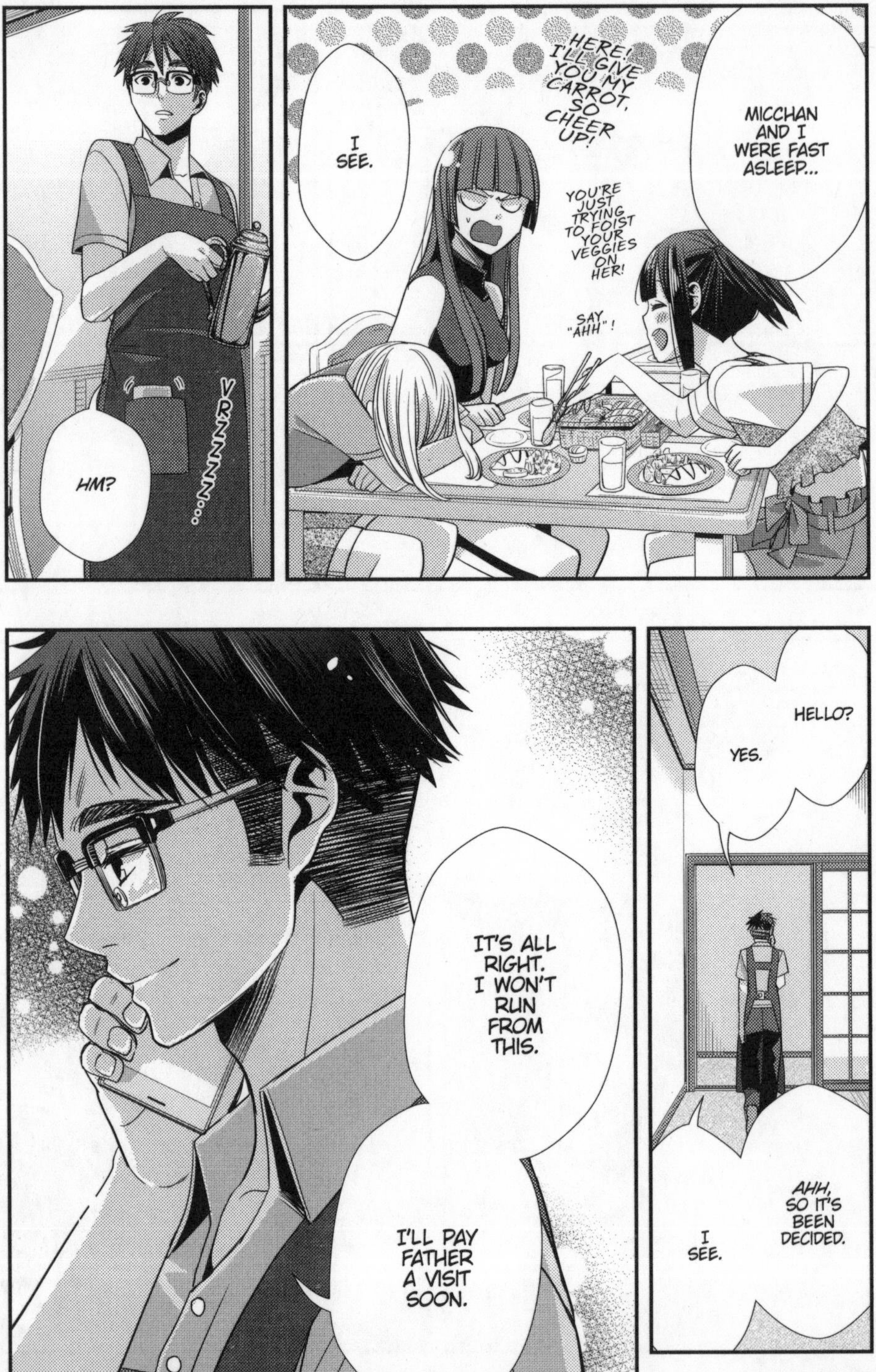
MICCHAN AND I WERE FAST ASLEEP...
HERE! I'LL GIVE YOU MY CARROT, SO CHEER UP!
YOU'RE JUST TRYING TO FOIST YOUR VEGGIES ON HER!
I SEE.
SAY "AHH"!
VRZZZZZZ...
HM?
HELLO?
YES.
AHH, SO IT'S BEEN DECIDED.
I SEE.
IT'S ALL RIGHT. I WON'T RUN FROM THIS.
I'LL PAY FATHER A VISIT SOON.

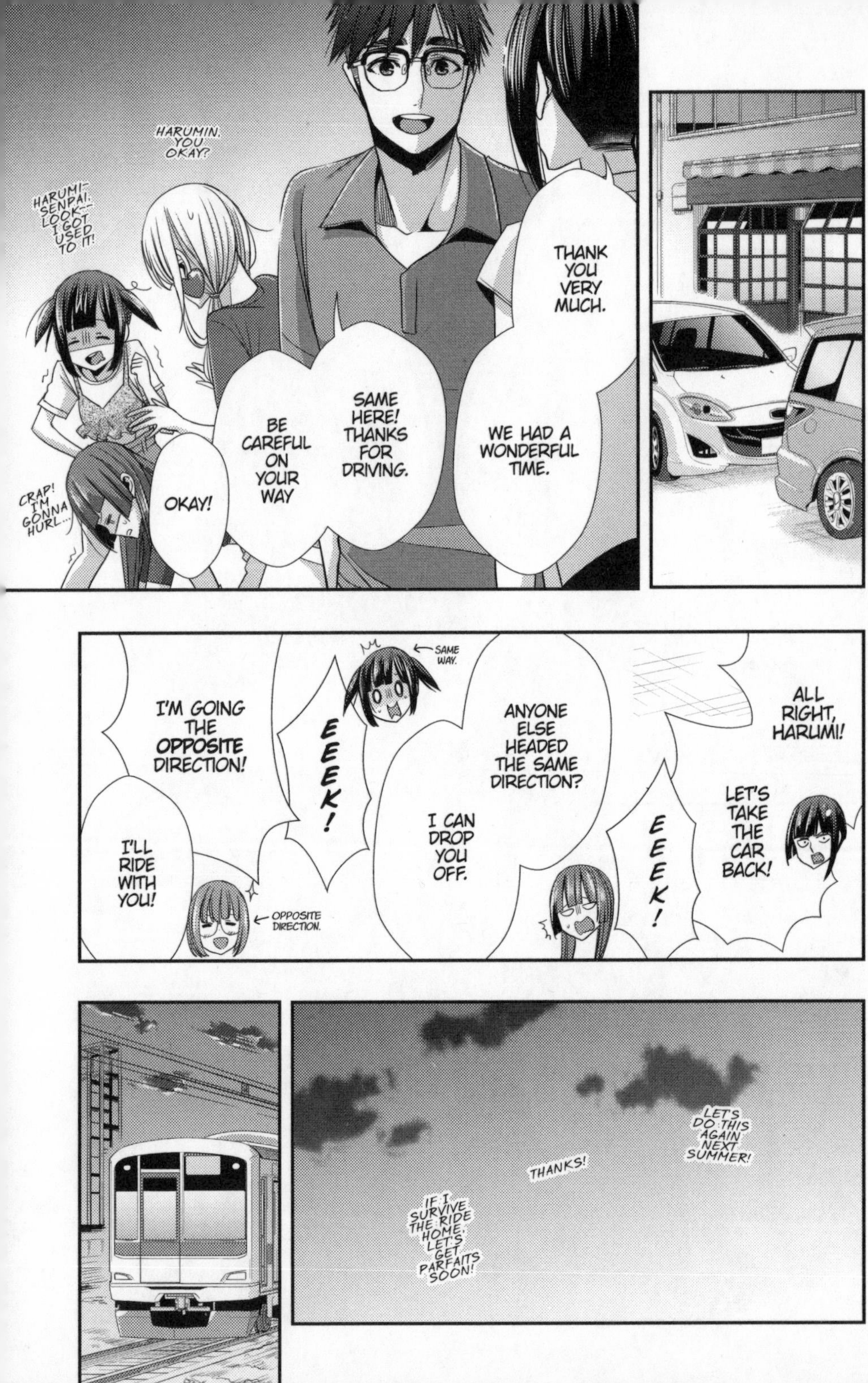
THANK YOU VERY MUCH.
WE HAD A WONDERFUL TIME.
SAME HERE! THANKS FOR DRIVING.
BE CAREFUL ON YOUR WAY
OKAY!
HARUMIN, YOU OKAY?
HARUMI-SENPAI, LOOK... I GOT USED TO IT!
CRAP! I'M GONNA HURL...
ALL RIGHT, HARUMI!
LET'S TAKE THE CAR BACK!
EEEK!
ANYONE ELSE HEADED THE SAME DIRECTION?
I CAN DROP YOU OFF.
SAME WAY.
EEEK!
I'M GOING THE OPPOSITE DIRECTION!
I'LL RIDE WITH YOU!
OPPOSITE DIRECTION.
LET'S DO THIS AGAIN NEXT SUMMER!
THANKS!
IF I SURVIVE THE RIDE HOME, LET'S GET PARFAITS SOON!

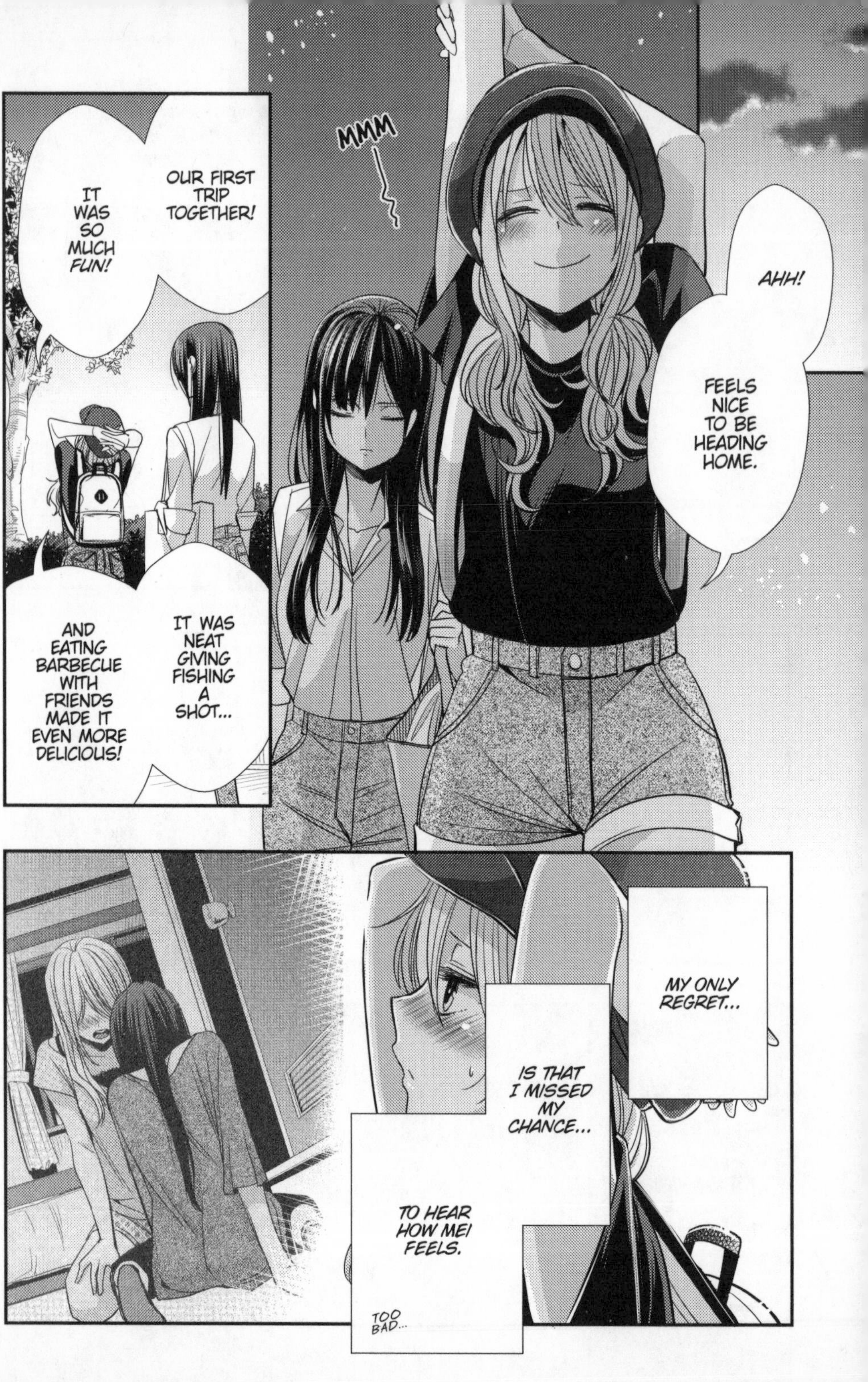
MMM
AHH!
FEELS NICE TO BE HEADING HOME.
OUR FIRST TRIP TOGETHER!
IT WAS SO MUCH FUN!
IT WAS NEAT GIVING FISHING A SHOT...
AND EATING BARBECUE WITH FRIENDS MADE IT EVEN MORE DELICIOUS!
MY ONLY REGRET...
IS THAT I MISSED MY CHANCE...
TO HEAR HOW MEI FEELS.
TOO BAD...

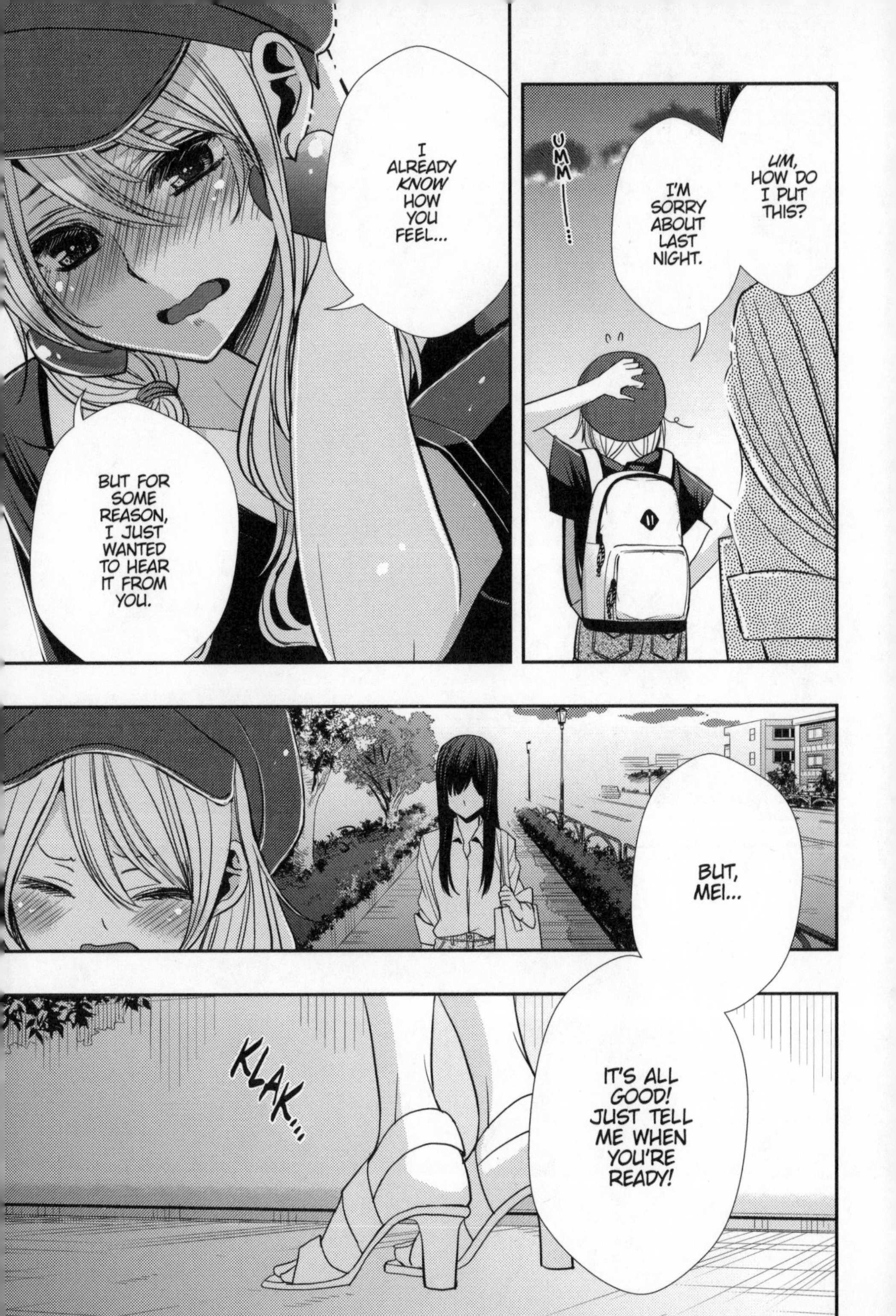
UM, HOW DO I PUT THIS?
I'M SORRY ABOUT LAST NIGHT.
UMM.....
I ALREADY *KNOW* HOW YOU FEEL...
BUT FOR SOME REASON, I JUST WANTED TO HEAR IT FROM YOU.
BUT, MEI...
IT'S ALL GOOD! JUST TELL ME WHEN YOU'RE READY!
KLAK...

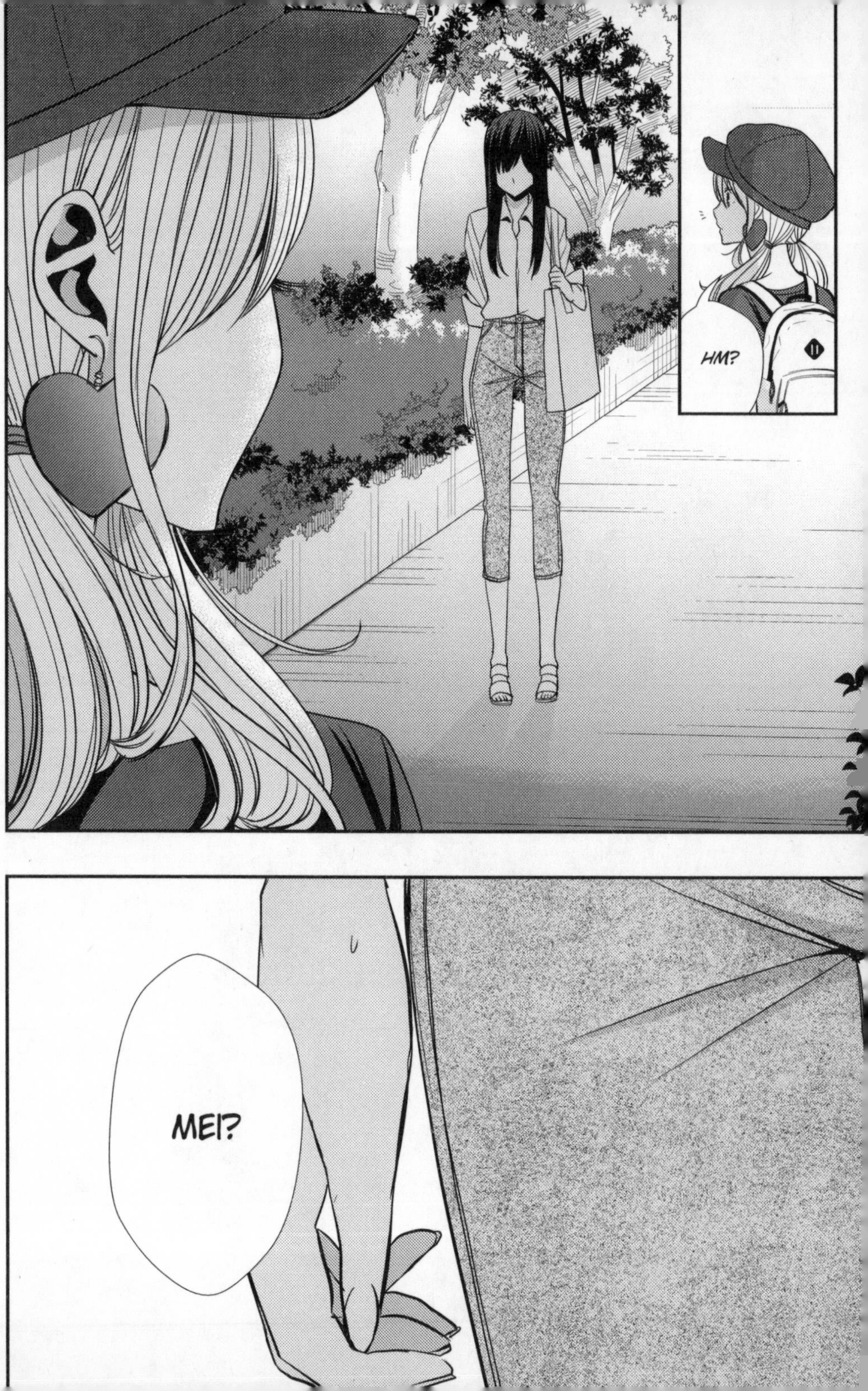
HM?
MEI?

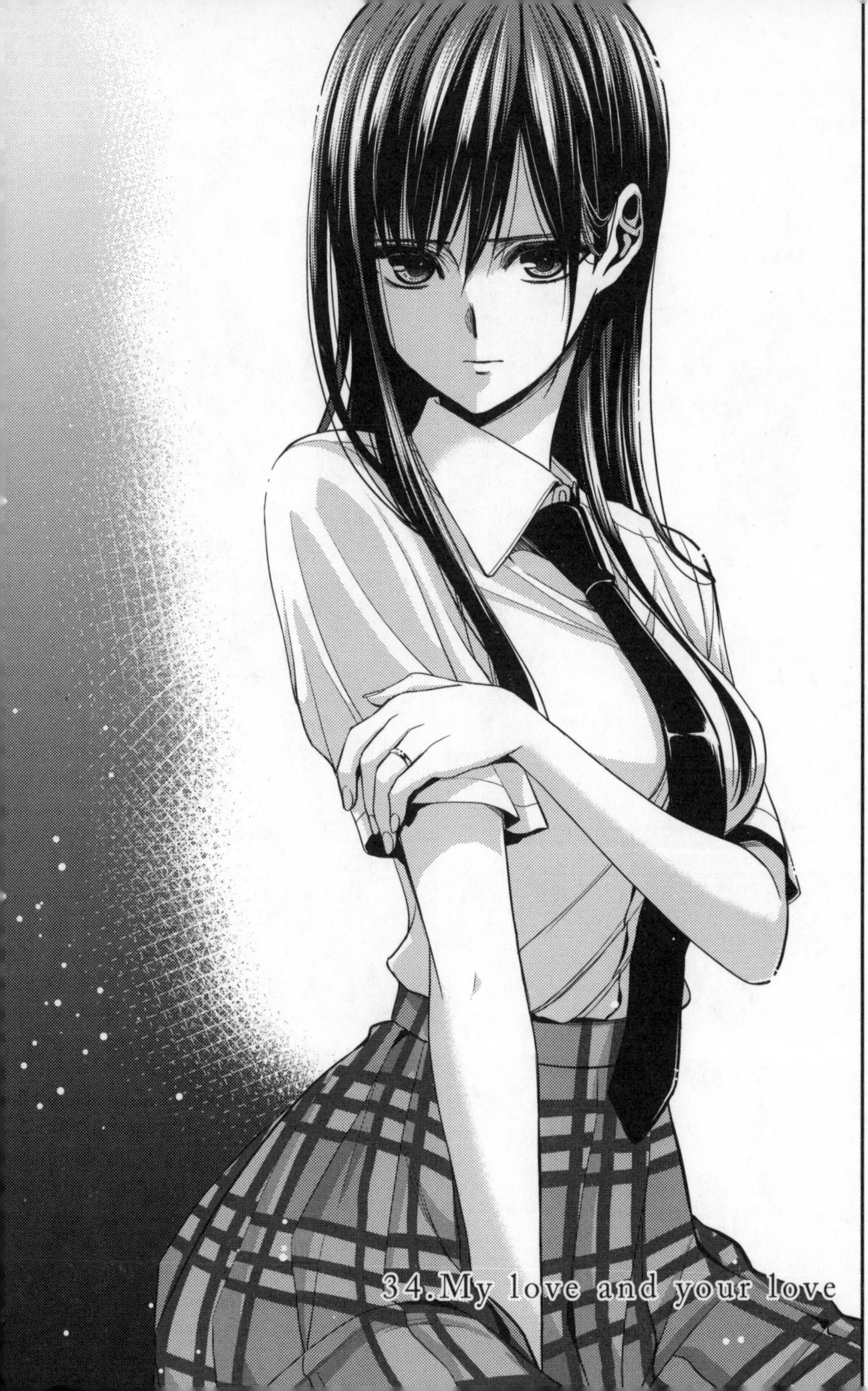

34.My love and your love

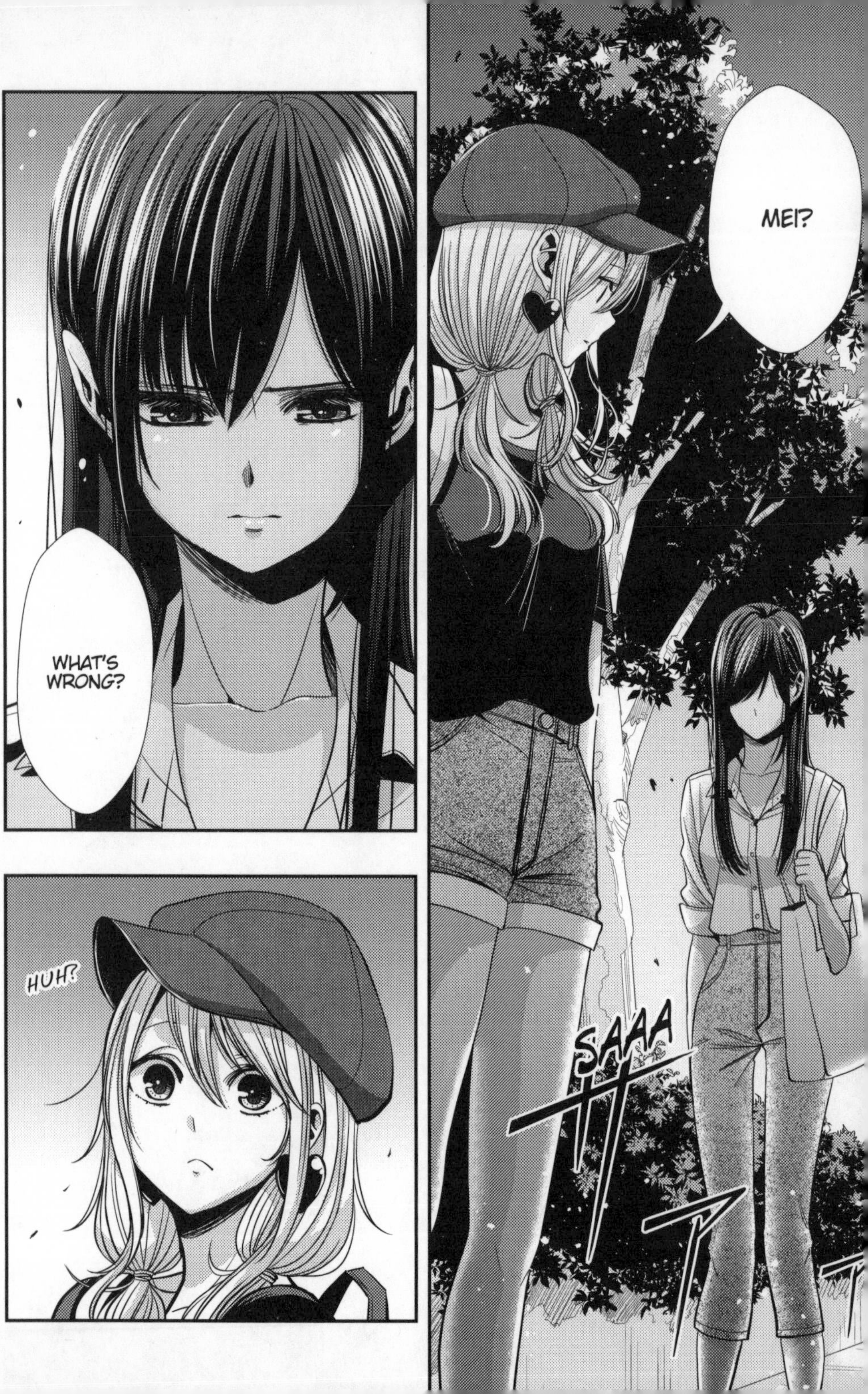
MEI?
SAAA
WHAT'S WRONG?
HUH?

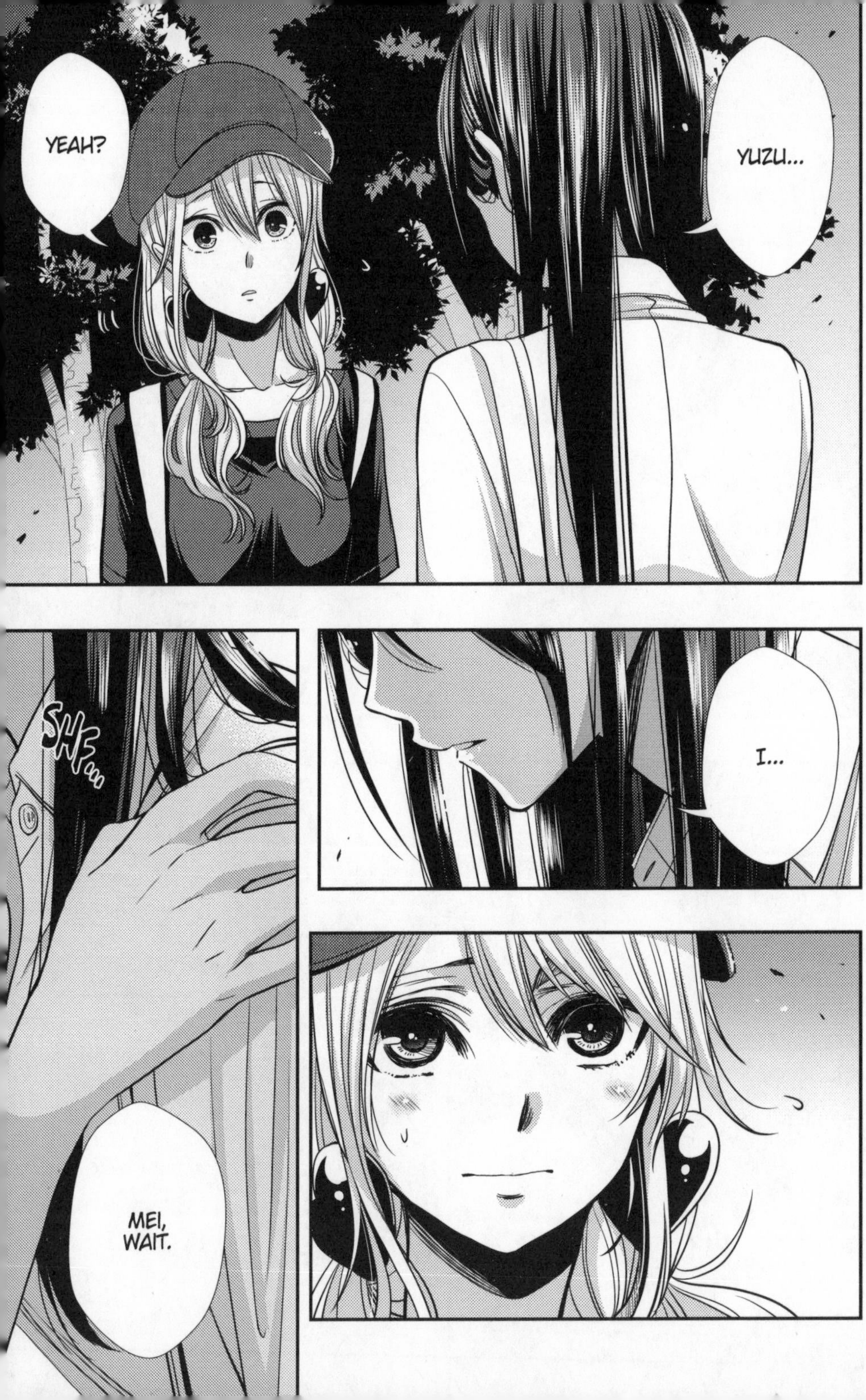
YUZU...
YEAH?
I...
SHF...
MEI,
WAIT.

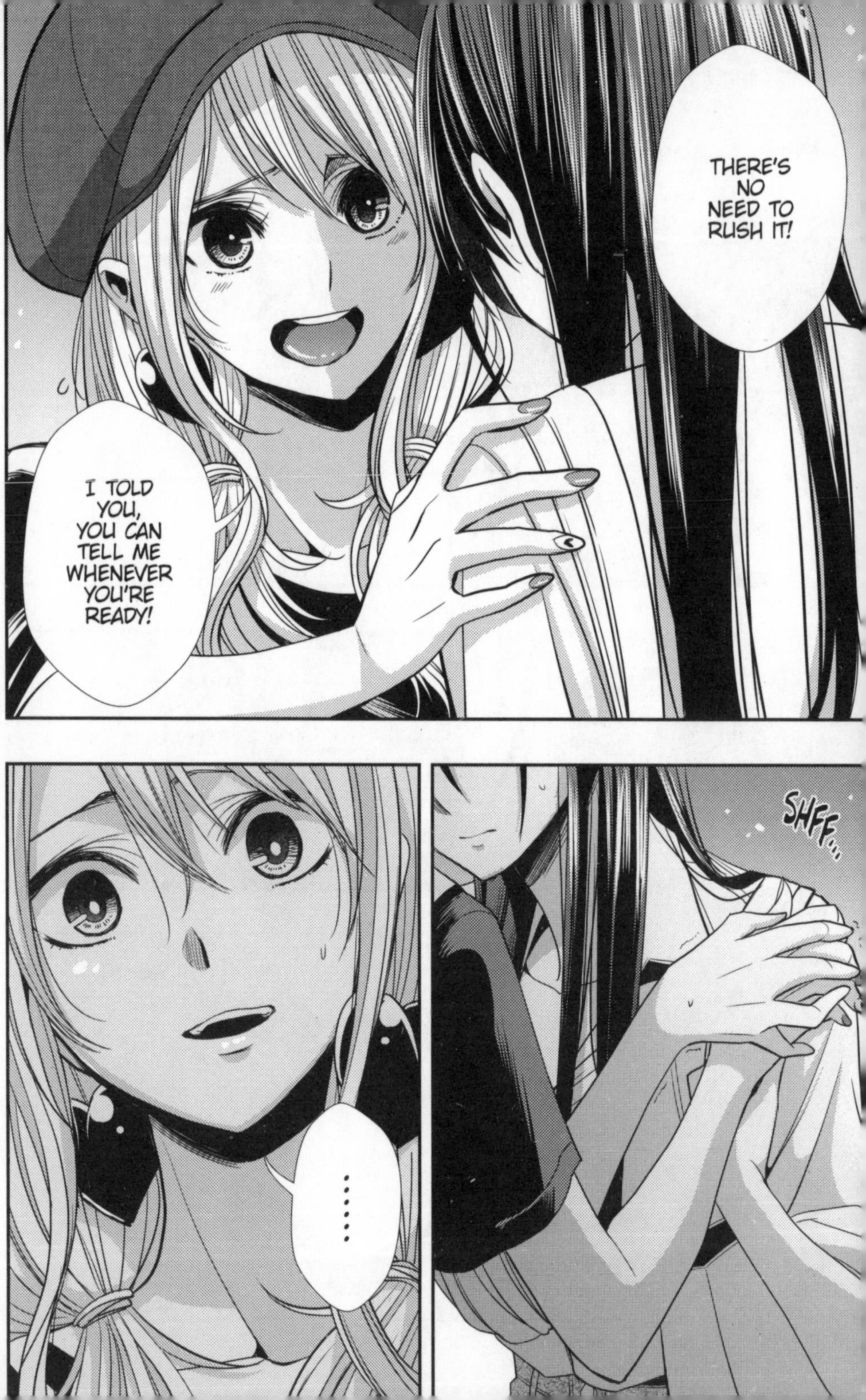
THERE'S NO NEED TO RUSH IT!
I TOLD YOU, YOU CAN TELL ME WHENEVER YOU'RE READY!
SHFF...
......

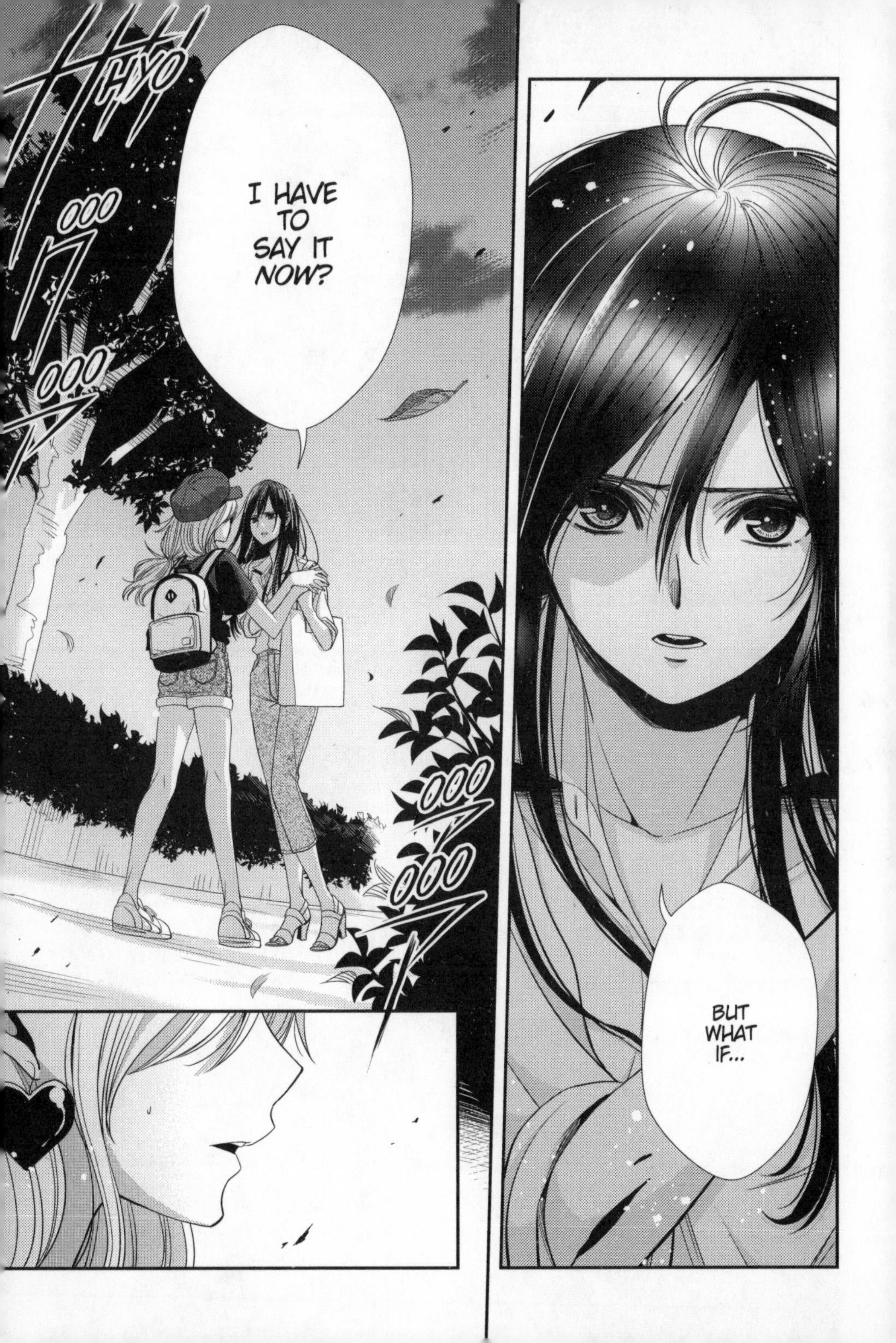
BUT WHAT IF...
I HAVE TO SAY IT NOW?

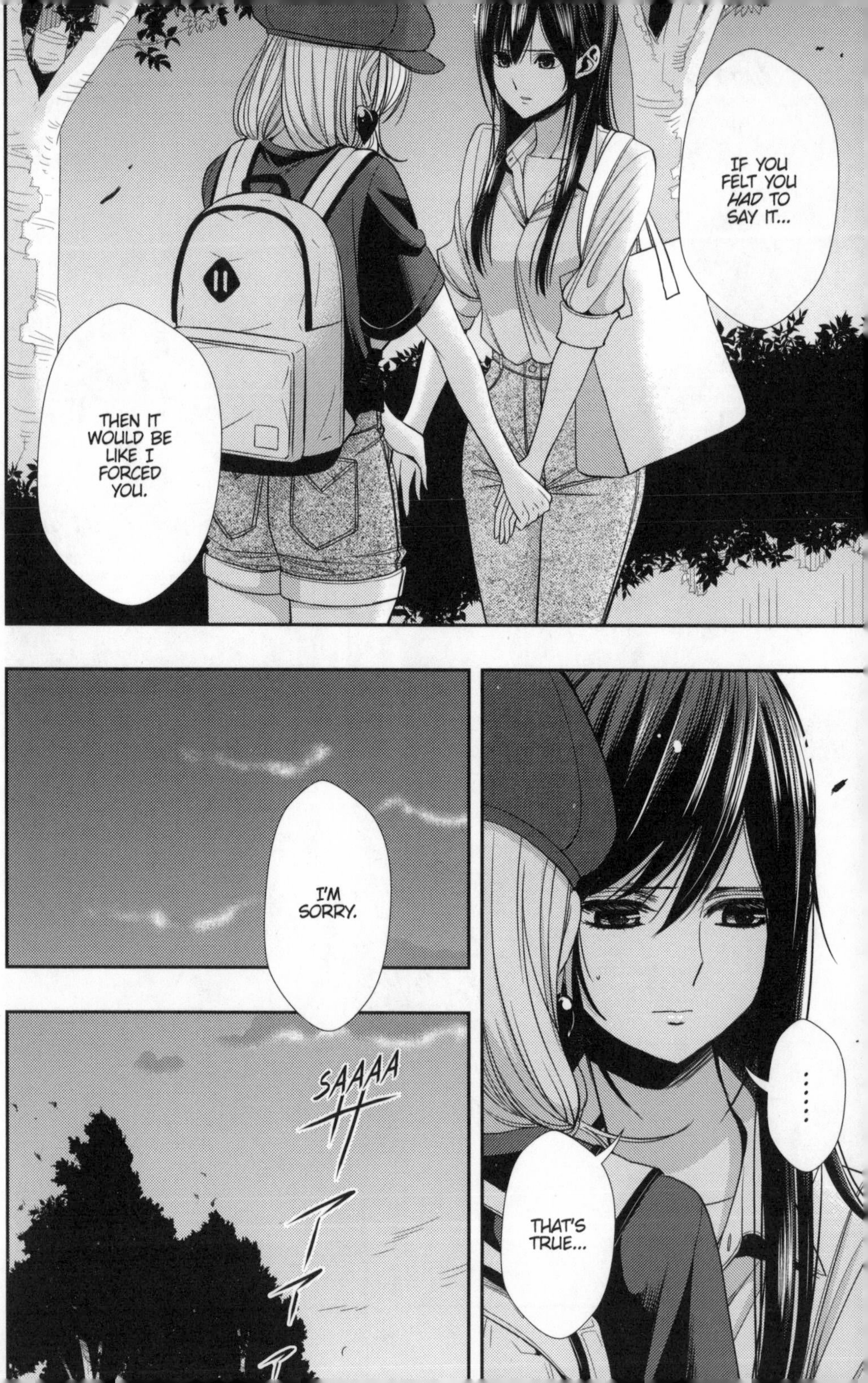
IF YOU FELT YOU *HAD* TO SAY IT...
THEN IT WOULD BE LIKE I FORCED YOU.
......
THAT'S TRUE...
I'M SORRY.
SAAAAH

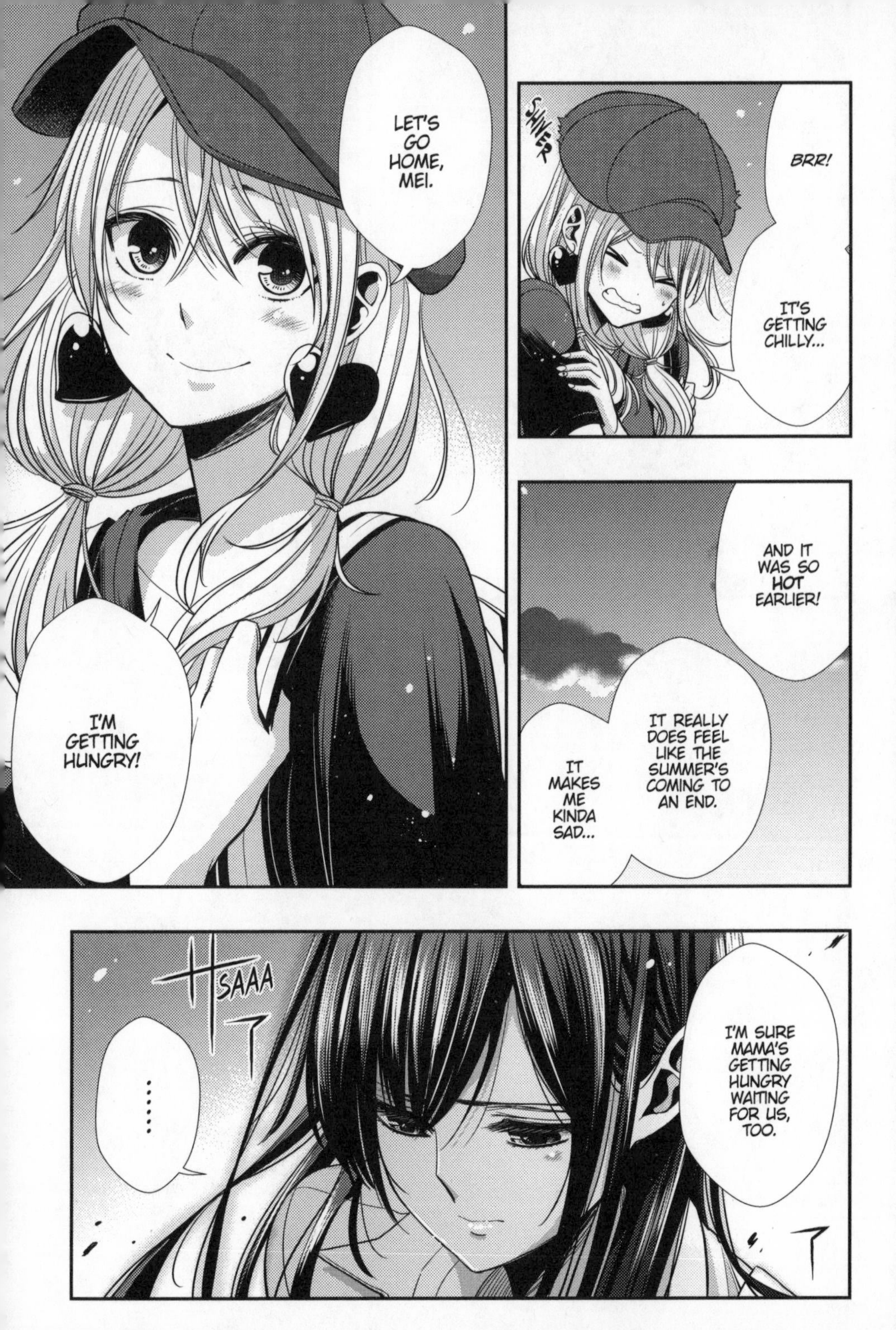
BRR!
SHIVER
IT'S GETTING CHILLY...
AND IT WAS SO HOT EARLIER!
IT REALLY DOES FEEL LIKE THE SUMMER'S COMING TO AN END.
IT MAKES ME KINDA SAD...
LET'S GO HOME, MEI.
I'M GETTING HUNGRY!
I'M SURE MAMA'S GETTING HUNGRY WAITING FOR US, TOO.
SAAA
......

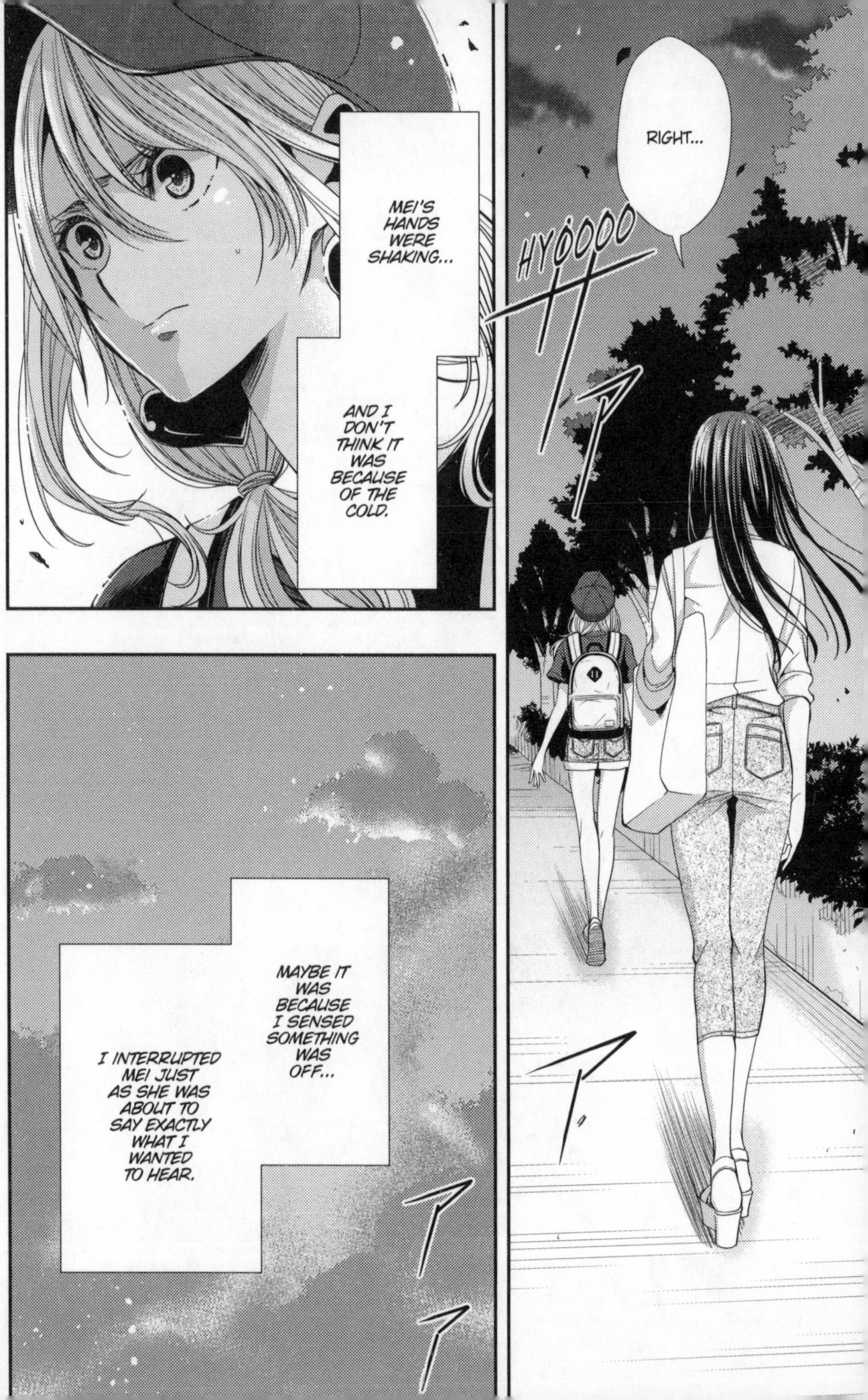
RIGHT...
HYOOOO
MEI'S HANDS WERE SHAKING...
AND I DON'T THINK IT WAS BECAUSE OF THE COLD.
MAYBE IT WAS BECAUSE I SENSED SOMETHING WAS OFF...
I INTERRUPTED MEI JUST AS SHE WAS ABOUT TO SAY EXACTLY WHAT I WANTED TO HEAR.

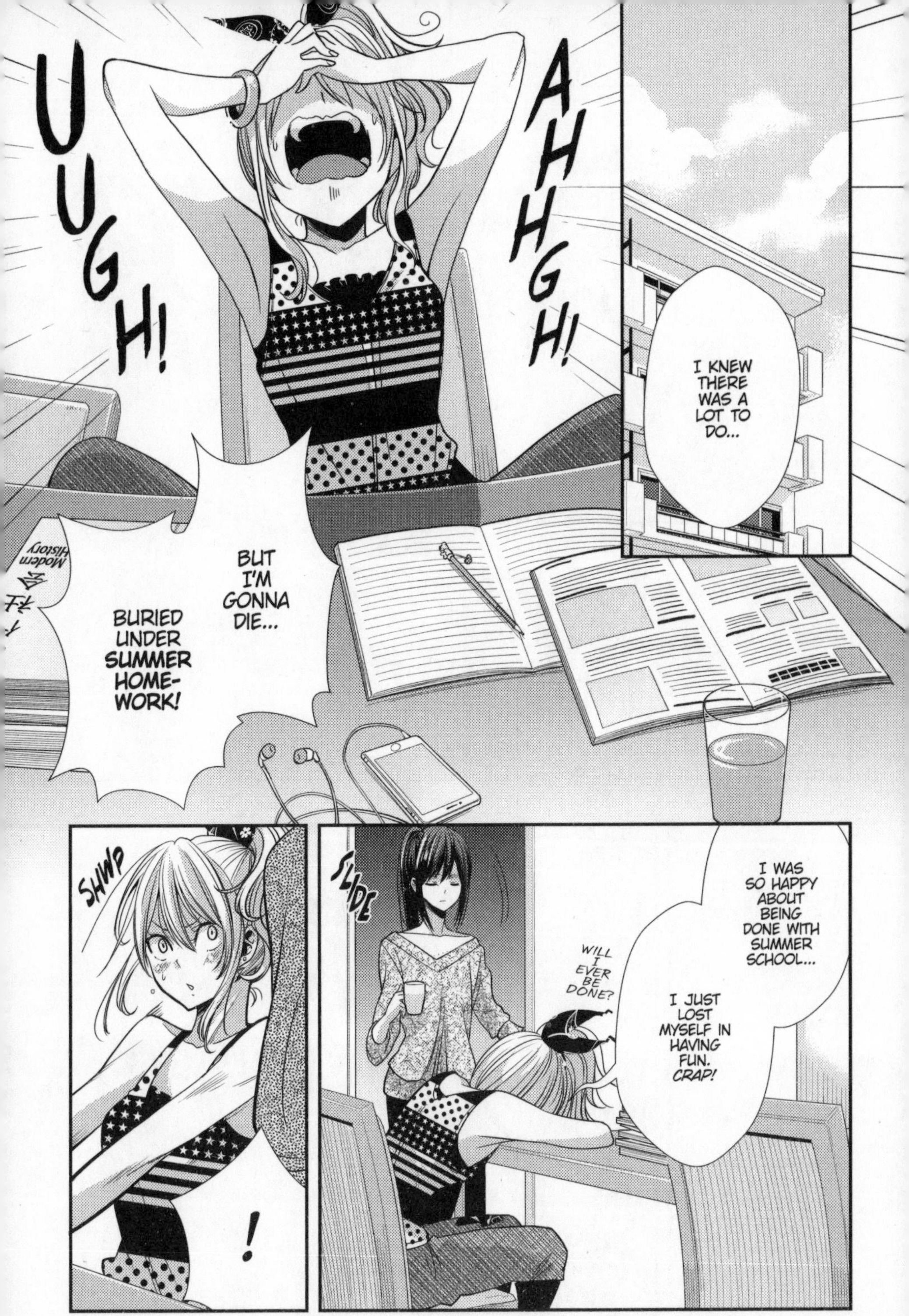
I KNEW THERE WAS A LOT TO DO...
AHHGH!
UUGH!
BUT I'M GONNA DIE...
BURIED UNDER SUMMER HOME-WORK!
Modern History
I WAS SO HAPPY ABOUT BEING DONE WITH SUMMER SCHOOL...
I JUST LOST MYSELF IN HAVING FUN. CRAP!
WILL I EVER BE DONE?
SLIDE
SHWP
!

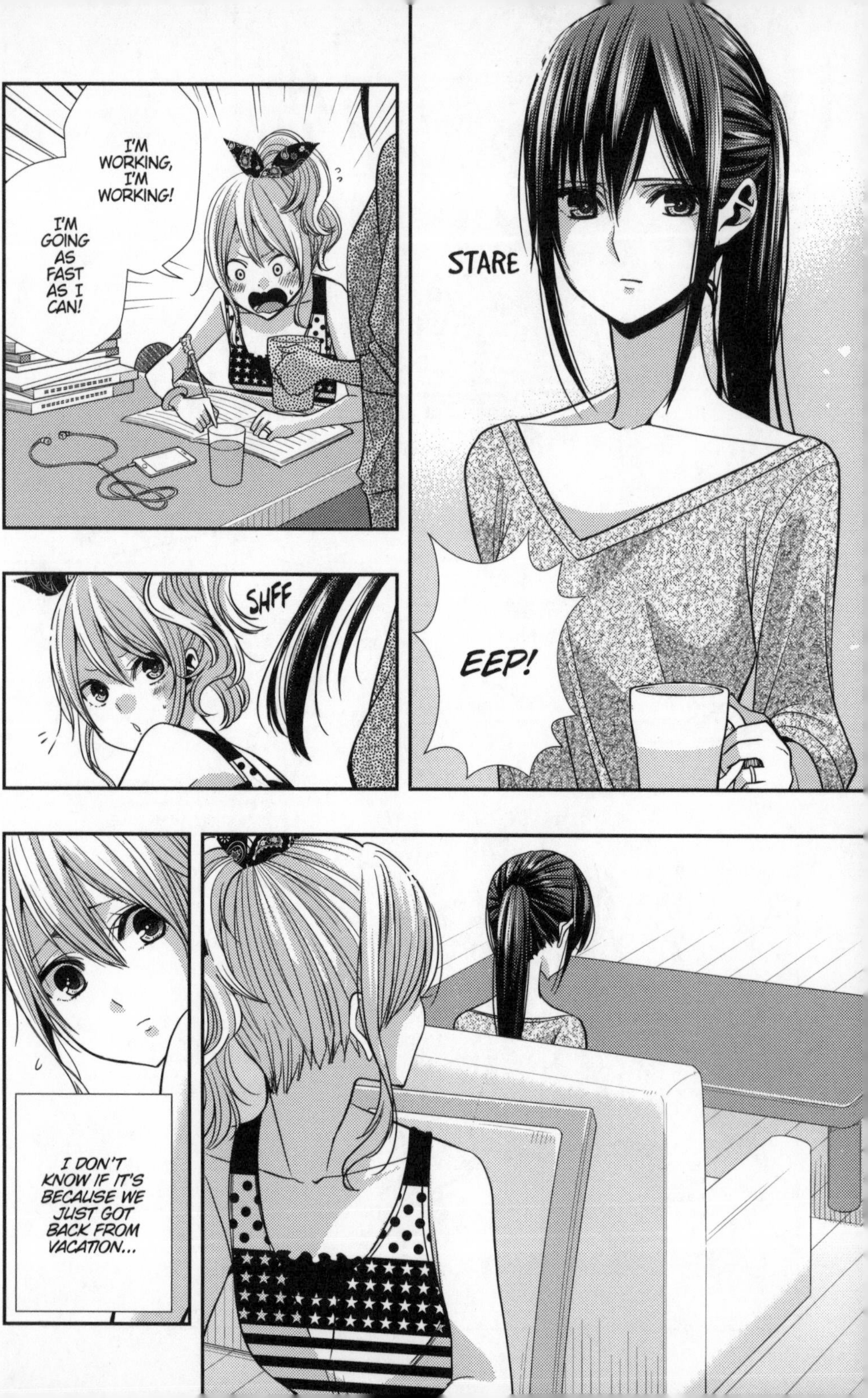
STARE
EEP!
I'M WORKING, I'M WORKING!
I'M GOING AS FAST AS I CAN!
SHFF
I DON'T KNOW IF IT'S BECAUSE WE JUST GOT BACK FROM VACATION...

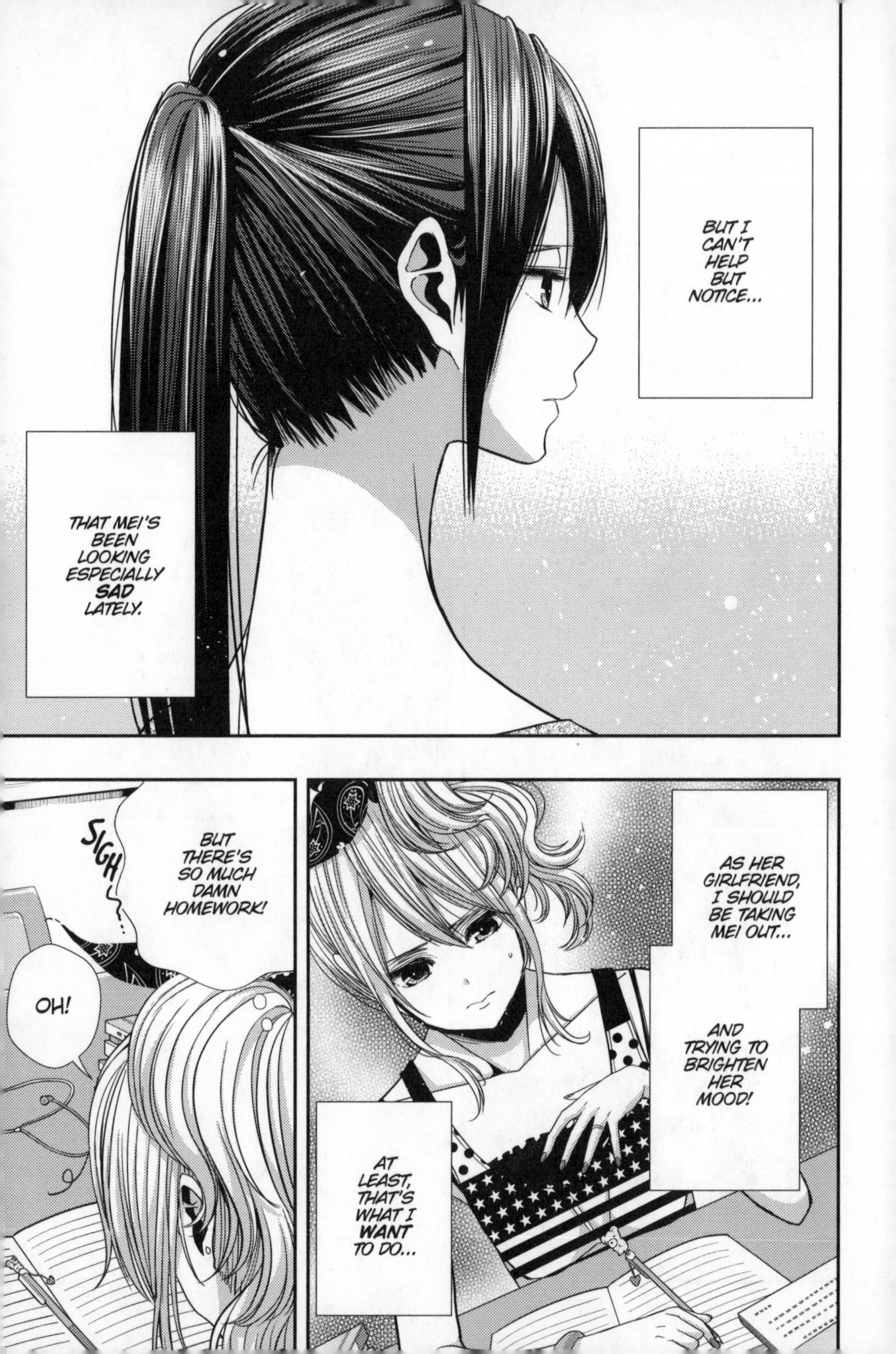
BUT I CAN'T HELP BUT NOTICE...
THAT MEI'S BEEN LOOKING ESPECIALLY SAD LATELY.
AS HER GIRLFRIEND, I SHOULD BE TAKING MEI OUT...
AND TRYING TO BRIGHTEN HER MOOD!
AT LEAST, THAT'S WHAT I WANT TO DO...
BUT THERE'S SO MUCH DAMN HOMEWORK!
SIGH...
OH!

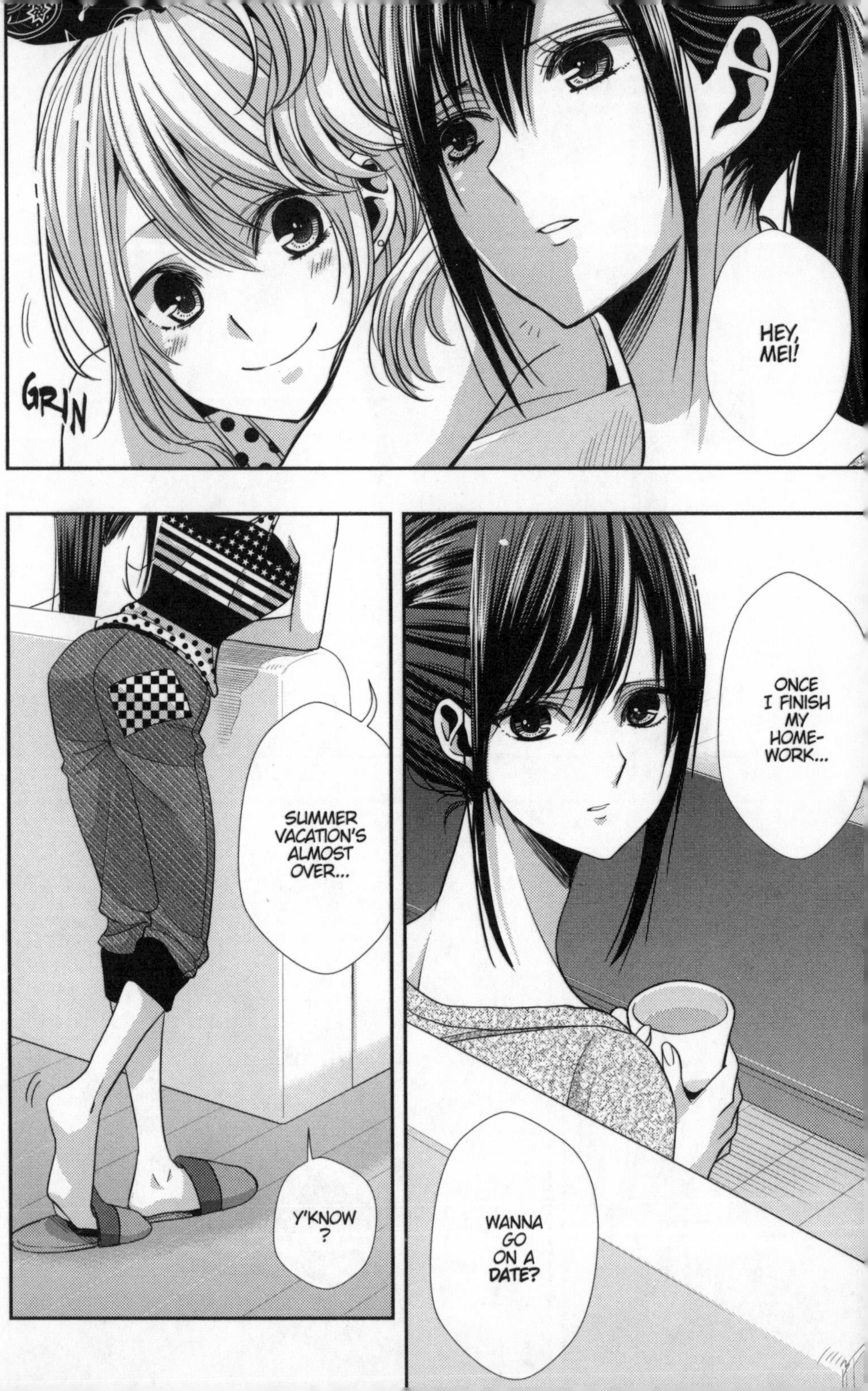
HEY, MEI!
GRIN
ONCE I FINISH MY HOME-WORK...
WANNA GO ON A DATE?
SUMMER VACATION'S ALMOST OVER...
Y'KNOW?

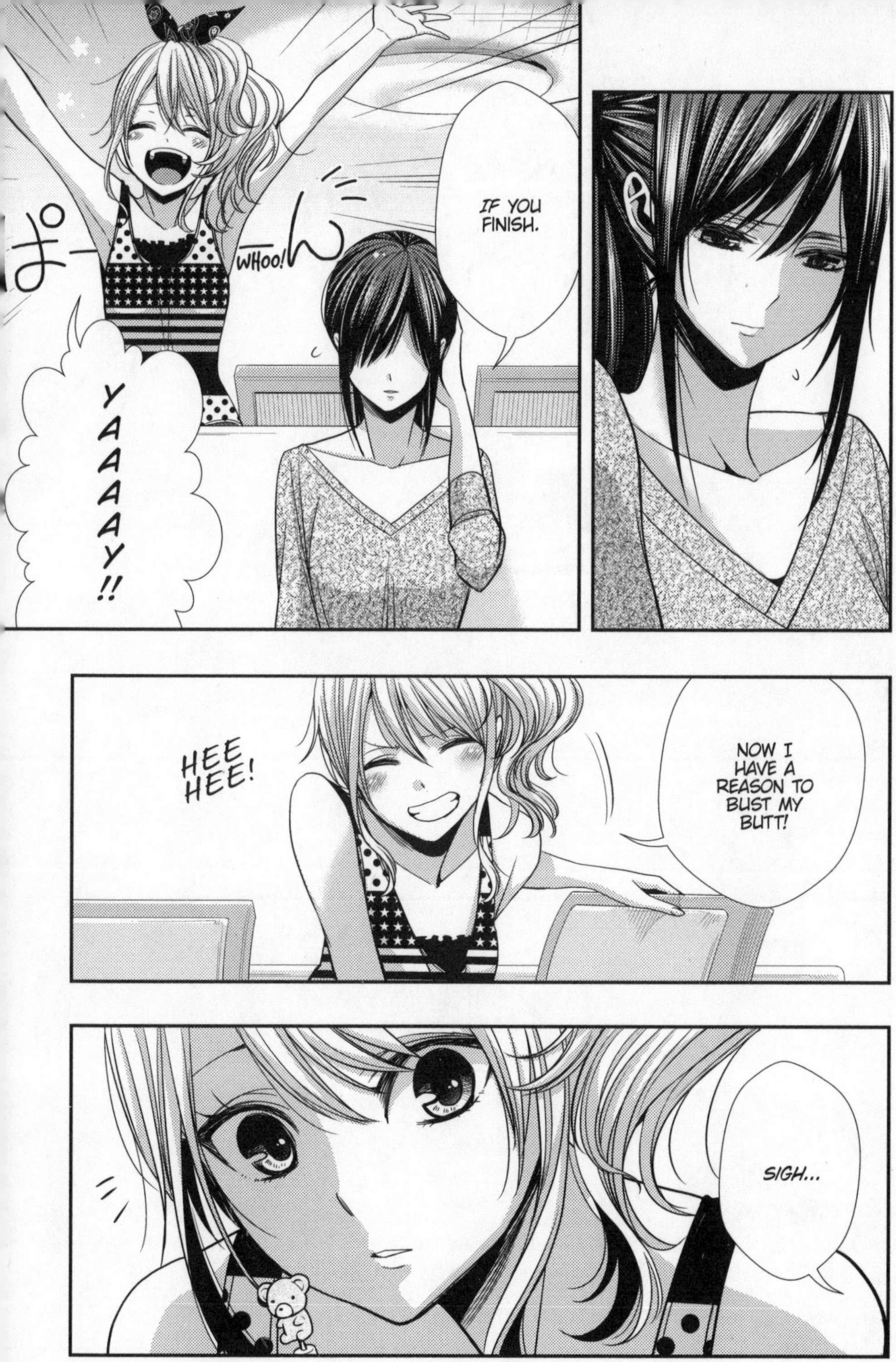
IF YOU FINISH.
ぽーん
WHOO!
YAAAAAY!!
NOW I HAVE A REASON TO BUST MY BUTT!
HEE HEE!
SIGH...

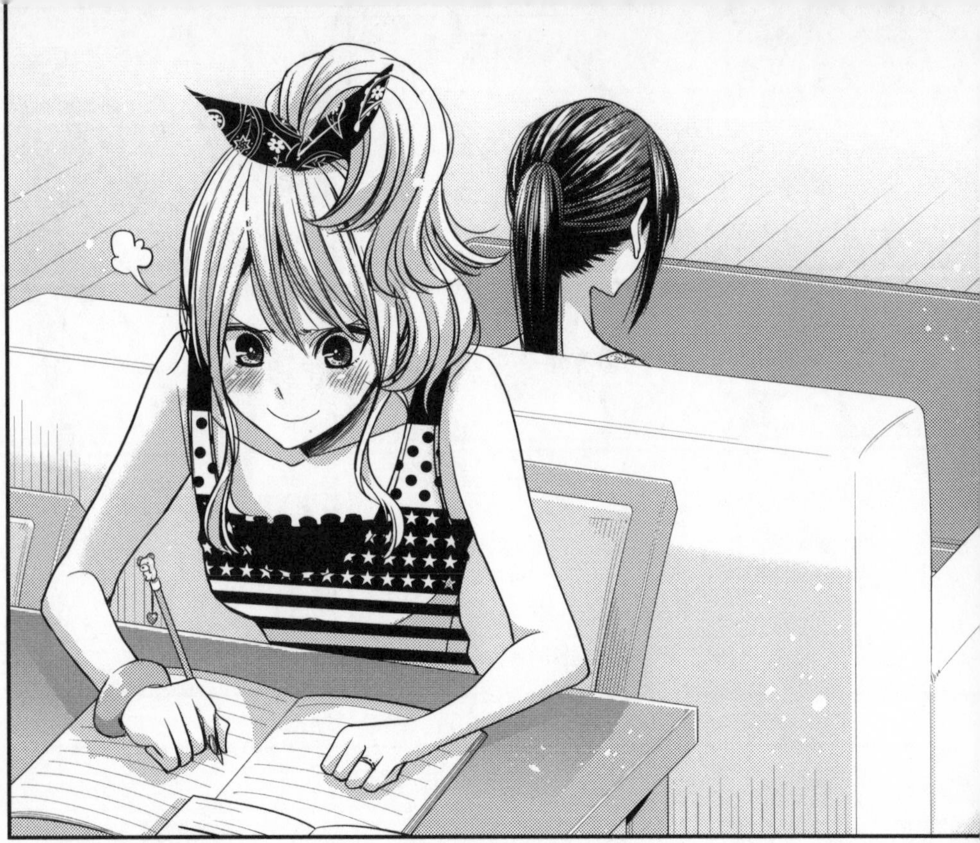
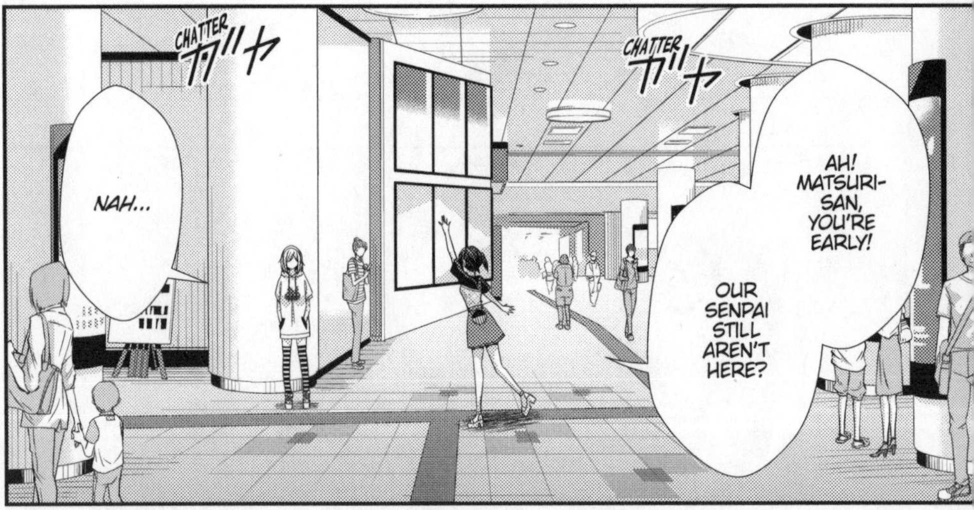
CHATTER
ガヤ
CHATTER
ガヤ
AH! MATSURI-SAN, YOU'RE EARLY!
OUR SENPAI STILL AREN'T HERE?
NAH...

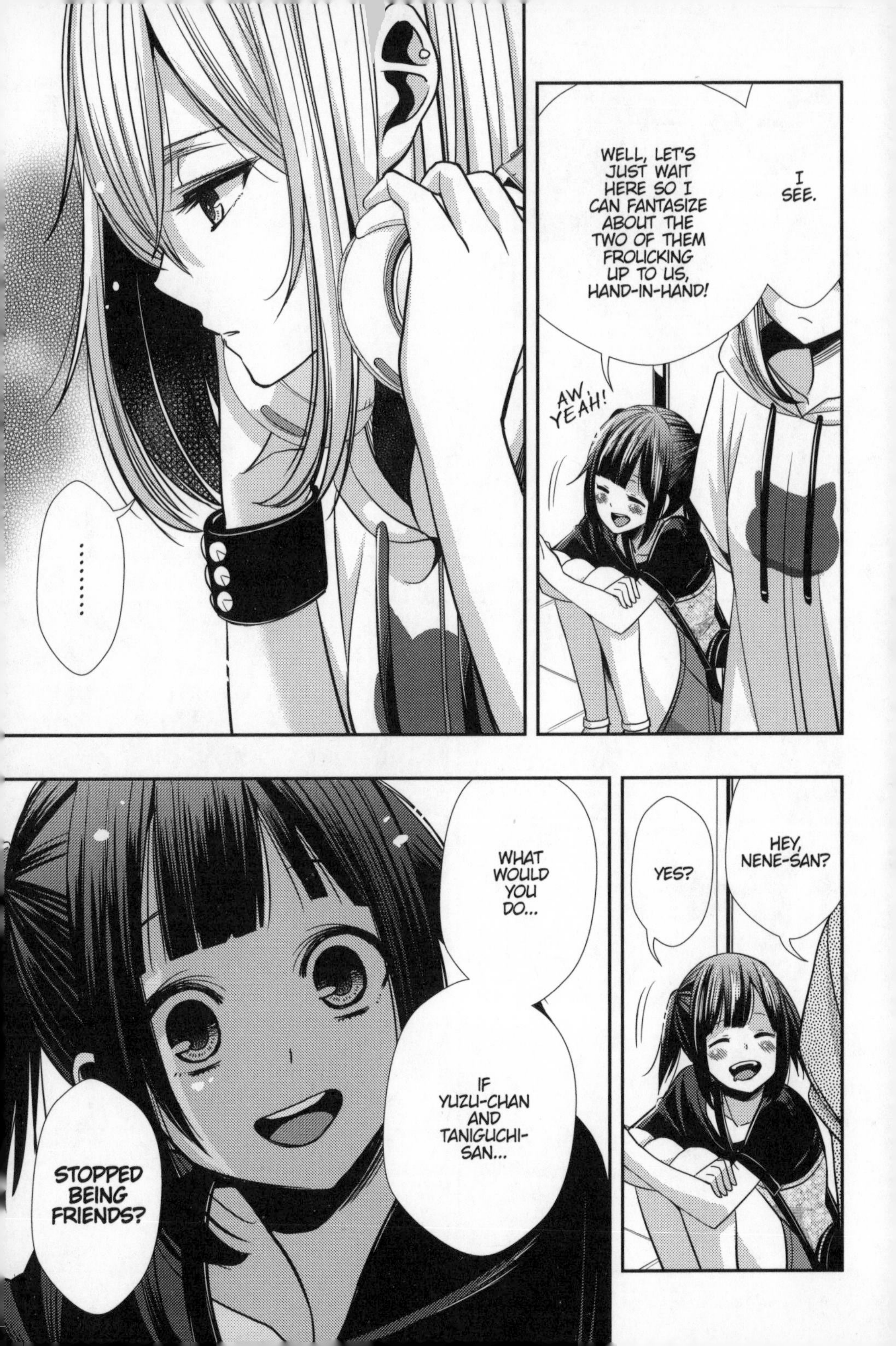
I SEE.
WELL, LET'S JUST WAIT HERE SO I CAN FANTASIZE ABOUT THE TWO OF THEM FROLICKING UP TO US, HAND-IN-HAND!
AW, YEAH!
......
HEY, NENE-SAN?
YES?
WHAT WOULD YOU DO...
IF YUZU-CHAN AND TANIGUCHI-SAN...
STOPPED BEING FRIENDS?

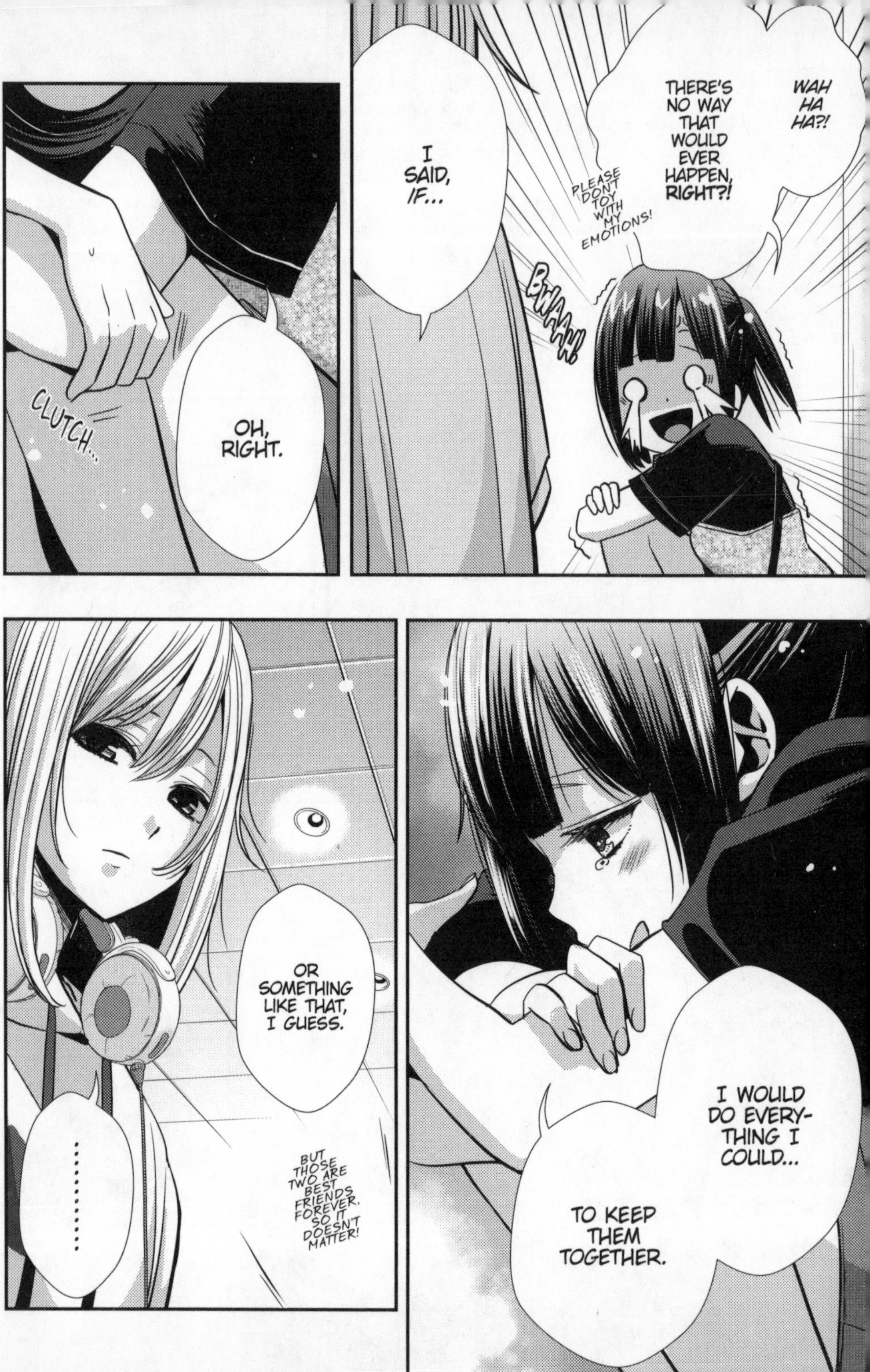
THERE'S NO WAY THAT WOULD EVER HAPPEN, RIGHT?!
WAH HA HA?!
PLEASE DON'T TOY WITH MY EMOTIONS!
BWAAH!
I SAID, IF...
OH, RIGHT.
CLUTCH...
I WOULD DO EVERY-THING I COULD...
TO KEEP THEM TOGETHER.
OR SOMETHING LIKE THAT, I GUESS.
BUT THOSE TWO ARE BEST FRIENDS FOREVER, SO IT DOESN'T MATTER!
......

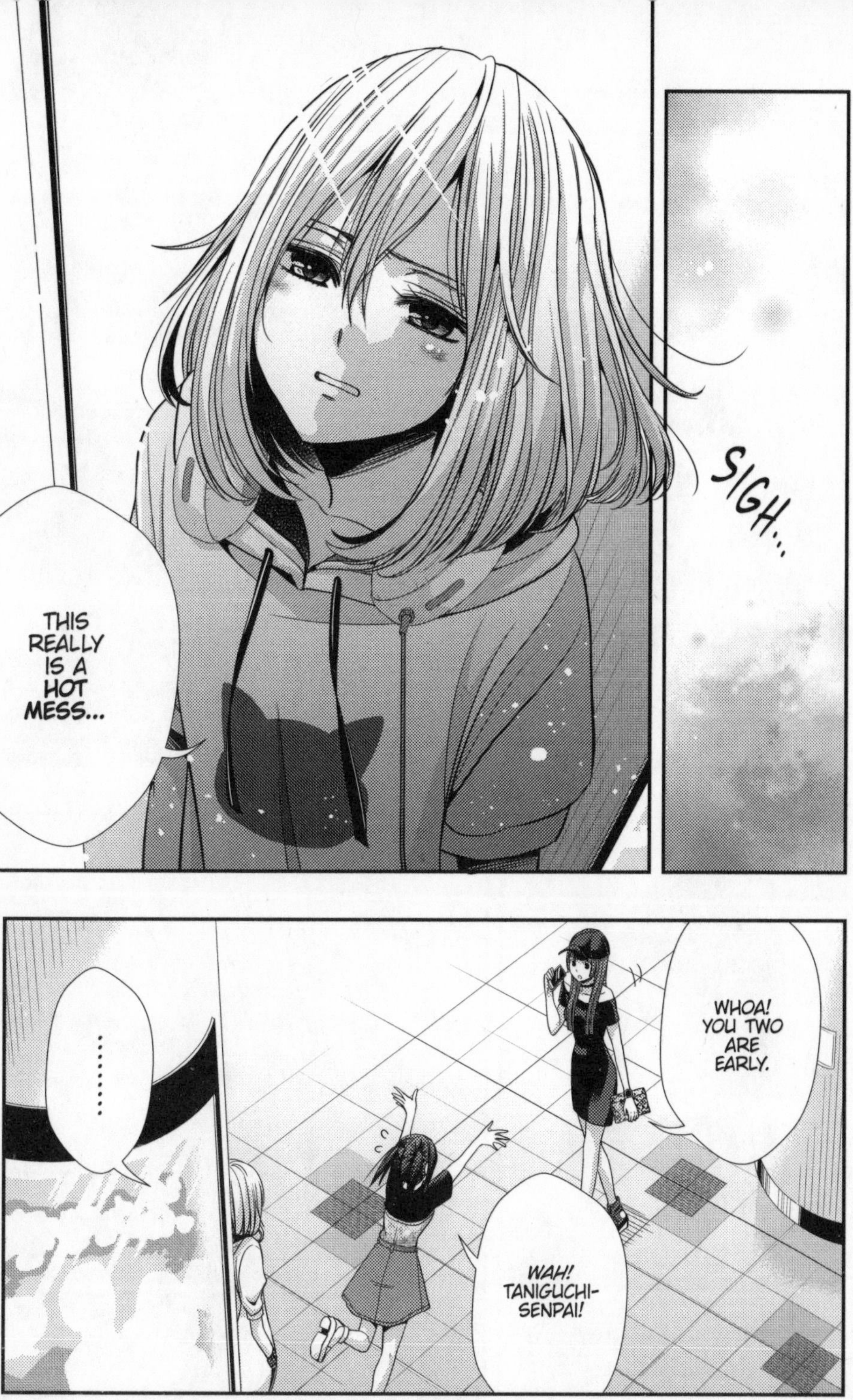
SIGH...
THIS REALLY IS A HOT MESS...
WHOA! YOU TWO ARE EARLY.
WAH! TANIGUCHI-SENPAI!
......

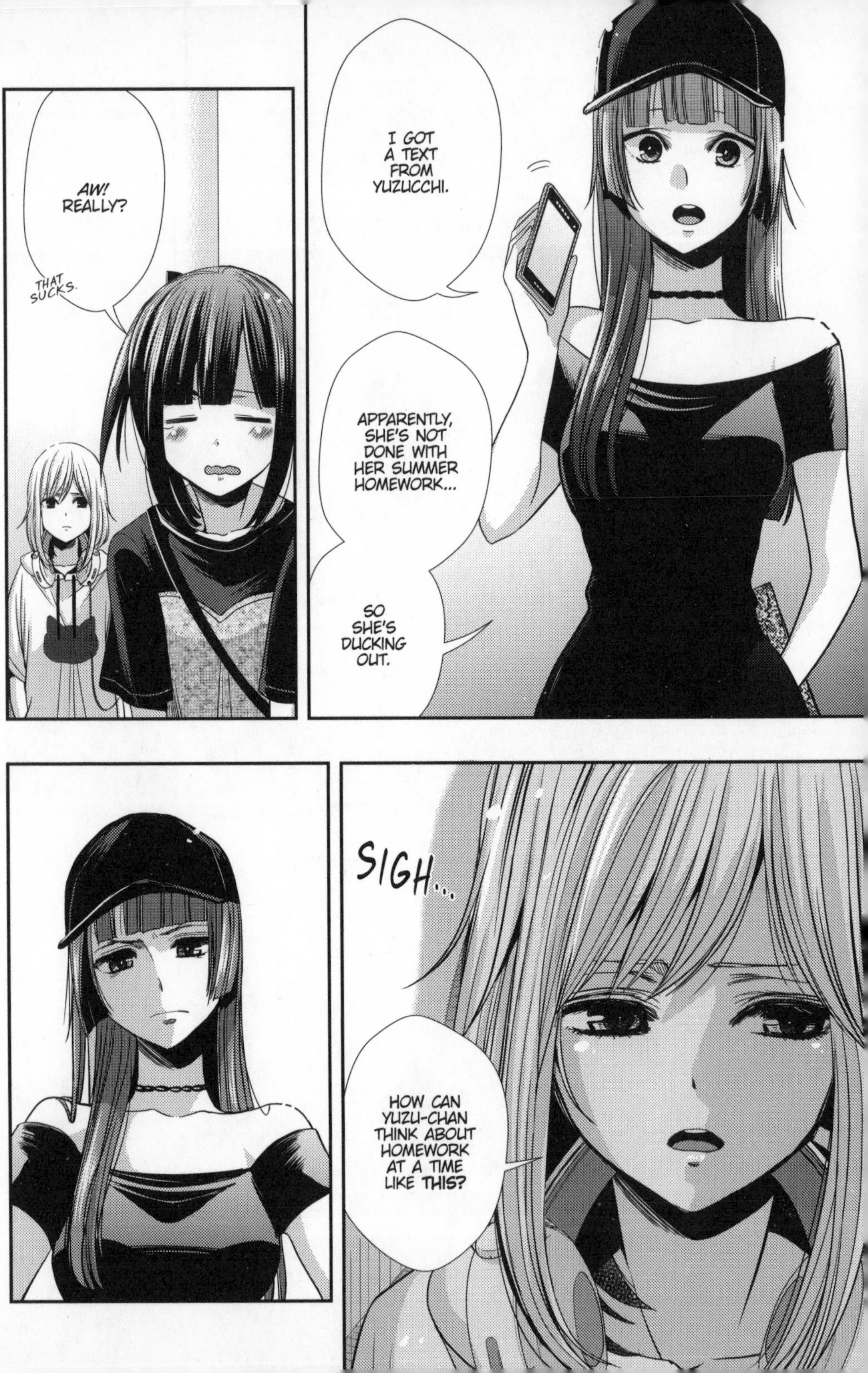
I GOT A TEXT FROM YUZUCCHI.
APPARENTLY, SHE'S NOT DONE WITH HER SUMMER HOMEWORK...
SO SHE'S DUCKING OUT.
AW! REALLY?
THAT SUCKS.
SIGH...
HOW CAN YUZU-CHAN THINK ABOUT HOMEWORK AT A TIME LIKE THIS?

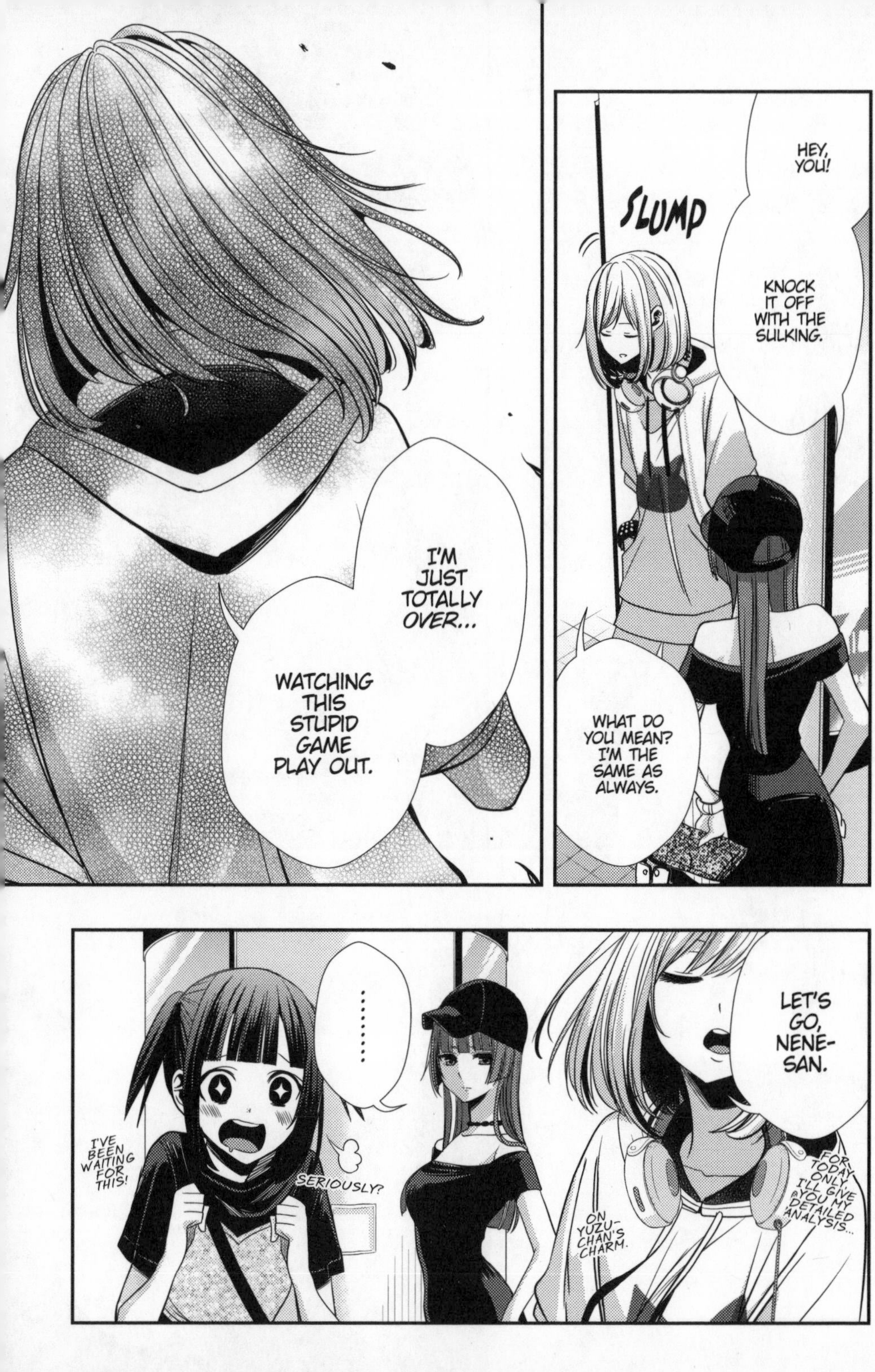
HEY, YOU!
SLUMP
KNOCK IT OFF WITH THE SULKING.
WHAT DO YOU MEAN? I'M THE SAME AS ALWAYS.
I'M JUST TOTALLY OVER...
WATCHING THIS STUPID GAME PLAY OUT.
LET'S GO, NENE-SAN.
FOR TODAY ONLY, I'LL GIVE YOU MY DETAILED ANALYSIS...
ON YUZU-CHAN'S CHARM.
....
SERIOUSLY?
I'VE BEEN WAITING FOR THIS!

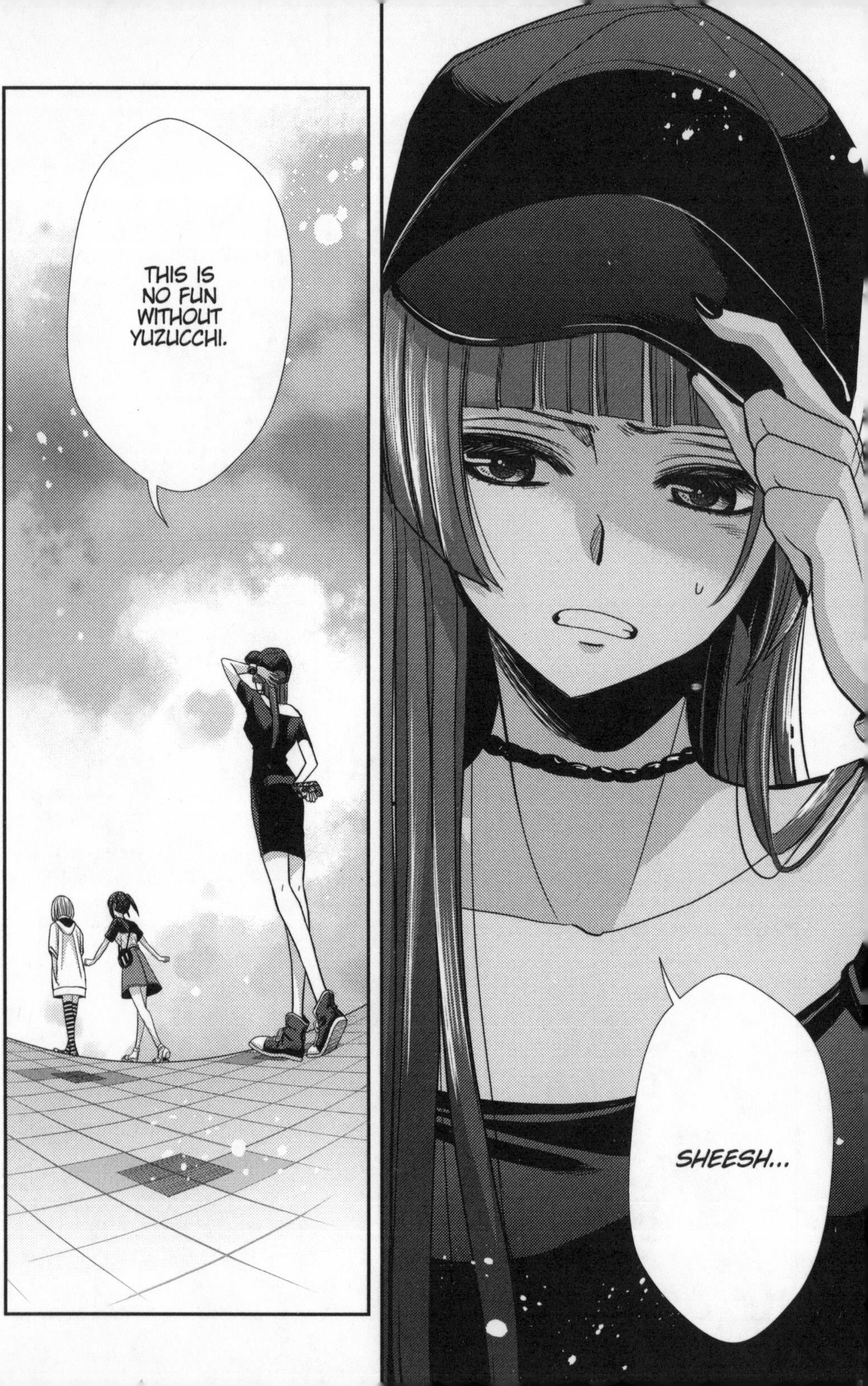
SHEESH...
THIS IS NO FUN WITHOUT YUZUCCHI.

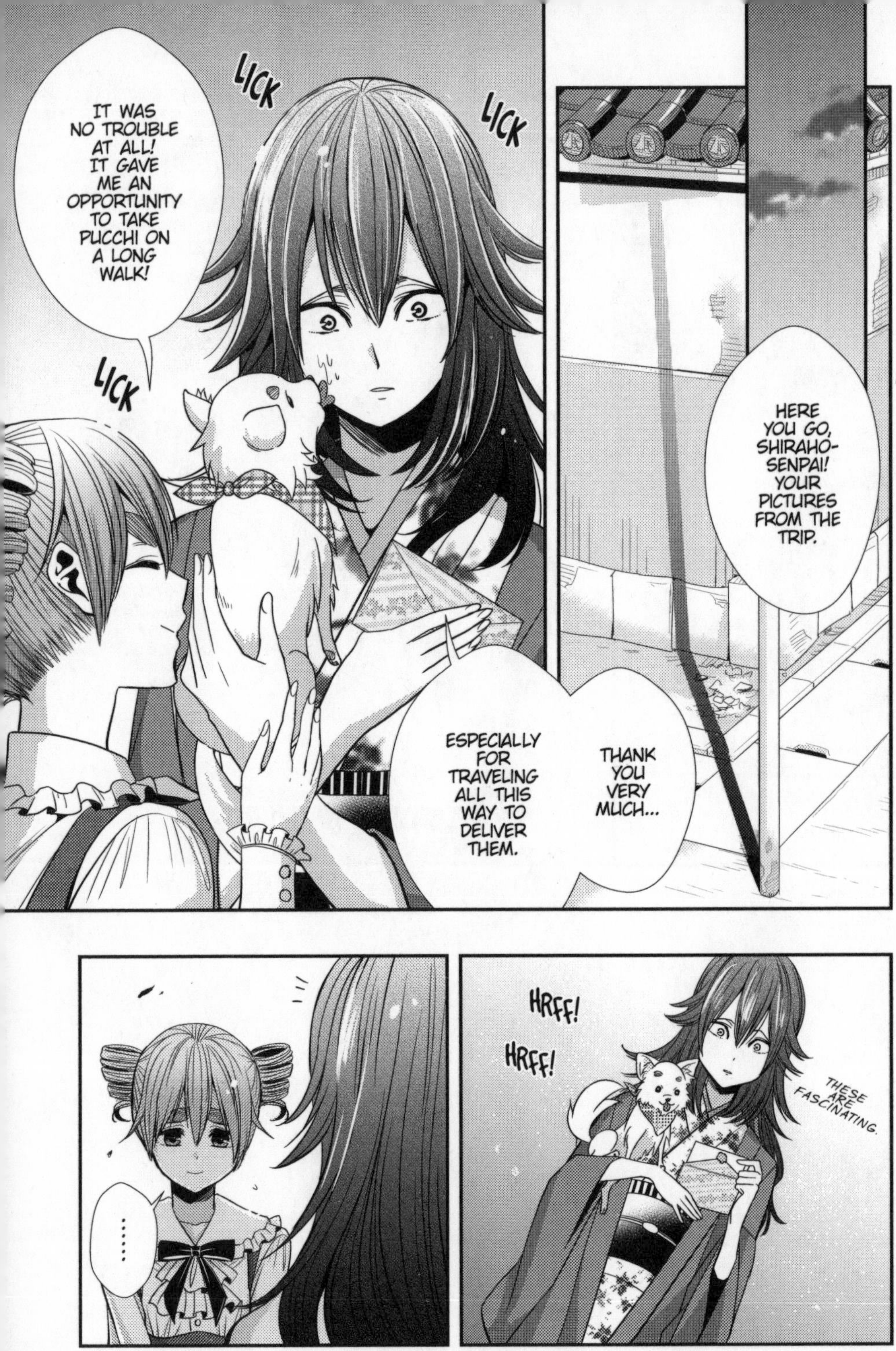
HERE YOU GO, SHIRAHO-SENPAI! YOUR PICTURES FROM THE TRIP.
THANK YOU VERY MUCH...
ESPECIALLY FOR TRAVELING ALL THIS WAY TO DELIVER THEM.
LICK
LICK
IT WAS NO TROUBLE AT ALL! IT GAVE ME AN OPPORTUNITY TO TAKE PUCCHI ON A LONG WALK!
LICK
HRFF!
HRFF!
THESE ARE FASCINATING.
......

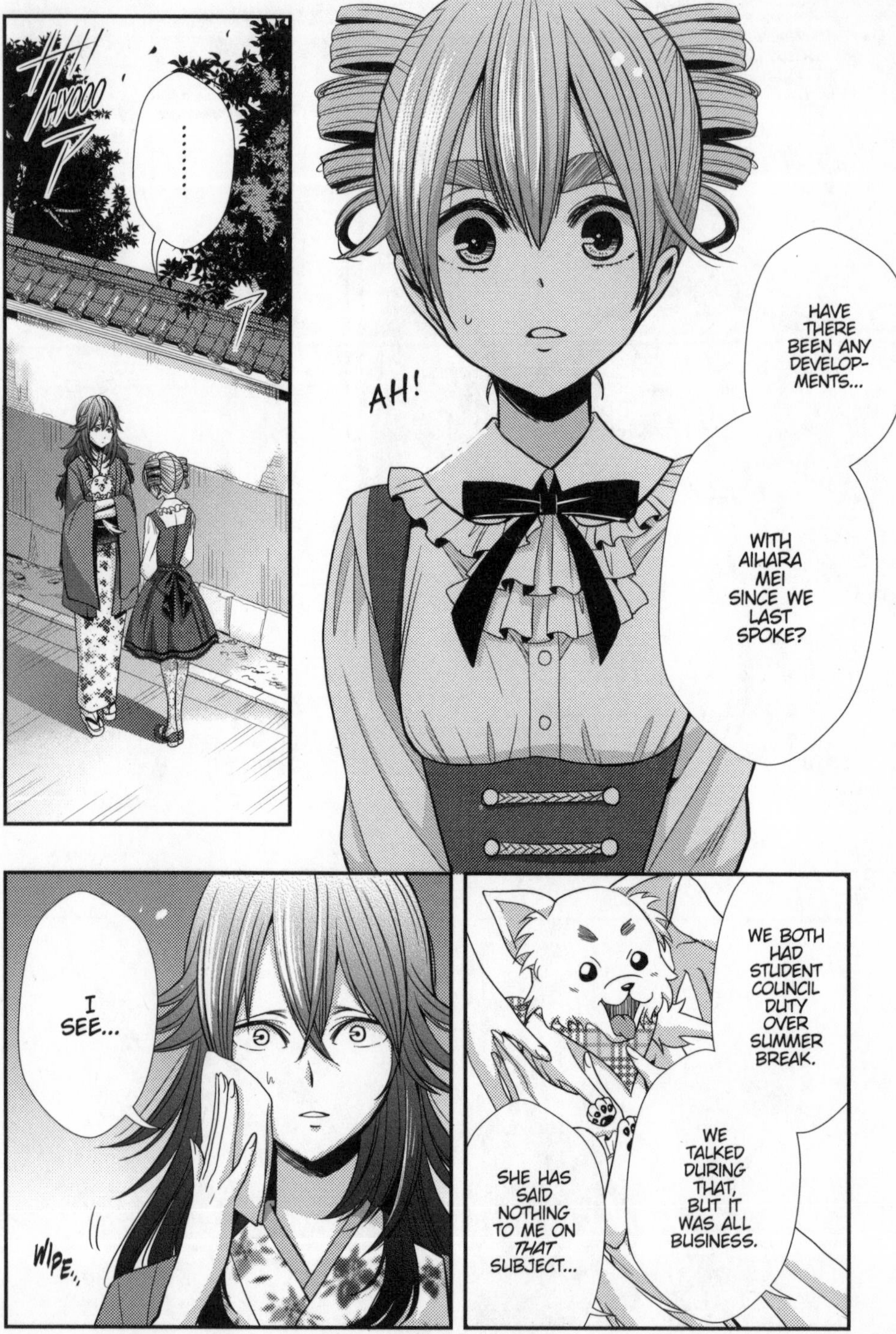
AH!
HAVE THERE BEEN ANY DEVELOPMENTS...
WITH AIHARA MEI SINCE WE LAST SPOKE?
HYOOO
......
WE BOTH HAD STUDENT COUNCIL DUTY OVER SUMMER BREAK.
WE TALKED DURING THAT, BUT IT WAS ALL BUSINESS.
SHE HAS SAID NOTHING TO ME ON *THAT* SUBJECT...
I SEE...
WIPE...

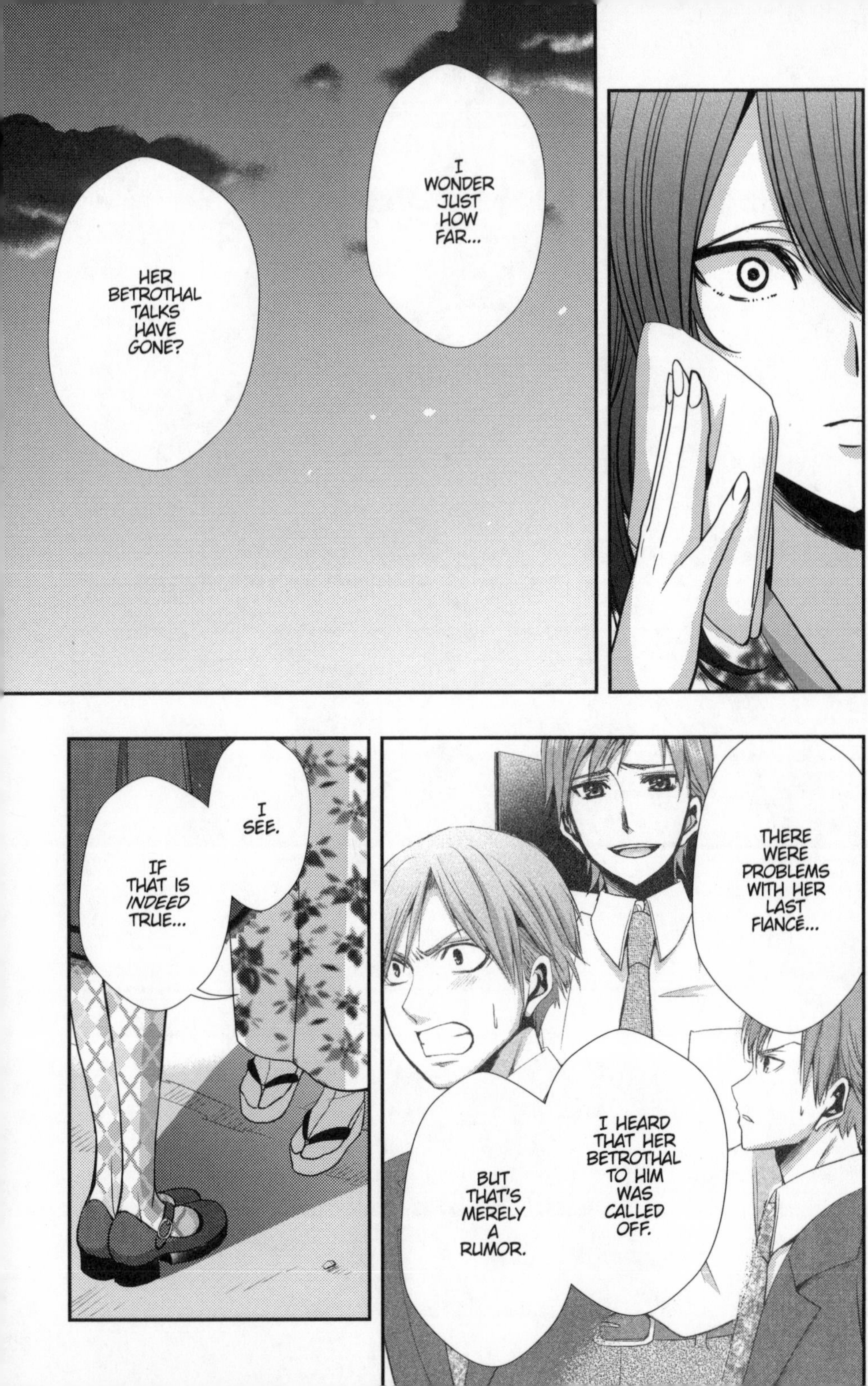
I WONDER JUST HOW FAR...
HER BETROTHAL TALKS HAVE GONE?
THERE WERE PROBLEMS WITH HER LAST FIANCÉ...
I HEARD THAT HER BETROTHAL TO HIM WAS CALLED OFF.
BUT THAT'S MERELY A RUMOR.
I SEE.
IF THAT IS *INDEED* TRUE...

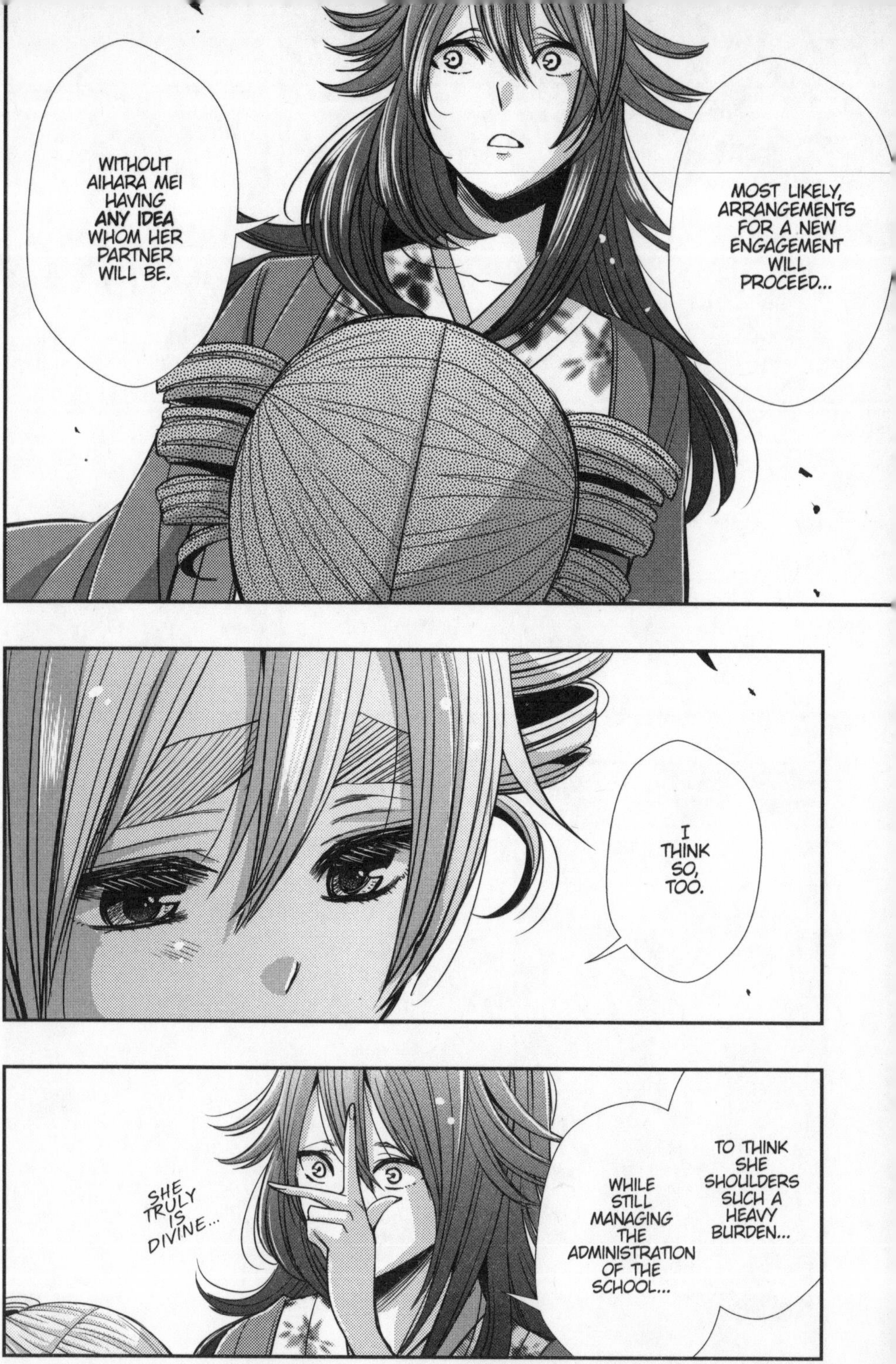
MOST LIKELY, ARRANGEMENTS FOR A NEW ENGAGEMENT WILL PROCEED...
WITHOUT AIHARA MEI HAVING ANY IDEA WHOM HER PARTNER WILL BE.
I THINK SO, TOO.
TO THINK SHE SHOULDERS SUCH A HEAVY BURDEN...
WHILE STILL MANAGING THE ADMINISTRATION OF THE SCHOOL...
SHE TRULY IS DIVINE...

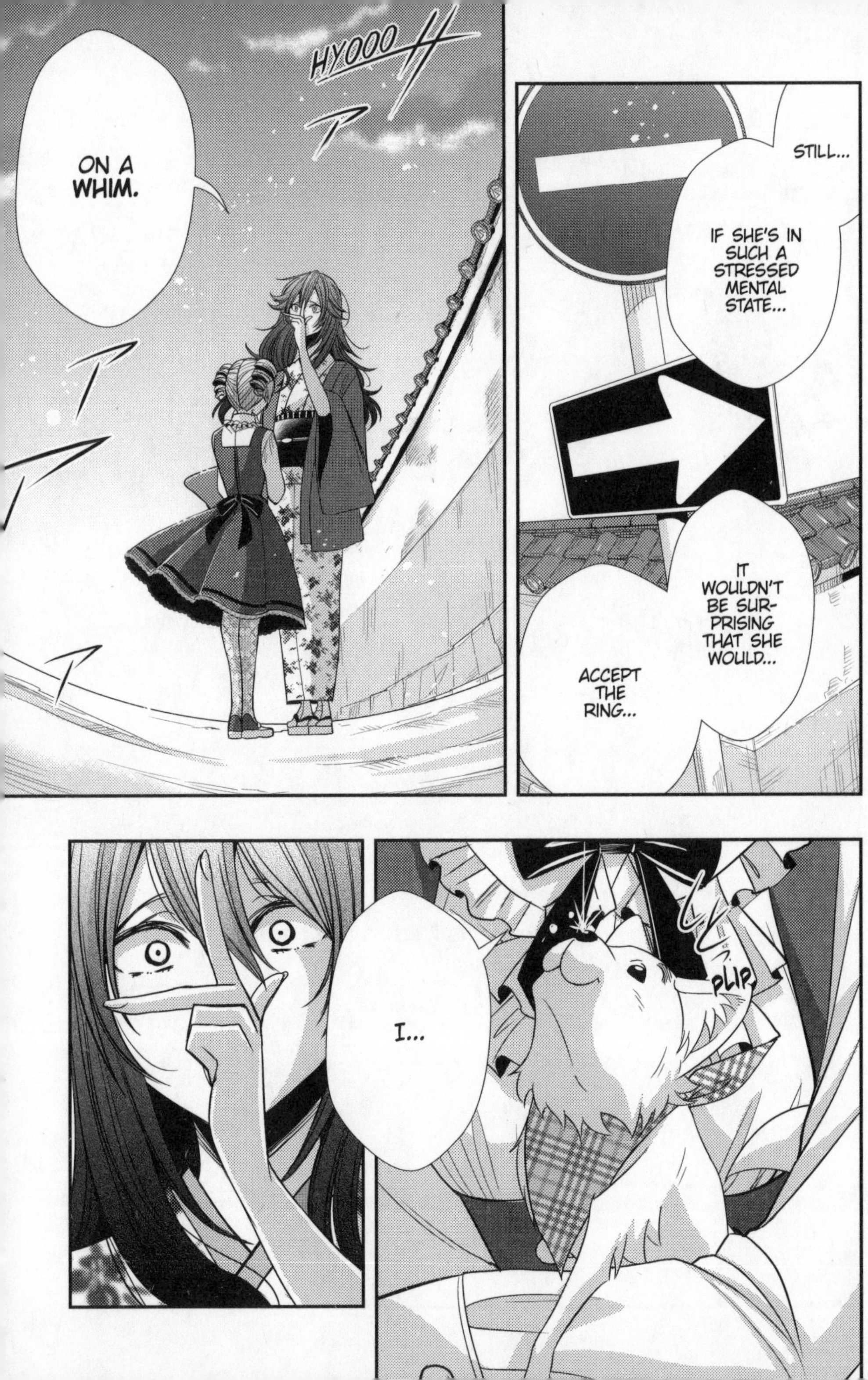
STILL...
IF SHE'S IN SUCH A STRESSED MENTAL STATE...
IT WOULDN'T BE SURPRISING THAT SHE WOULD...
ACCEPT THE RING...
HYOOOH
ON A WHIM.
PLIP
I...

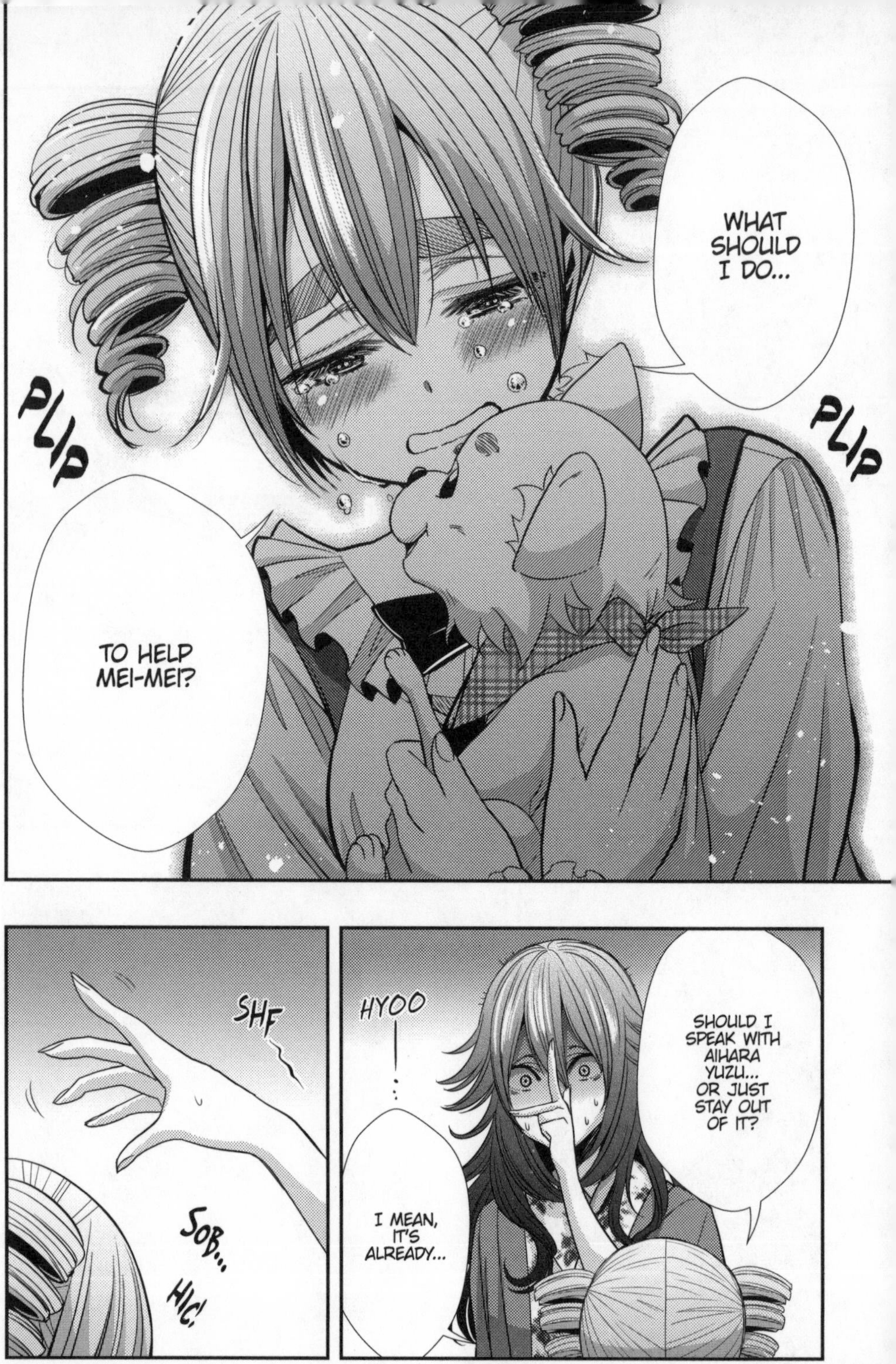

WHAT SHOULD I DO...
PLIP
PLIP
TO HELP MEI-MEI?
SHOULD I SPEAK WITH AIHARA YUZU... OR JUST STAY OUT OF IT?
HYOO
I MEAN, IT'S ALREADY...
SHF
SOB...
HIC!

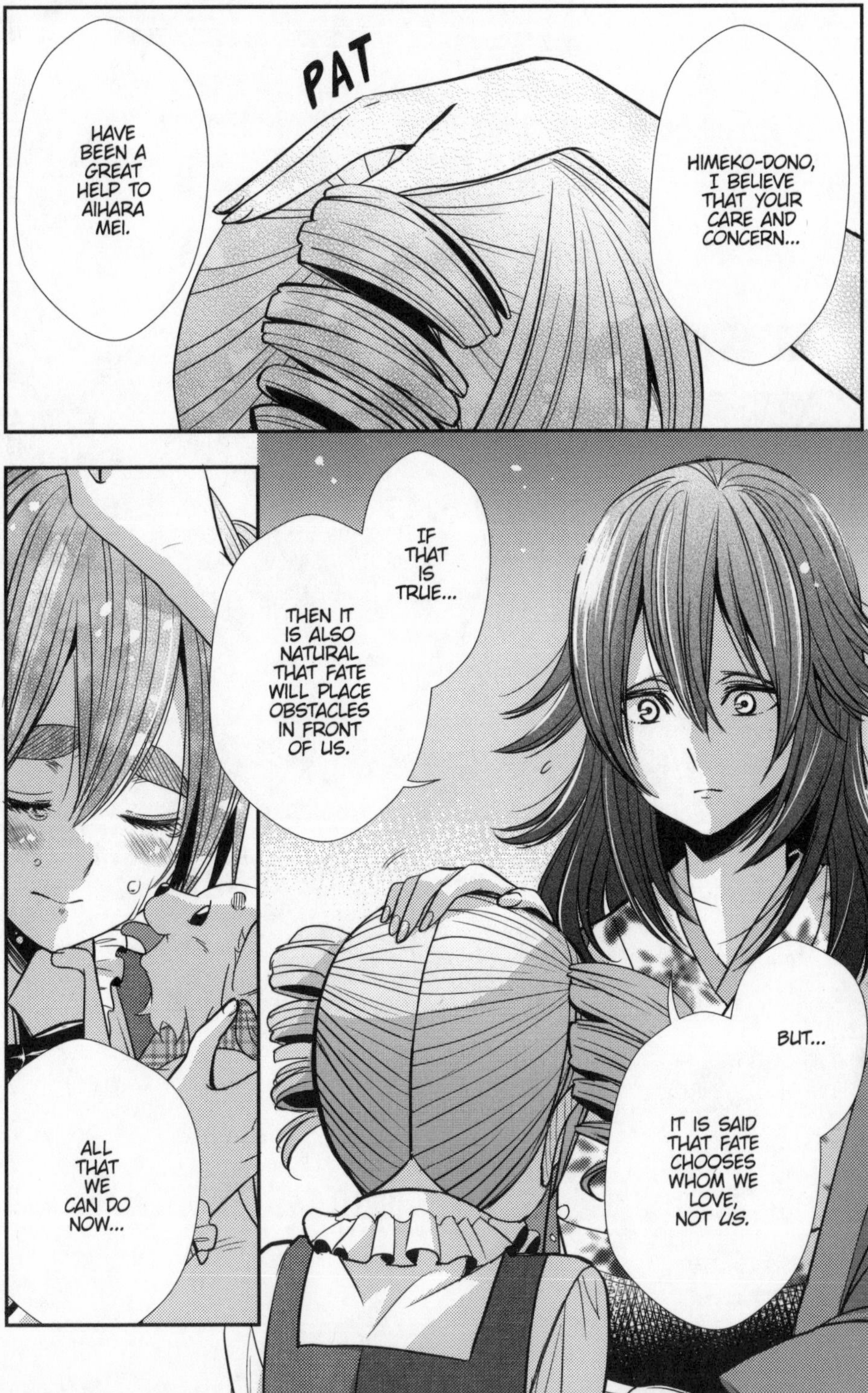
HIMEKO-DONO, I BELIEVE THAT YOUR CARE AND CONCERN...
PAT
HAVE BEEN A GREAT HELP TO AIHARA MEI.
BUT...
IT IS SAID THAT FATE CHOOSES WHOM WE LOVE, NOT US.
IF THAT IS TRUE...
THEN IT IS ALSO NATURAL THAT FATE WILL PLACE OBSTACLES IN FRONT OF US.
ALL THAT WE CAN DO NOW...

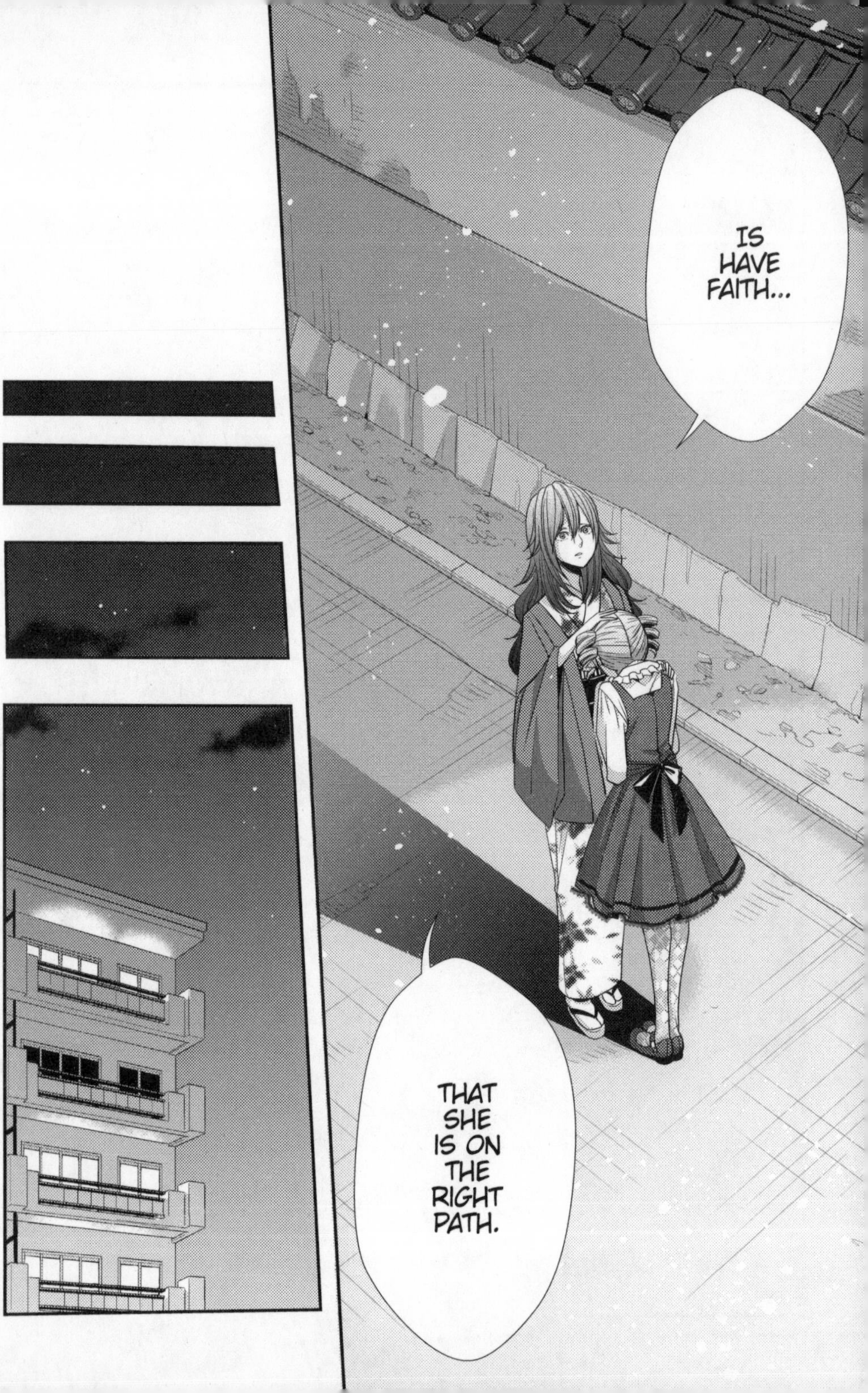
IS HAVE FAITH...
THAT SHE IS ON THE RIGHT PATH.

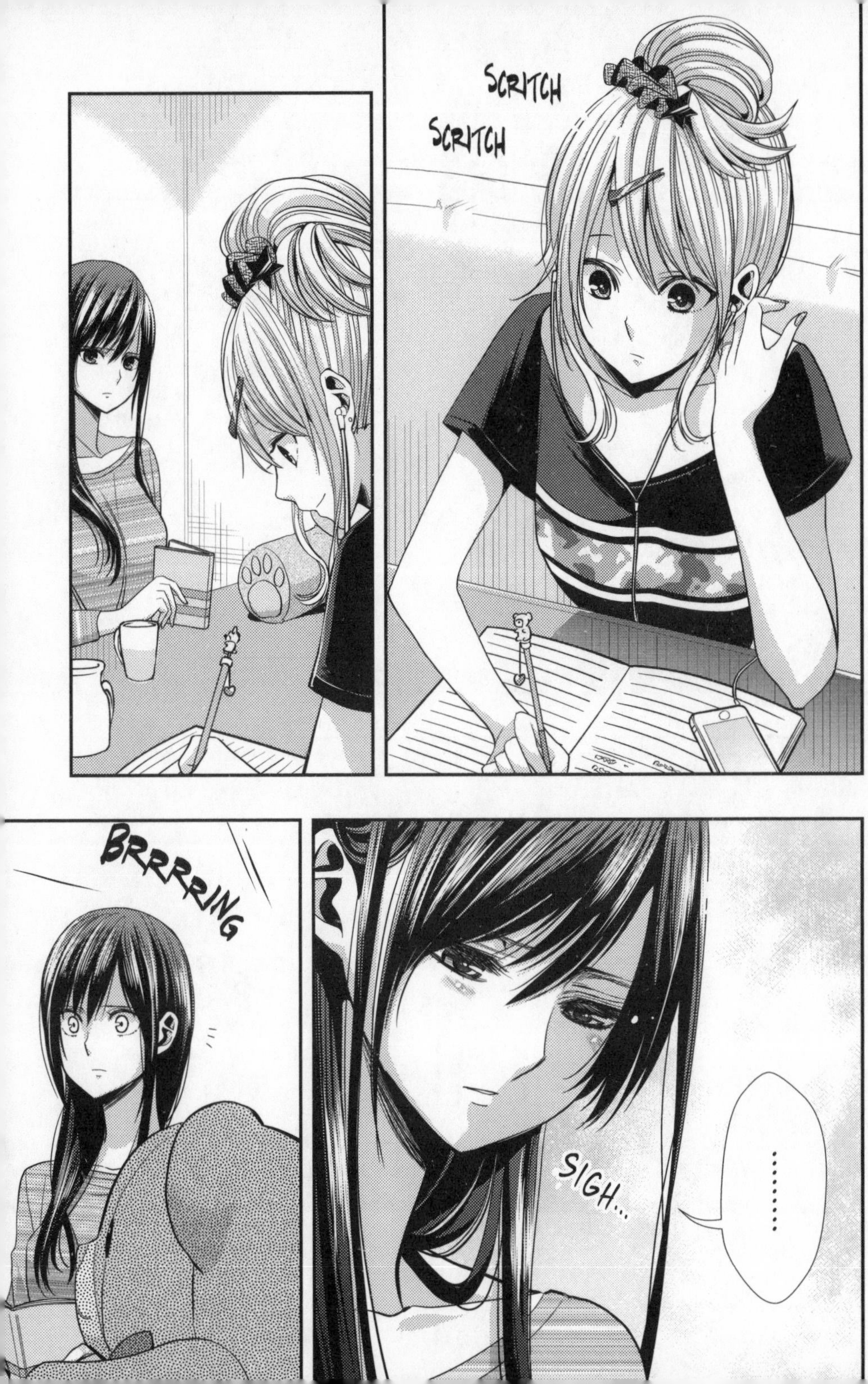
SCRITCH
SCRITCH
SIGH...
....
BRRRRING

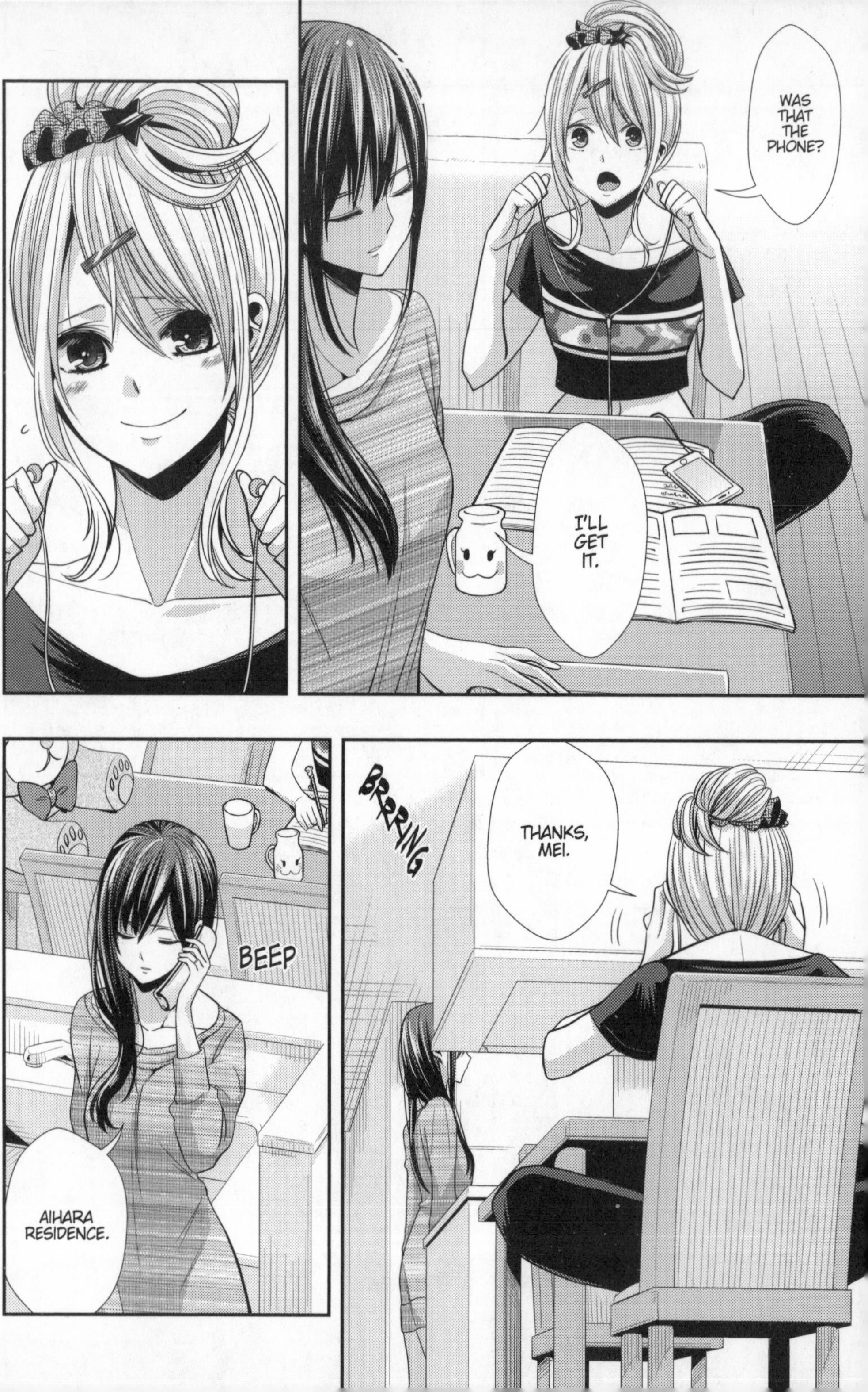
WAS THAT THE PHONE?
I'LL GET IT.
BRRRING
THANKS, MEI.
BEEP
AIHARA RESIDENCE.

GRAND-
FATHER?

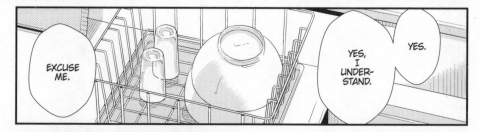

EXCUSE
ME.

YES,
I
UNDER-
STAND.

YES.

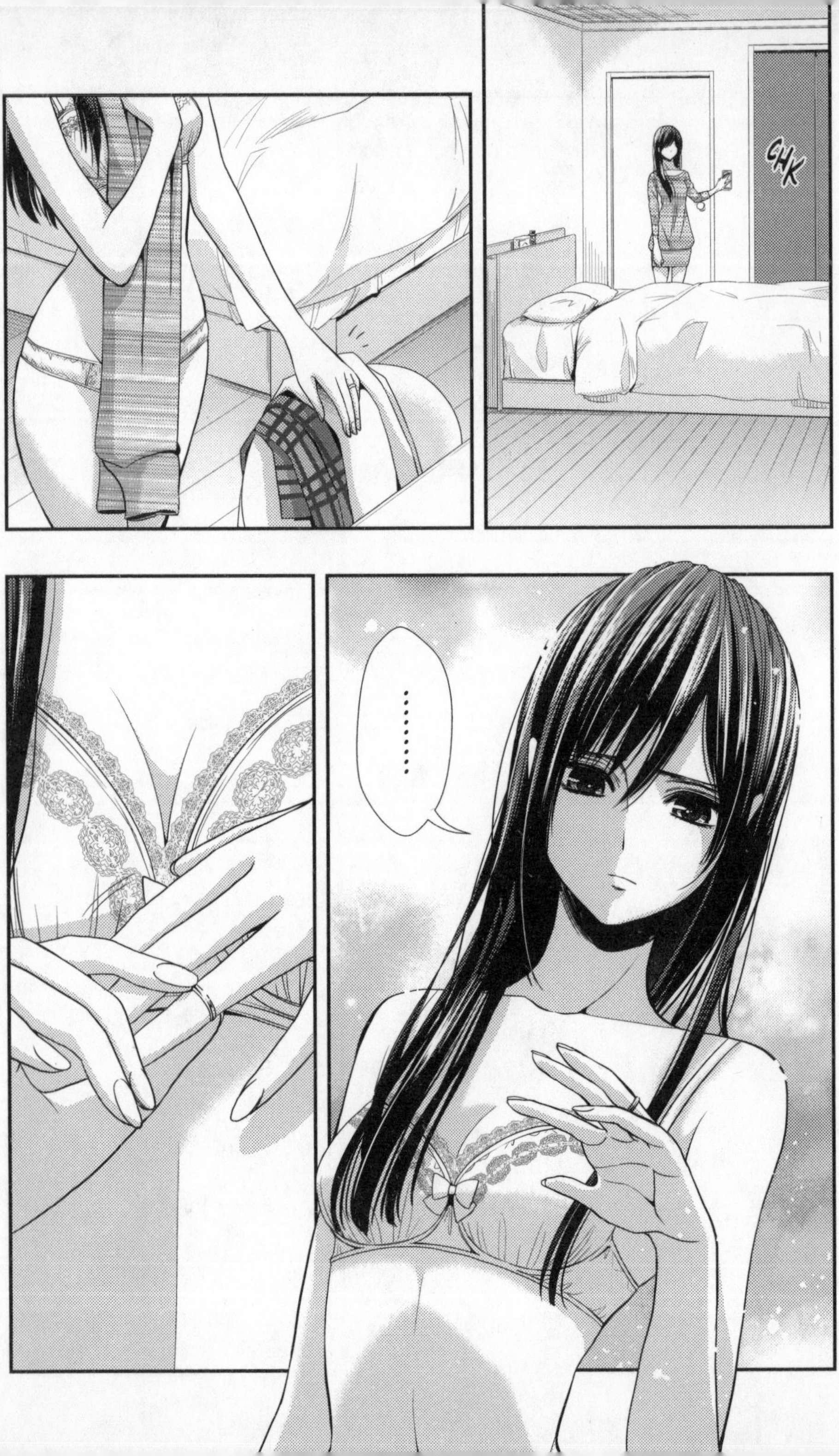
CHK
......

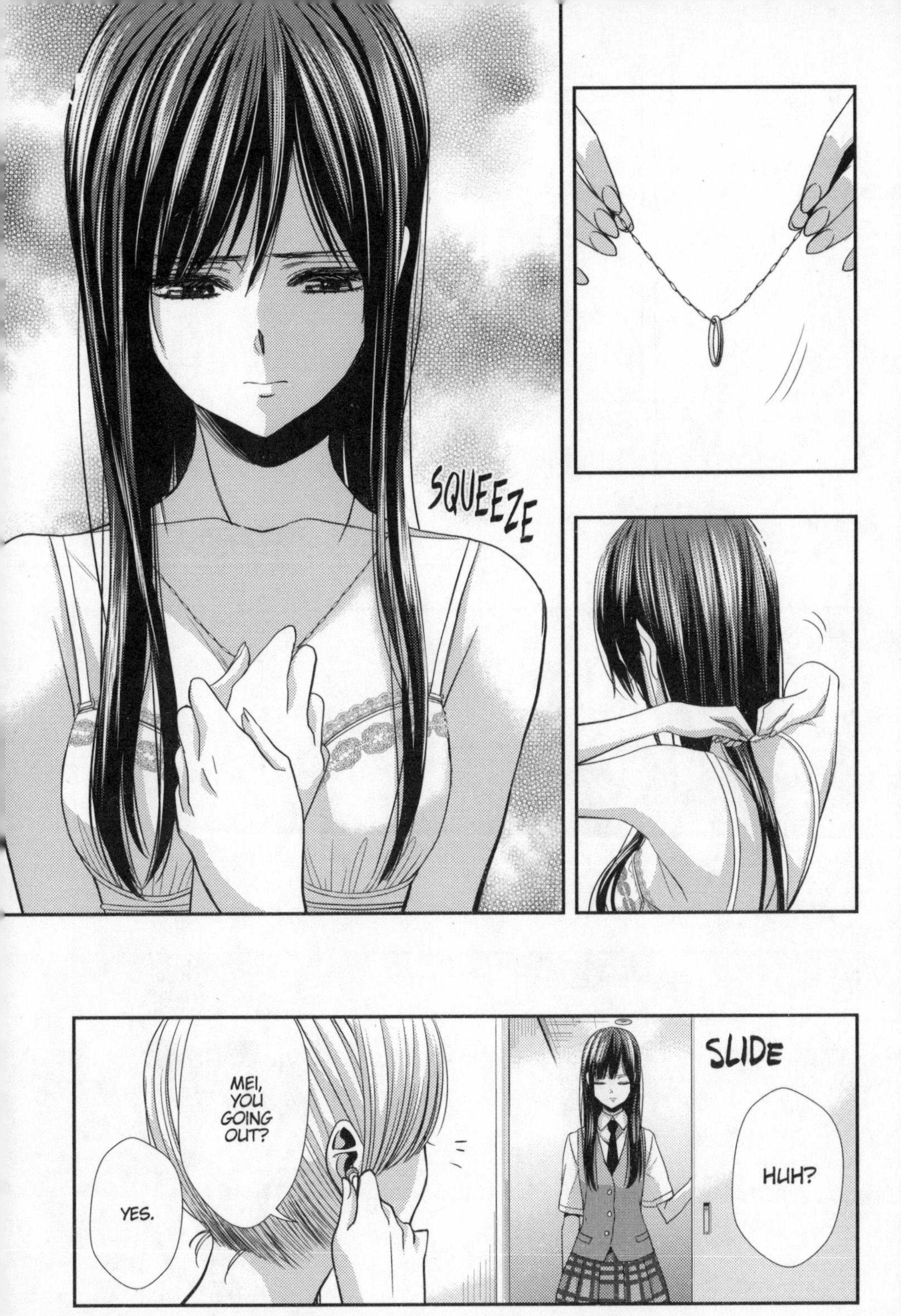
SQUEEZE
SLIDE
HUH?
MEI, YOU GOING OUT?
YES.

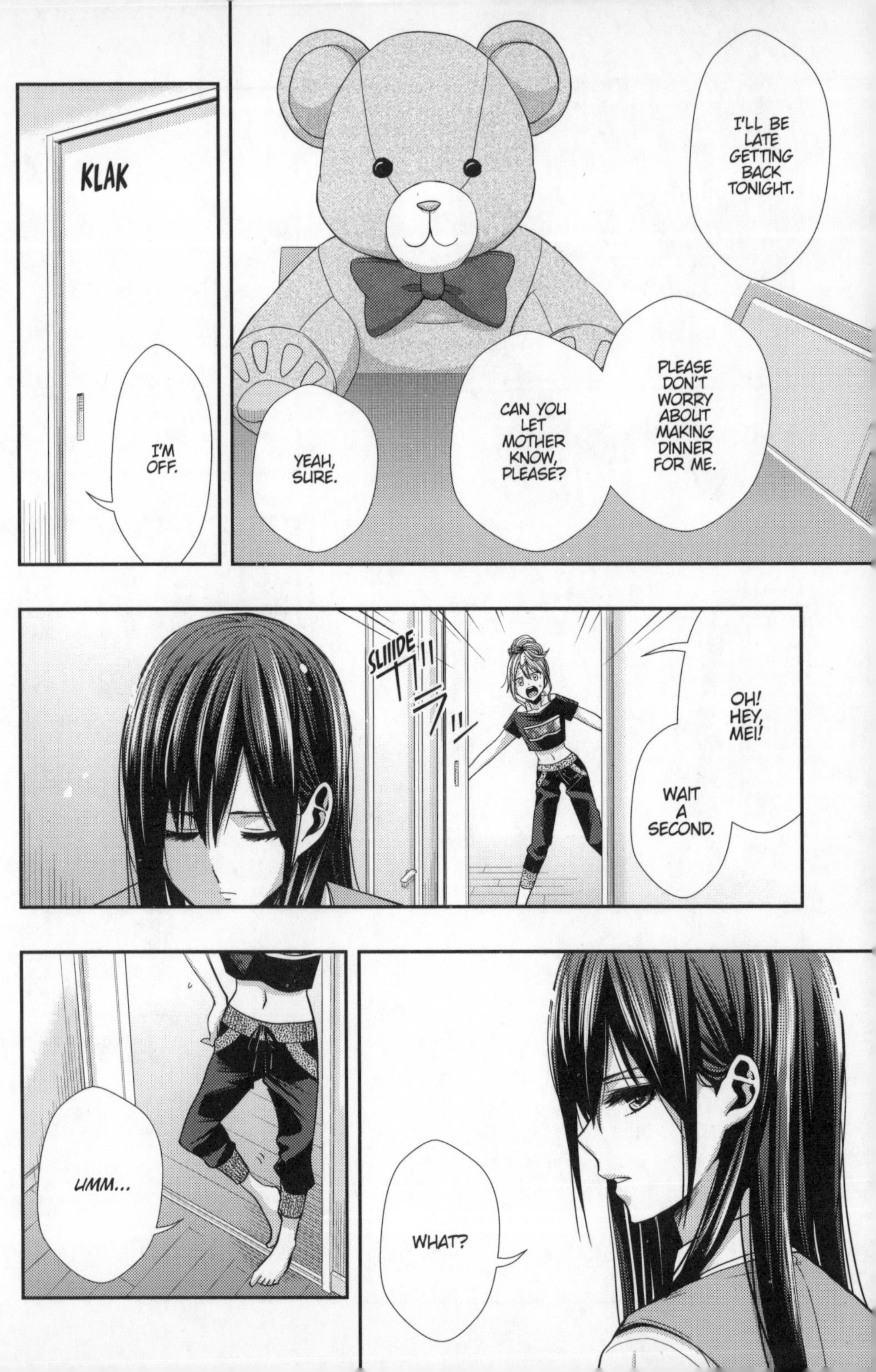
I'LL BE LATE GETTING BACK TONIGHT.
PLEASE DON'T WORRY ABOUT MAKING DINNER FOR ME.
CAN YOU LET MOTHER KNOW, PLEASE?
YEAH, SURE.
KLAK
I'M OFF.
OH! HEY, MEI!
WAIT A SECOND.
SLIIIDE
WHAT?
UMM...

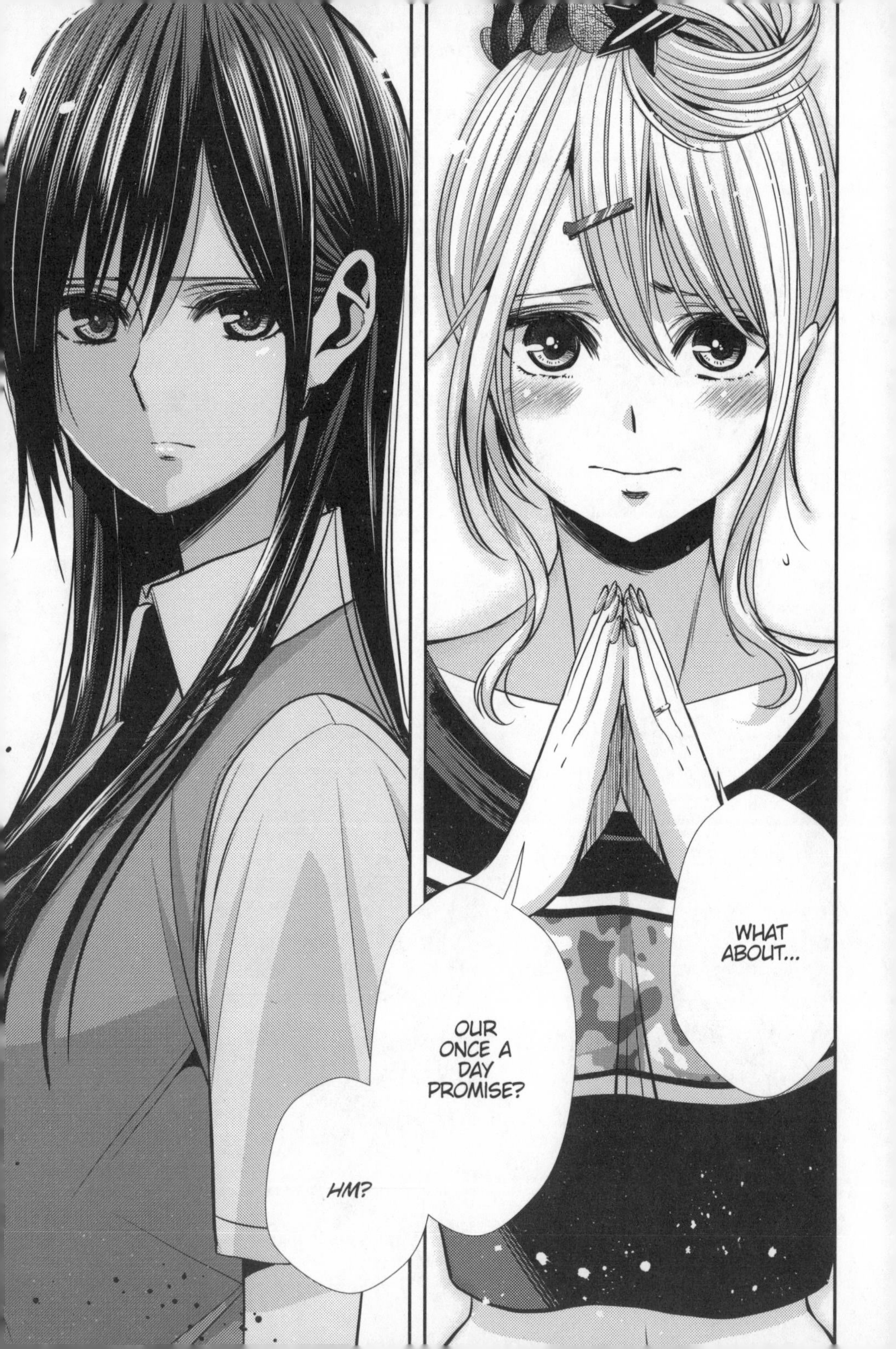
WHAT ABOUT...
OUR ONCE A DAY PROMISE?
HM?

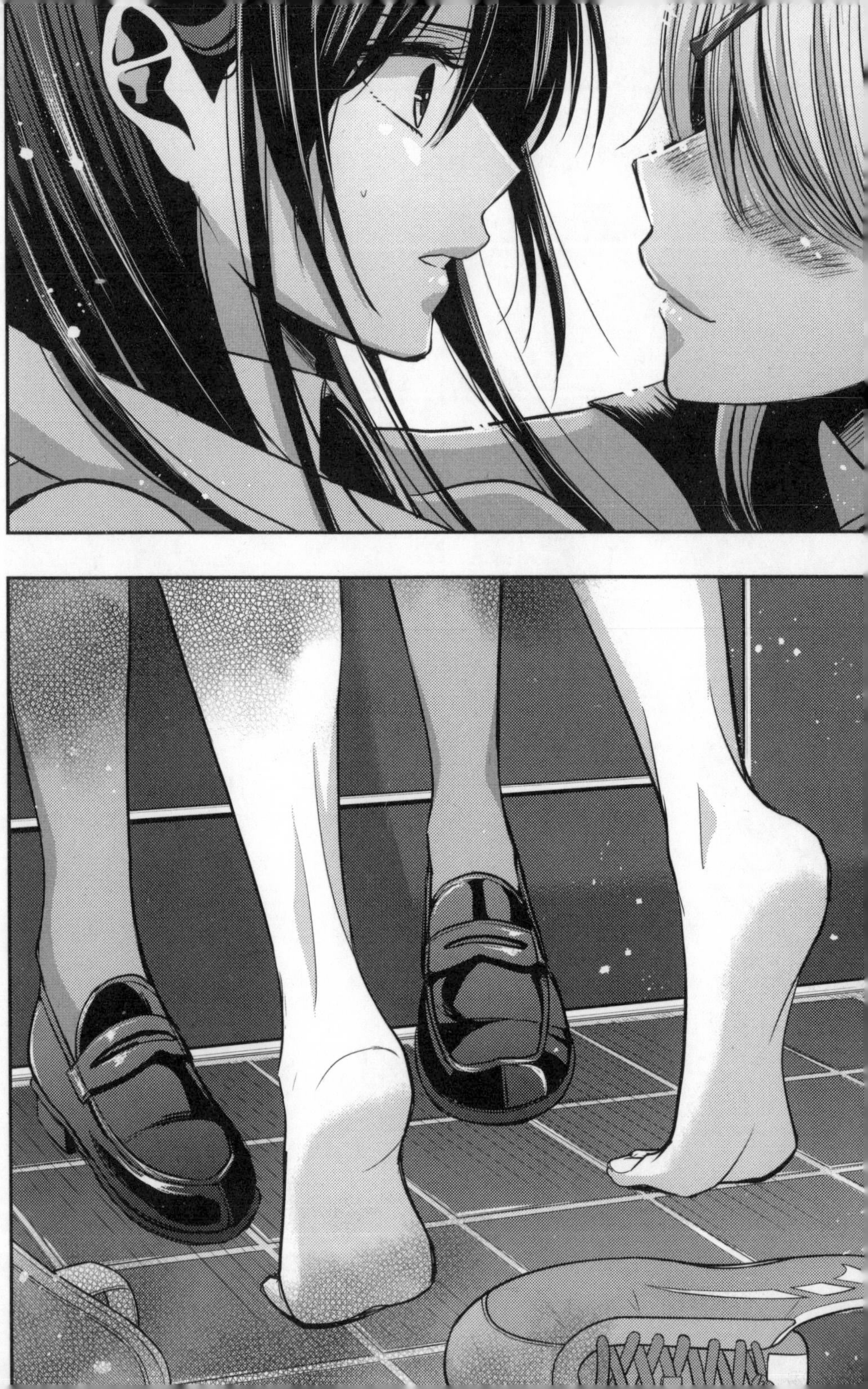

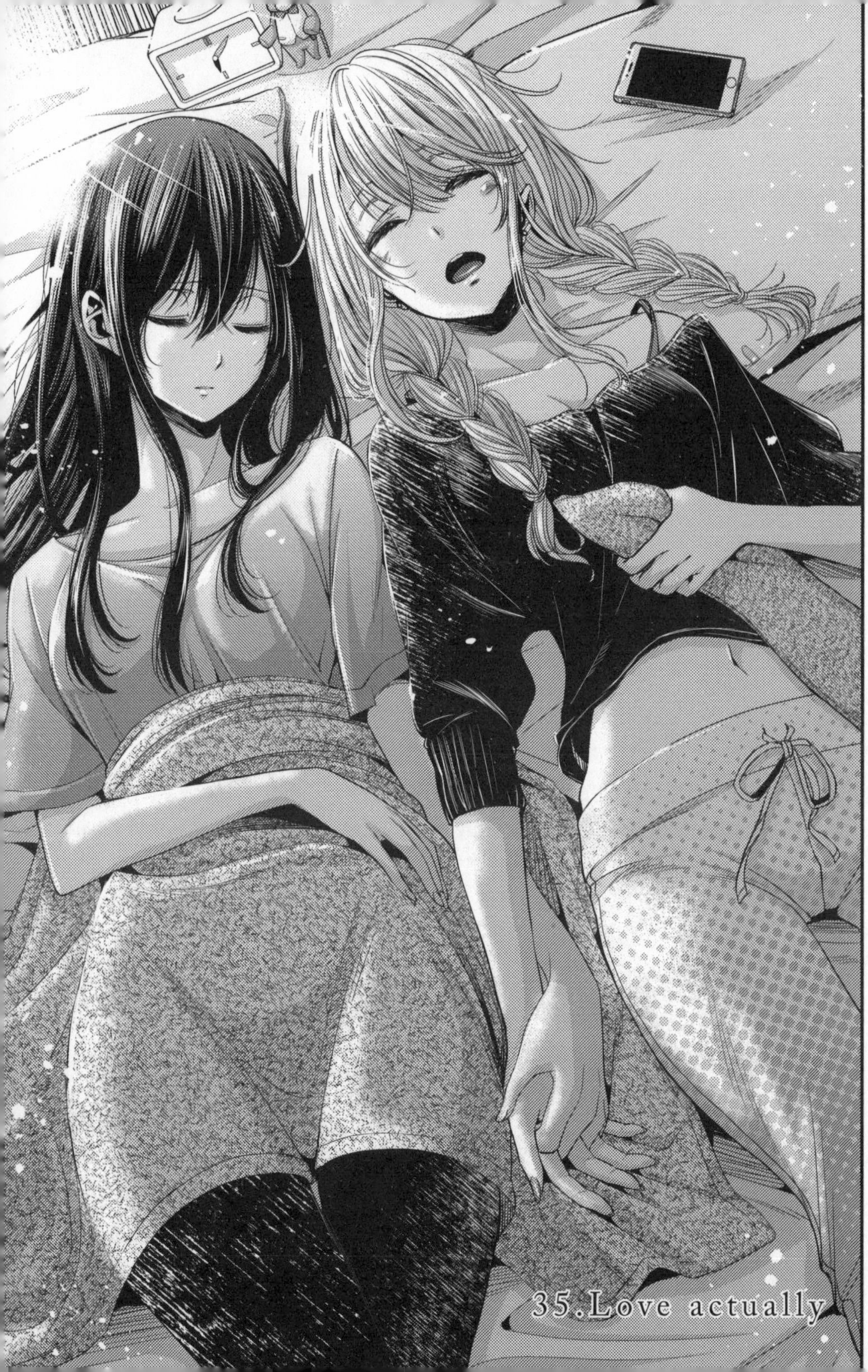
35. Love actually

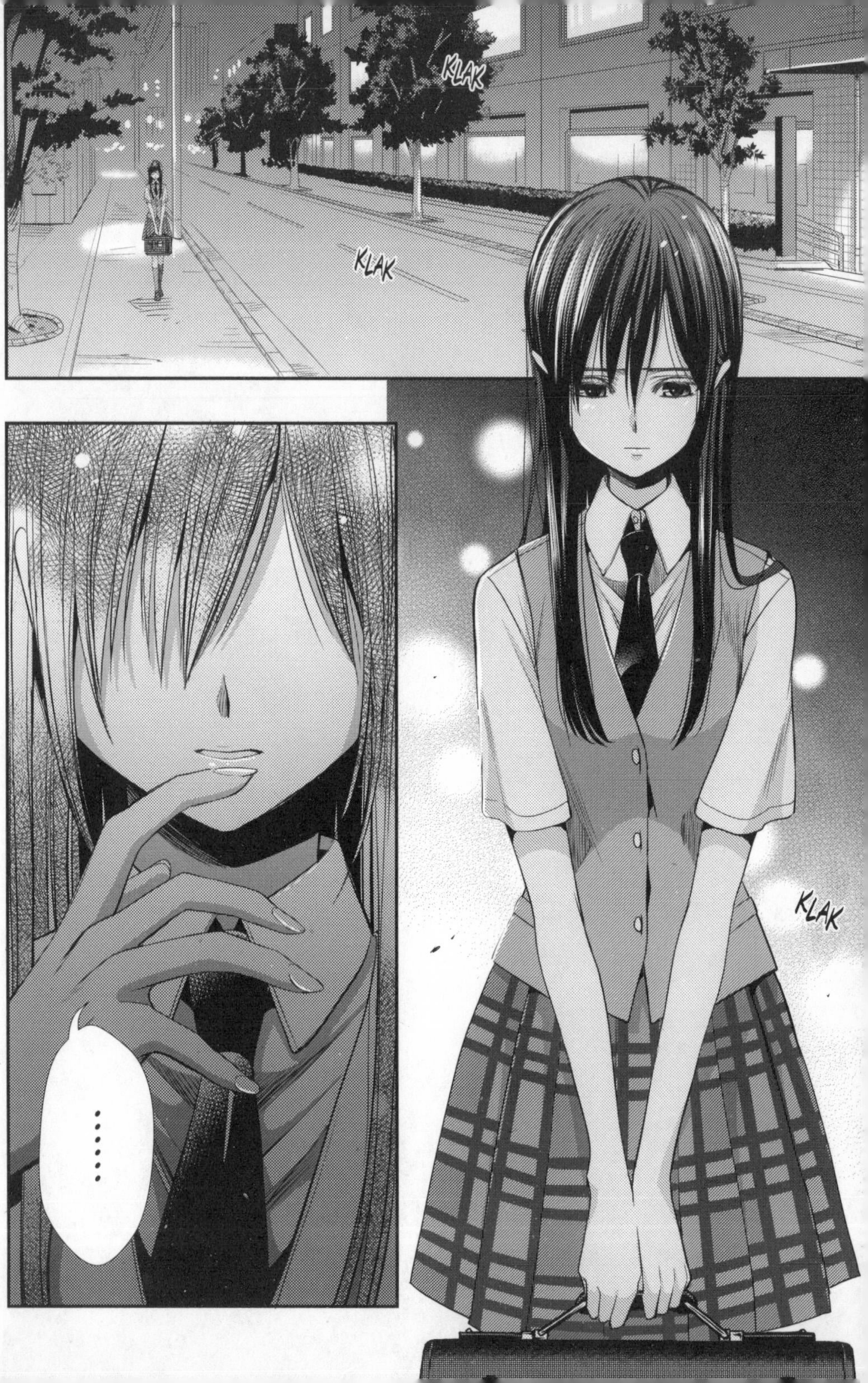
KLAK
KLAK
KLAK
......

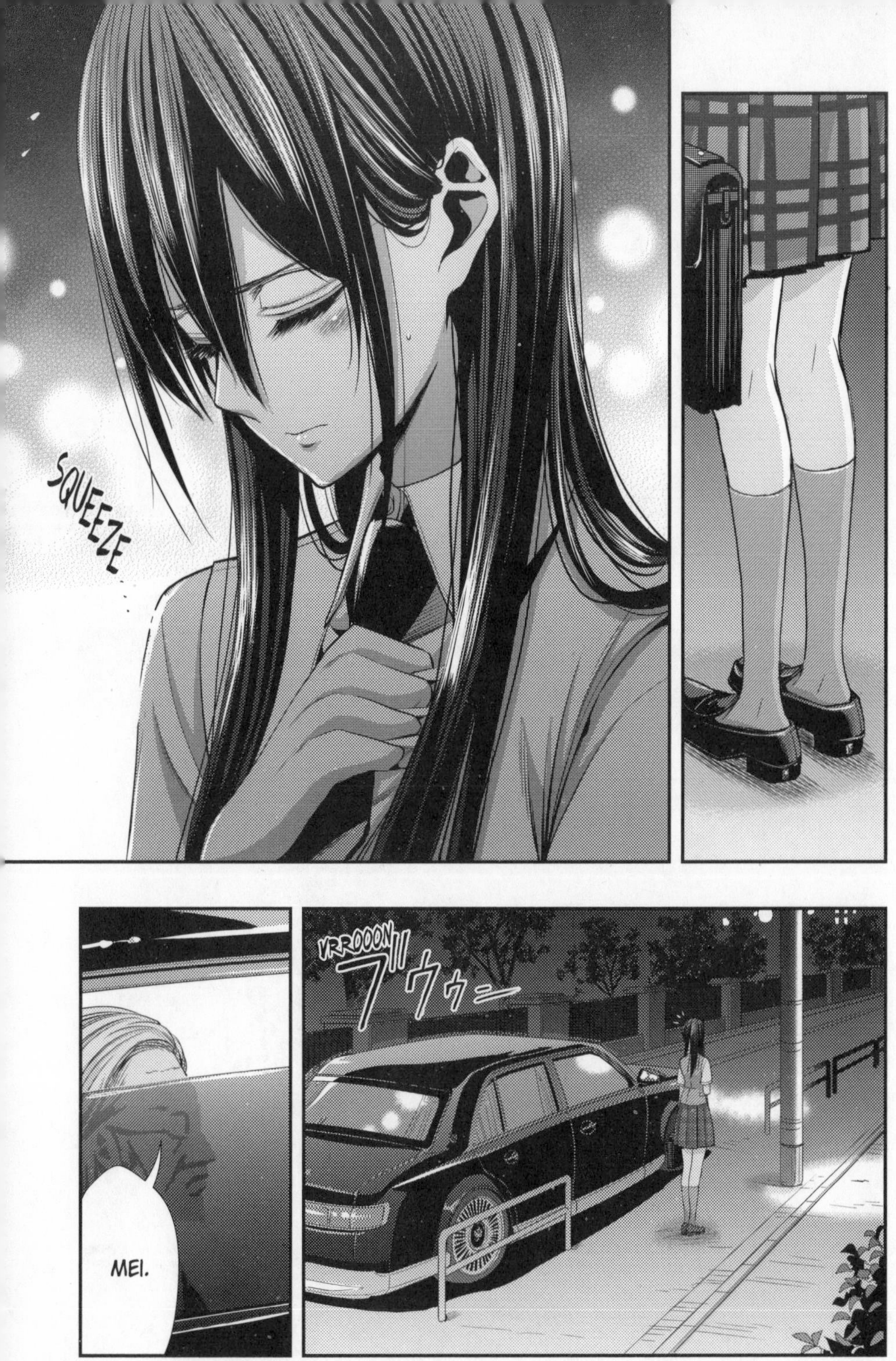
SQUEEZE
VRROOON
ブウゥ—
MEI.

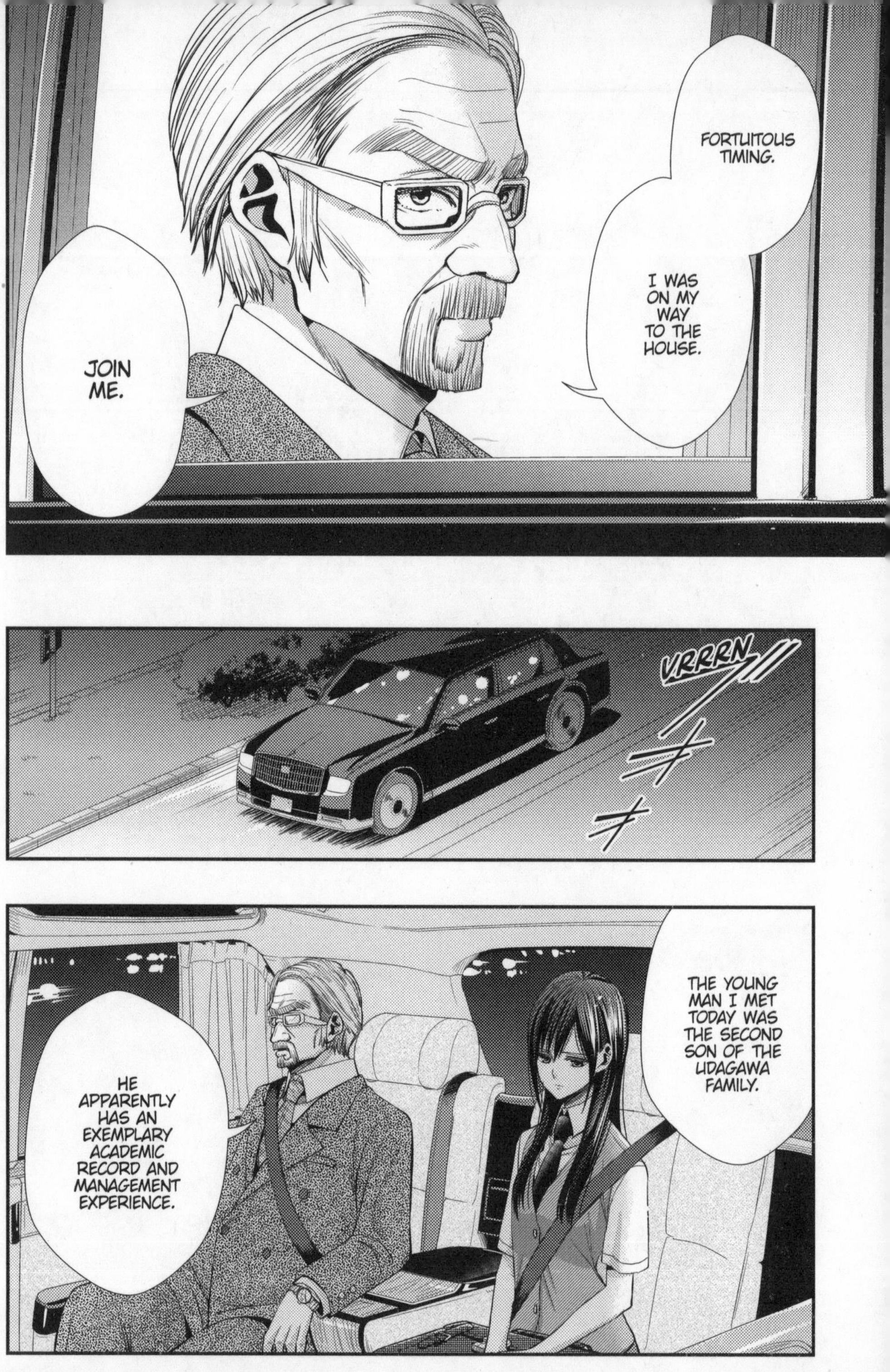
FORTUITOUS TIMING.
I WAS ON MY WAY TO THE HOUSE.
JOIN ME.
VRRRN
THE YOUNG MAN I MET TODAY WAS THE SECOND SON OF THE UDAGAWA FAMILY.
HE APPARENTLY HAS AN EXEMPLARY ACADEMIC RECORD AND MANAGEMENT EXPERIENCE.

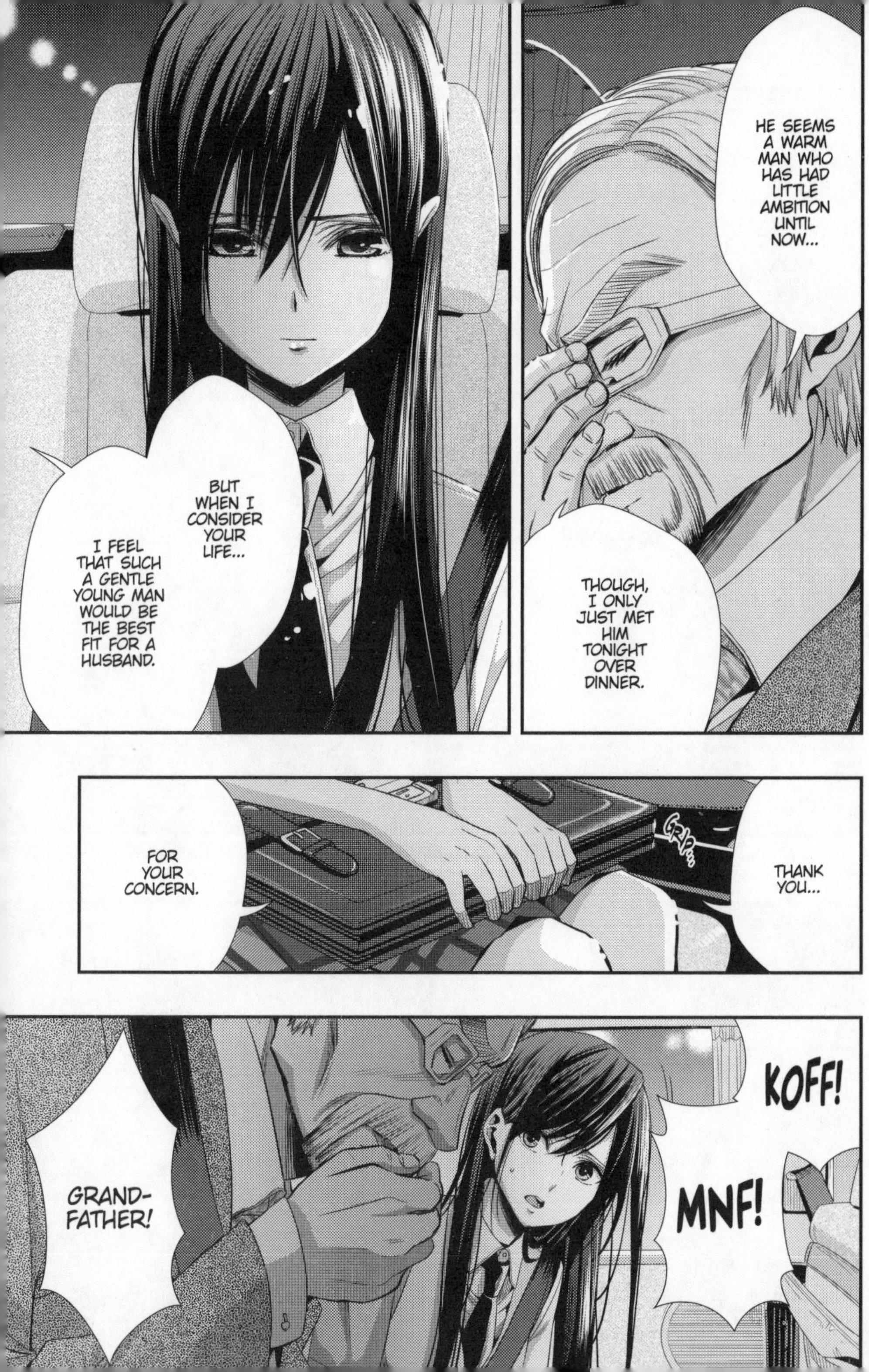
HE SEEMS A WARM MAN WHO HAS HAD LITTLE AMBITION UNTIL NOW...
THOUGH, I ONLY JUST MET HIM TONIGHT OVER DINNER.
BUT WHEN I CONSIDER YOUR LIFE...
I FEEL THAT SUCH A GENTLE YOUNG MAN WOULD BE THE BEST FIT FOR A HUSBAND.
THANK YOU...
GRIP...
FOR YOUR CONCERN.
KOFF!
MNF!
GRAND-FATHER!

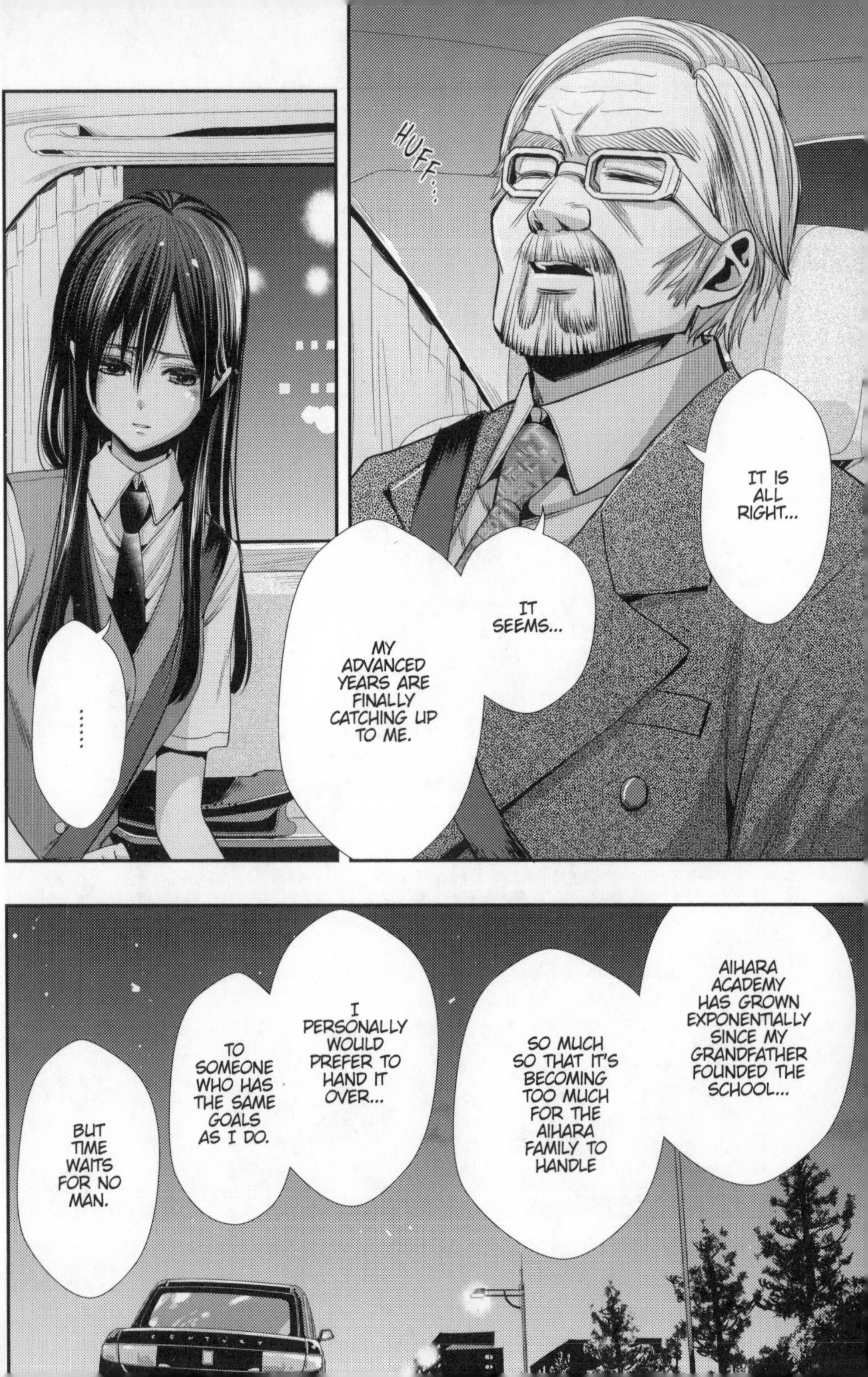
HUFF...
IT IS ALL RIGHT...
IT SEEMS...
MY ADVANCED YEARS ARE FINALLY CATCHING UP TO ME.
......
AIHARA ACADEMY HAS GROWN EXPONENTIALLY SINCE MY GRANDFATHER FOUNDED THE SCHOOL...
SO MUCH SO THAT IT'S BECOMING TOO MUCH FOR THE AIHARA FAMILY TO HANDLE
I PERSONALLY WOULD PREFER TO HAND IT OVER...
TO SOMEONE WHO HAS THE SAME GOALS AS I DO.
BUT TIME WAITS FOR NO MAN.

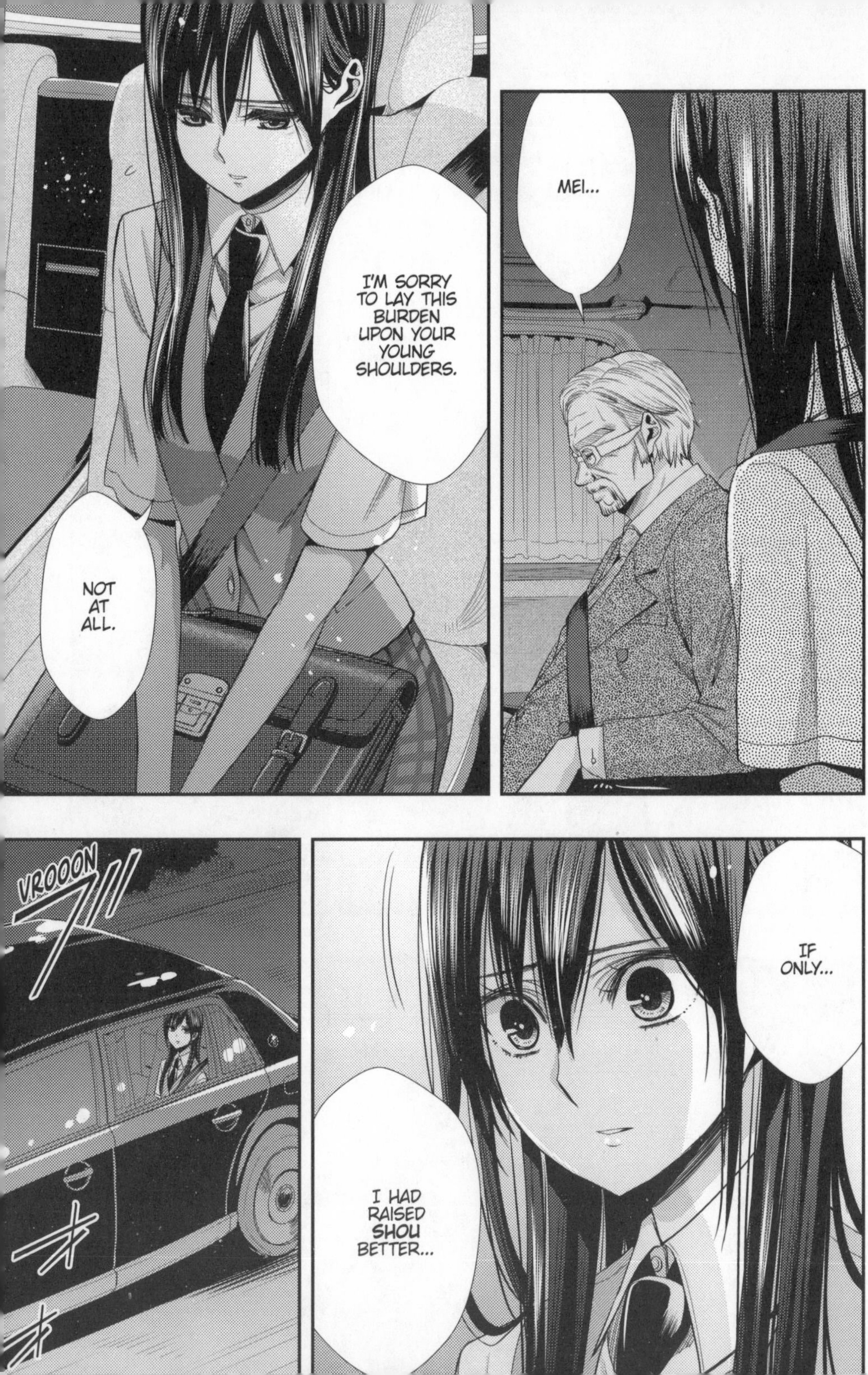
MEI...
I'M SORRY TO LAY THIS BURDEN UPON YOUR YOUNG SHOULDERS.
NOT AT ALL.
IF ONLY...
I HAD RAISED SHOU BETTER...
VROOON

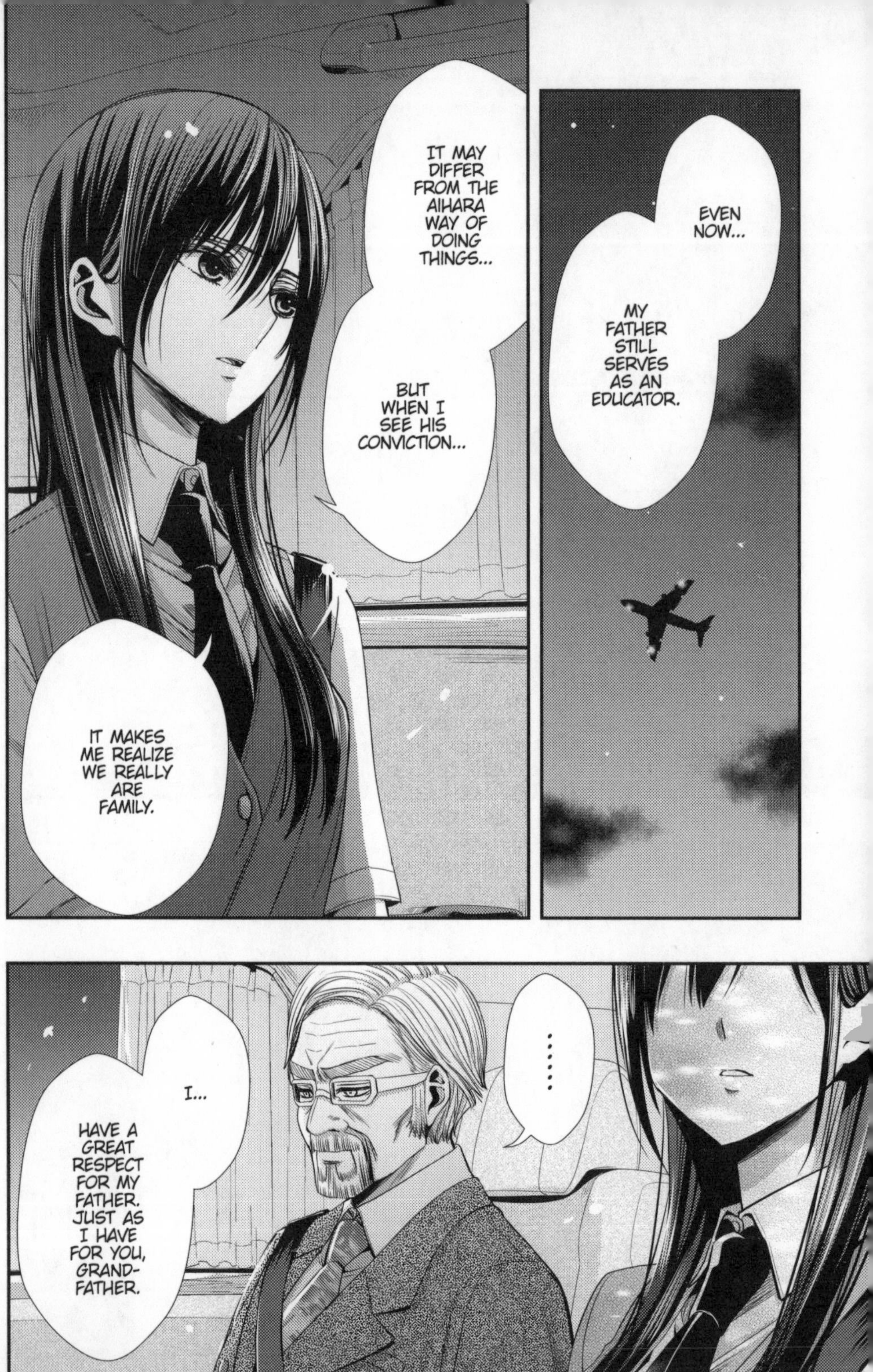
EVEN NOW...
MY FATHER STILL SERVES AS AN EDUCATOR.
IT MAY DIFFER FROM THE AIHARA WAY OF DOING THINGS...
BUT WHEN I SEE HIS CONVICTION...
IT MAKES ME REALIZE WE REALLY ARE FAMILY.
......
I...
HAVE A GREAT RESPECT FOR MY FATHER. JUST AS I HAVE FOR YOU, GRAND-FATHER.

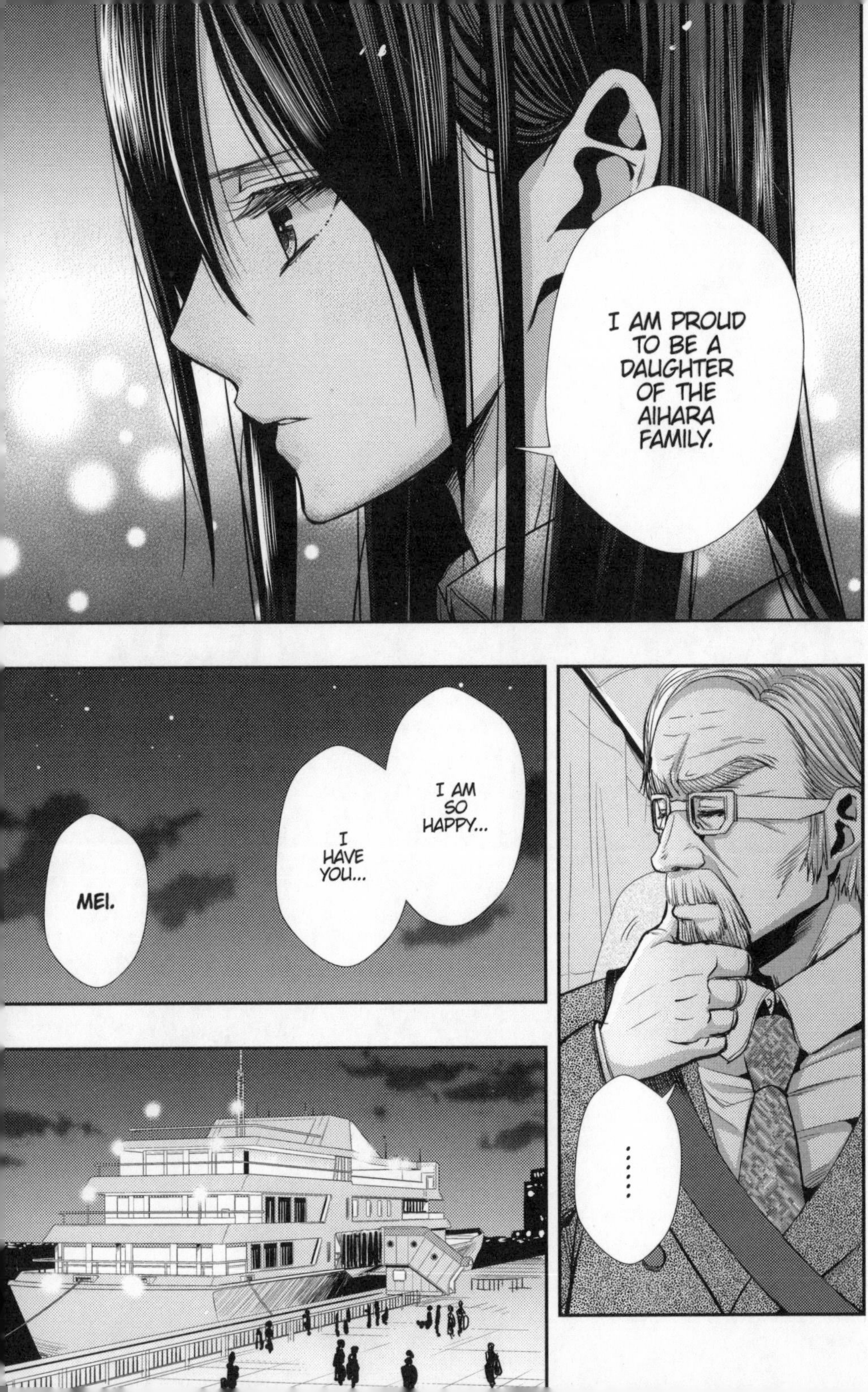
I AM PROUD TO BE A DAUGHTER OF THE AIHARA FAMILY.
......
I AM SO HAPPY...
I HAVE YOU...
MEI.

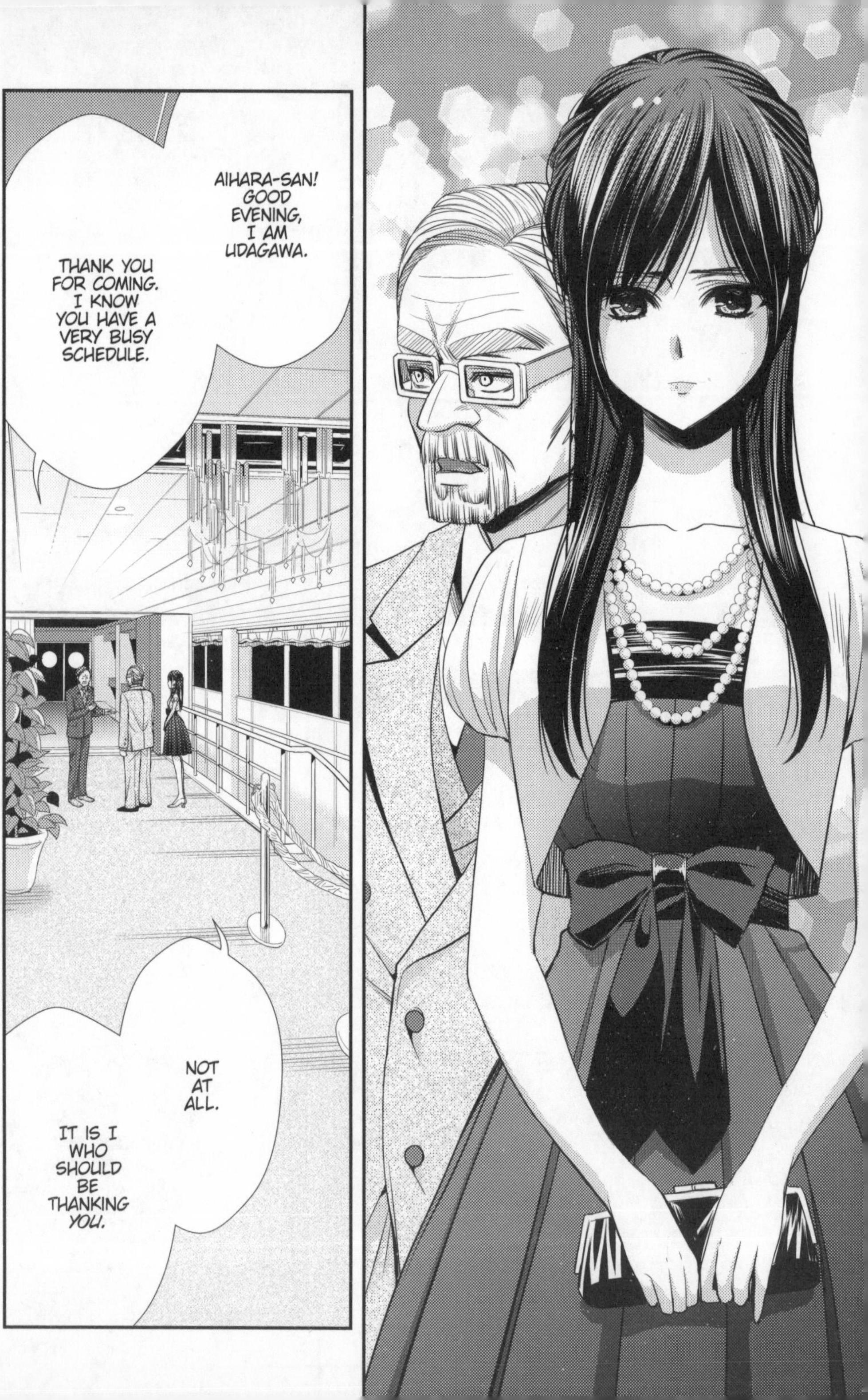
AIHARA-SAN! GOOD EVENING, I AM UDAGAWA.
THANK YOU FOR COMING. I KNOW YOU HAVE A VERY BUSY SCHEDULE.
NOT AT ALL.
IT IS I WHO SHOULD BE THANKING *YOU*.

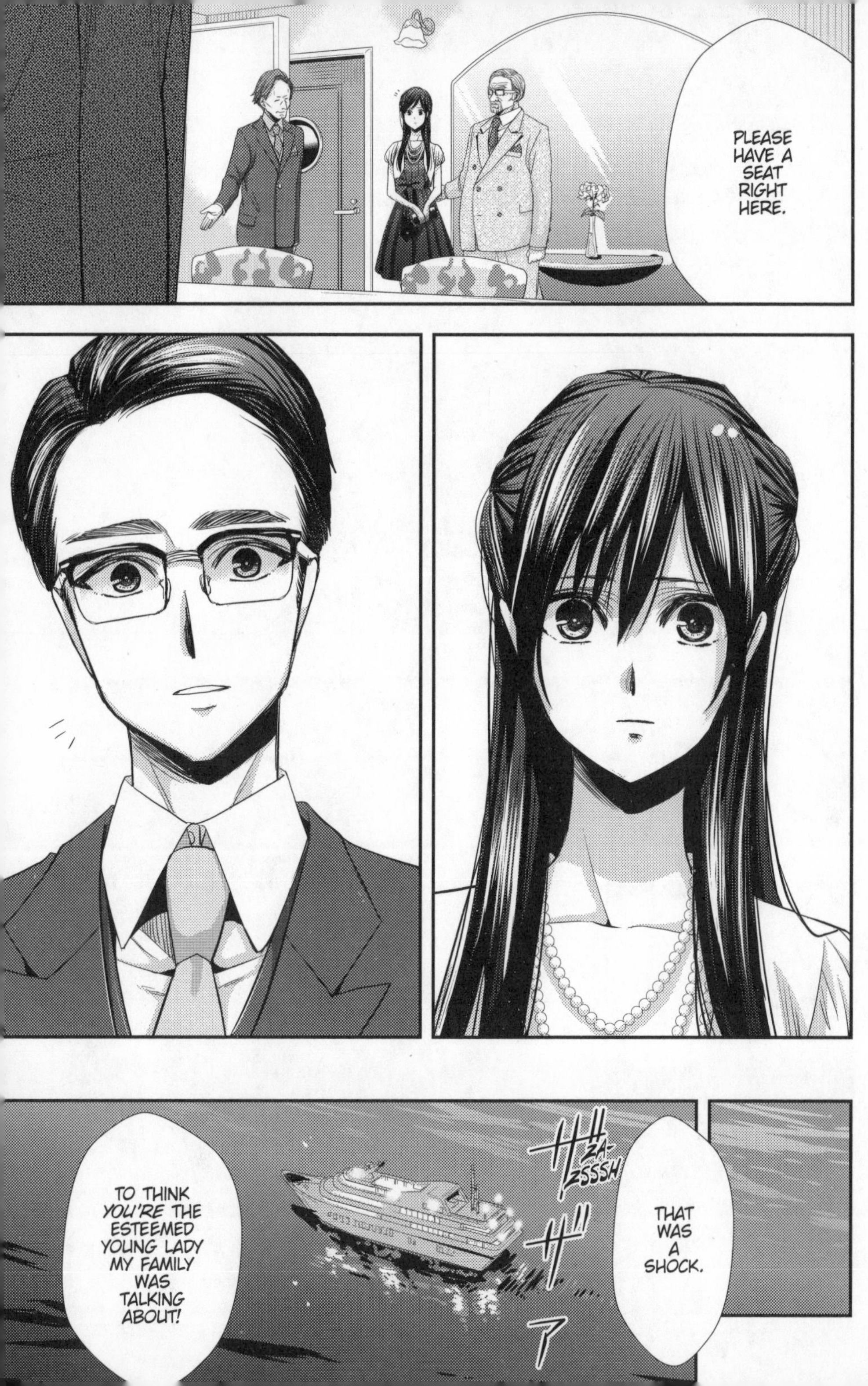
PLEASE HAVE A SEAT RIGHT HERE.
ZA-ZSSSH
THAT WAS A SHOCK.
TO THINK YOU'RE THE ESTEEMED YOUNG LADY MY FAMILY WAS TALKING ABOUT!

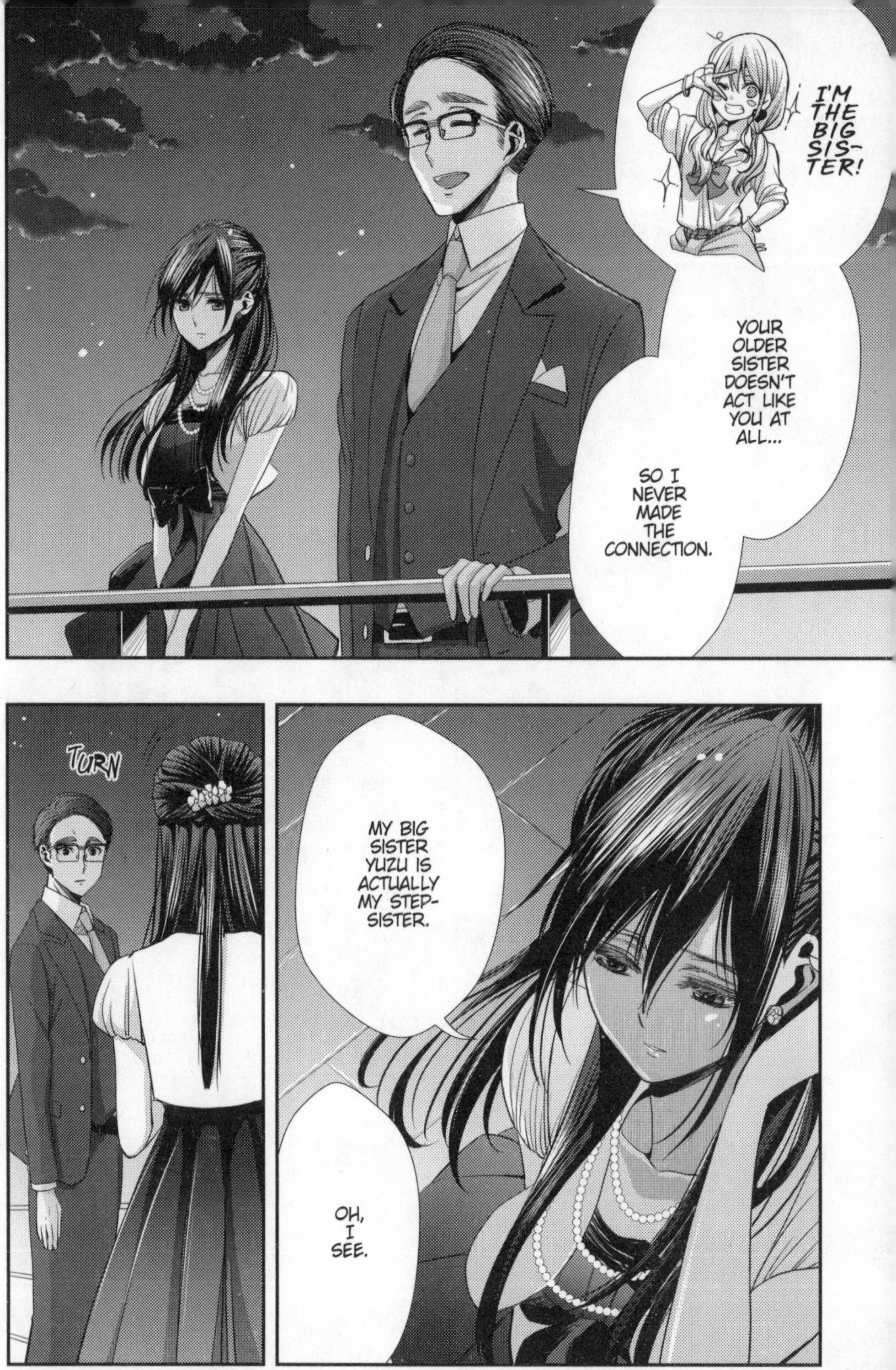
I'M THE BIG SIS-TER!
YOUR OLDER SISTER DOESN'T ACT LIKE YOU AT ALL...
SO I NEVER MADE THE CONNECTION.
MY BIG SISTER YUZU IS ACTUALLY MY STEP-SISTER.
OH, I SEE.
TURN

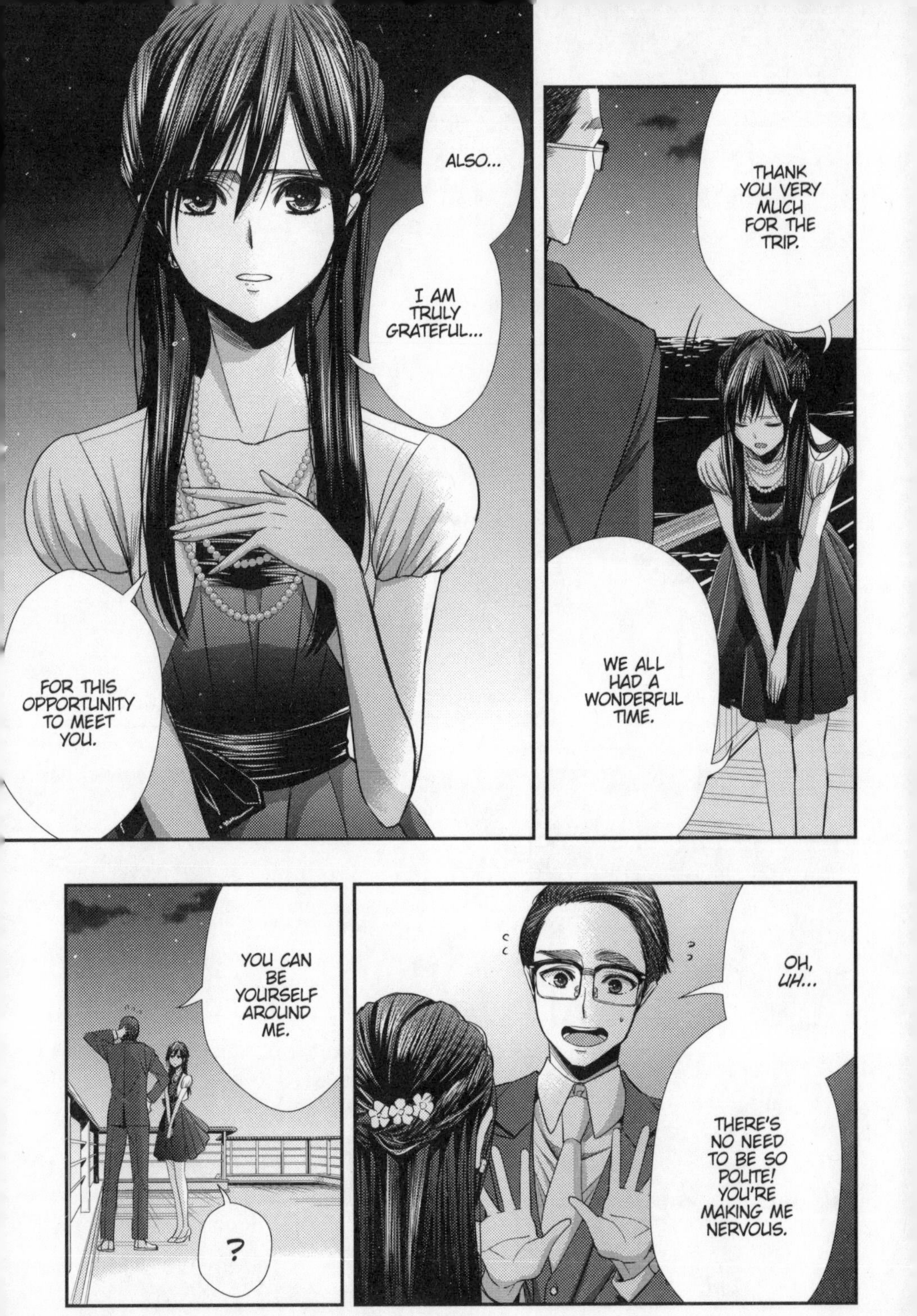
THANK YOU VERY MUCH FOR THE TRIP.
WE ALL HAD A WONDERFUL TIME.
ALSO...
I AM TRULY GRATEFUL...
FOR THIS OPPORTUNITY TO MEET YOU.
OH, UH...
THERE'S NO NEED TO BE SO POLITE! YOU'RE MAKING ME NERVOUS.
YOU CAN BE YOURSELF AROUND ME.
?

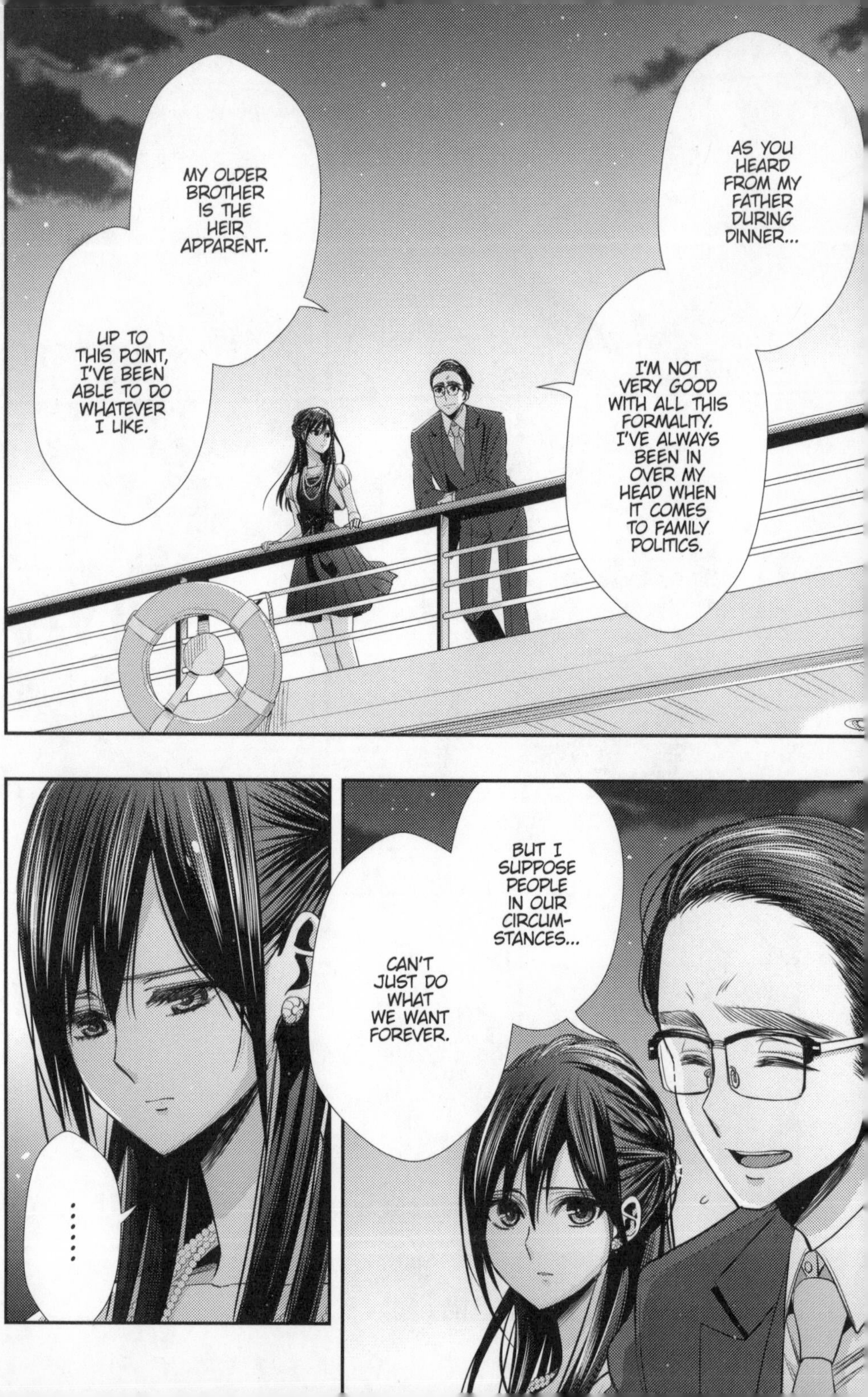
AS YOU HEARD FROM MY FATHER DURING DINNER...
I'M NOT VERY GOOD WITH ALL THIS FORMALITY. I'VE ALWAYS BEEN IN OVER MY HEAD WHEN IT COMES TO FAMILY POLITICS.
MY OLDER BROTHER IS THE HEIR APPARENT.
UP TO THIS POINT, I'VE BEEN ABLE TO DO WHATEVER I LIKE.
BUT I SUPPOSE PEOPLE IN OUR CIRCUM-STANCES...
CAN'T JUST DO WHAT WE WANT FOREVER.
......

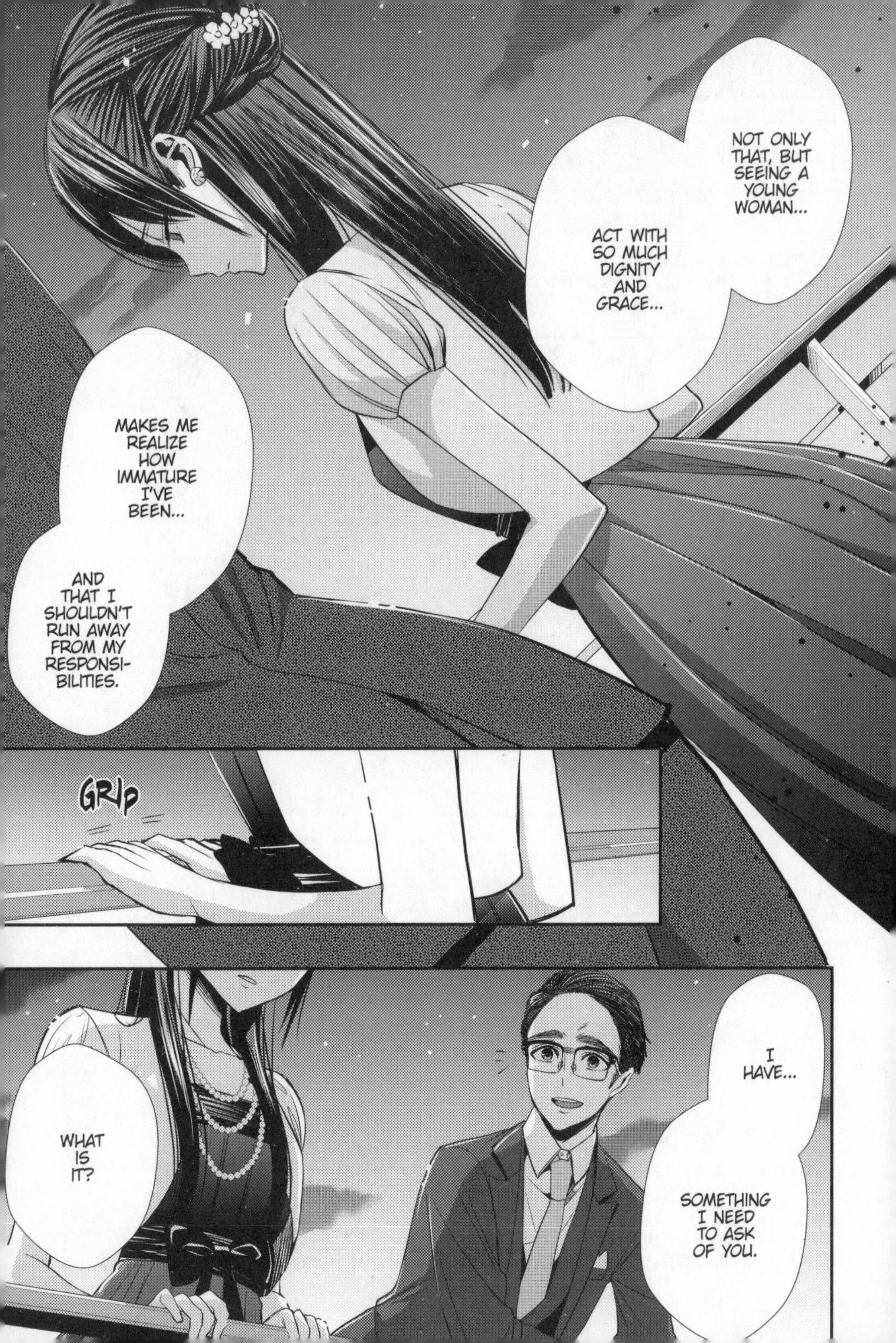
NOT ONLY THAT, BUT SEEING A YOUNG WOMAN...
ACT WITH SO MUCH DIGNITY AND GRACE...
MAKES ME REALIZE HOW IMMATURE I'VE BEEN...
AND THAT I SHOULDN'T RUN AWAY FROM MY RESPONSI-BILITIES.
GRIP
I HAVE...
SOMETHING I NEED TO ASK OF YOU.
WHAT IS IT?

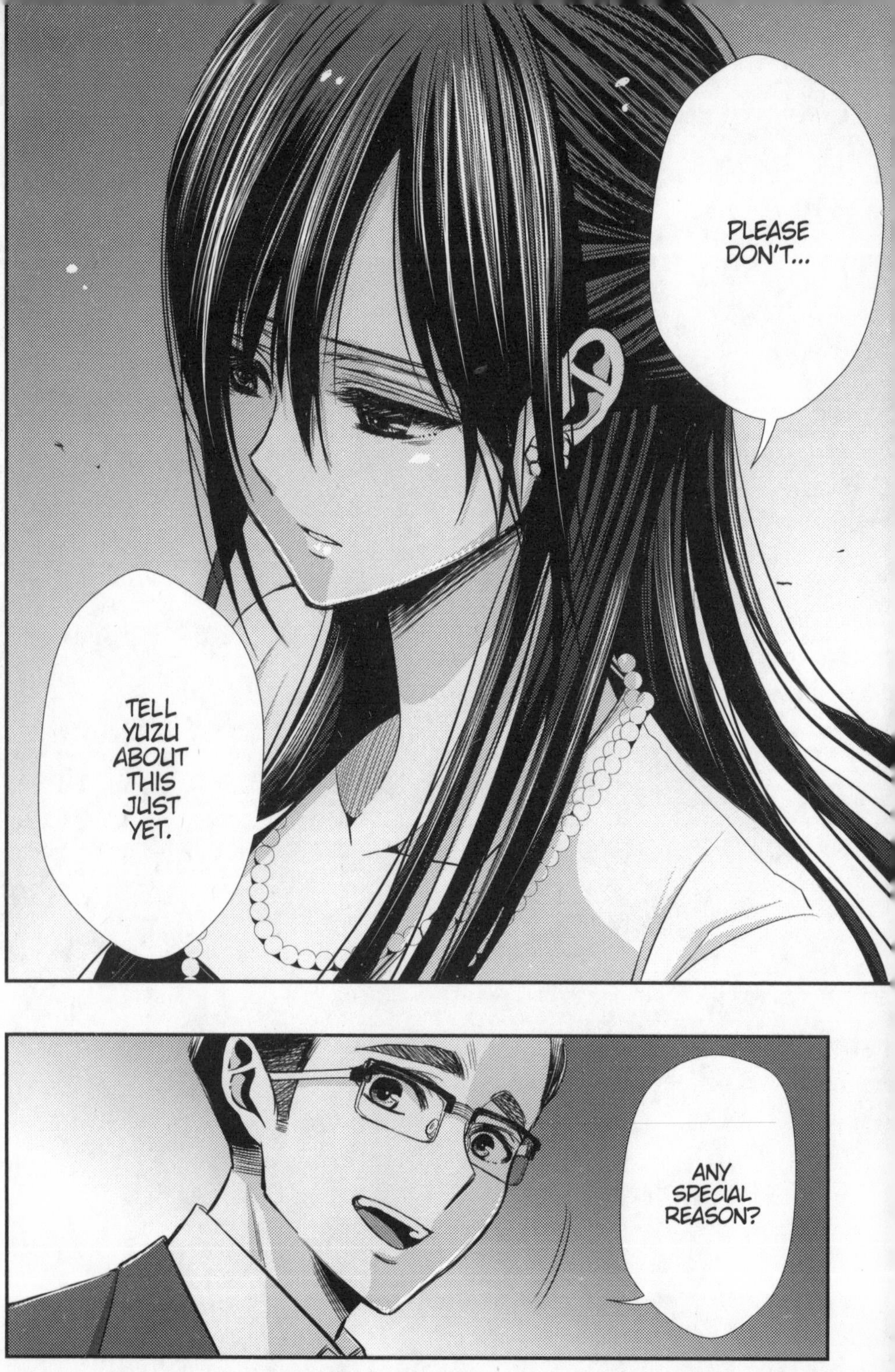
PLEASE DON'T...
TELL YUZU ABOUT THIS JUST YET.
ANY SPECIAL REASON?

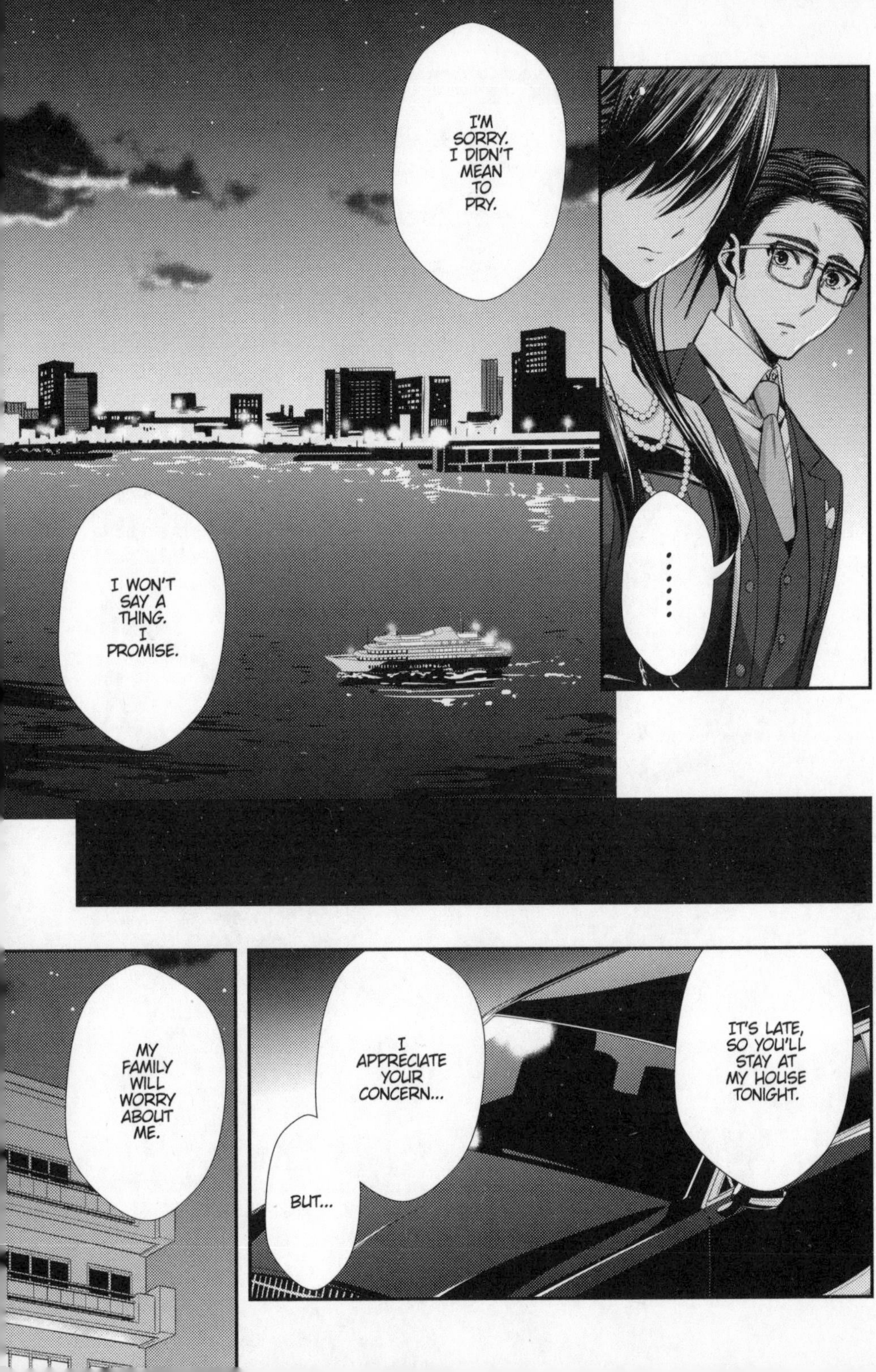
......
I'M SORRY. I DIDN'T MEAN TO PRY.
I WON'T SAY A THING. I PROMISE.
IT'S LATE, SO YOU'LL STAY AT MY HOUSE TONIGHT.
I APPRECIATE YOUR CONCERN...
BUT...
MY FAMILY WILL WORRY ABOUT ME.

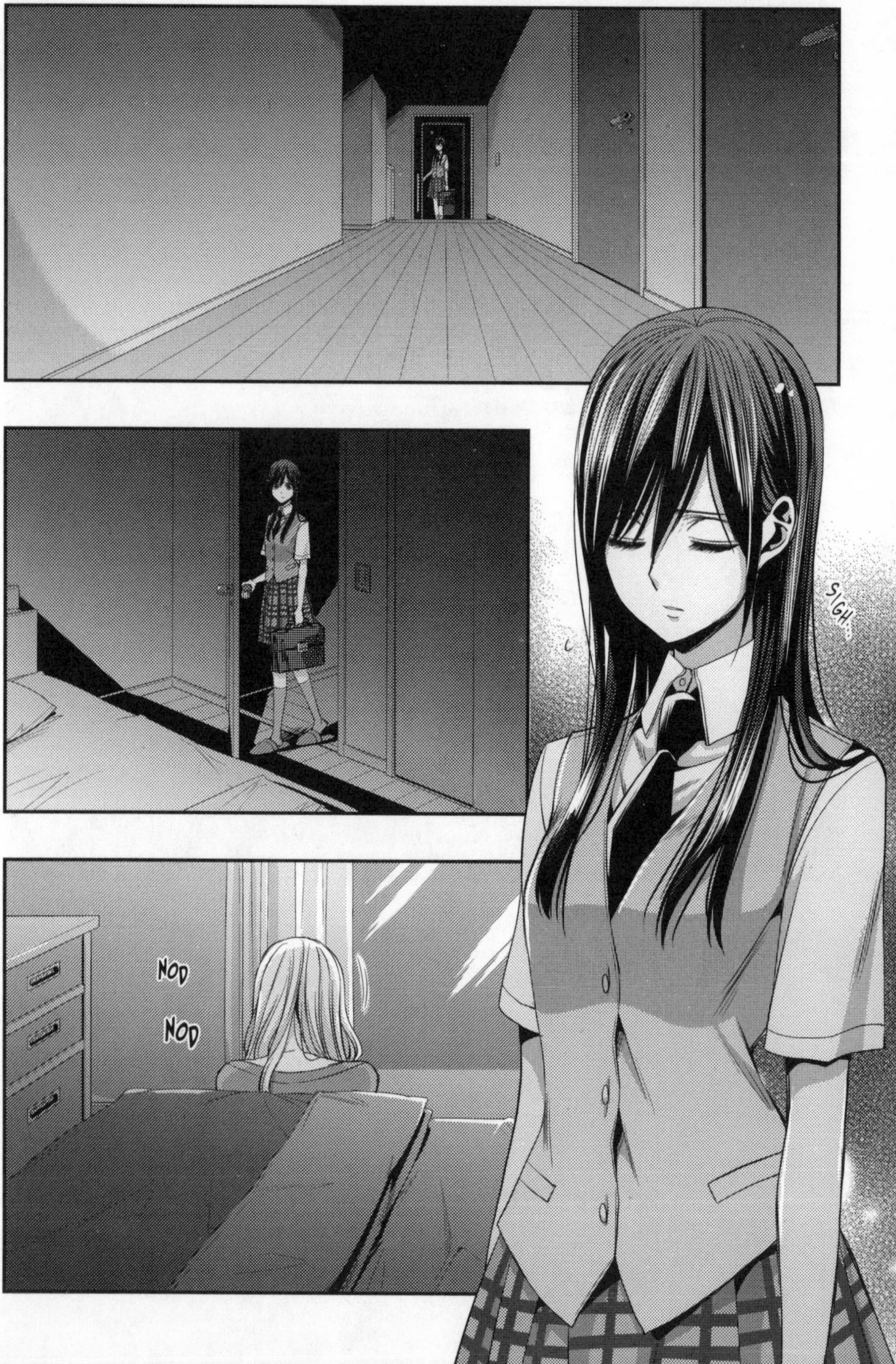
SIGH...
NOD
NOD

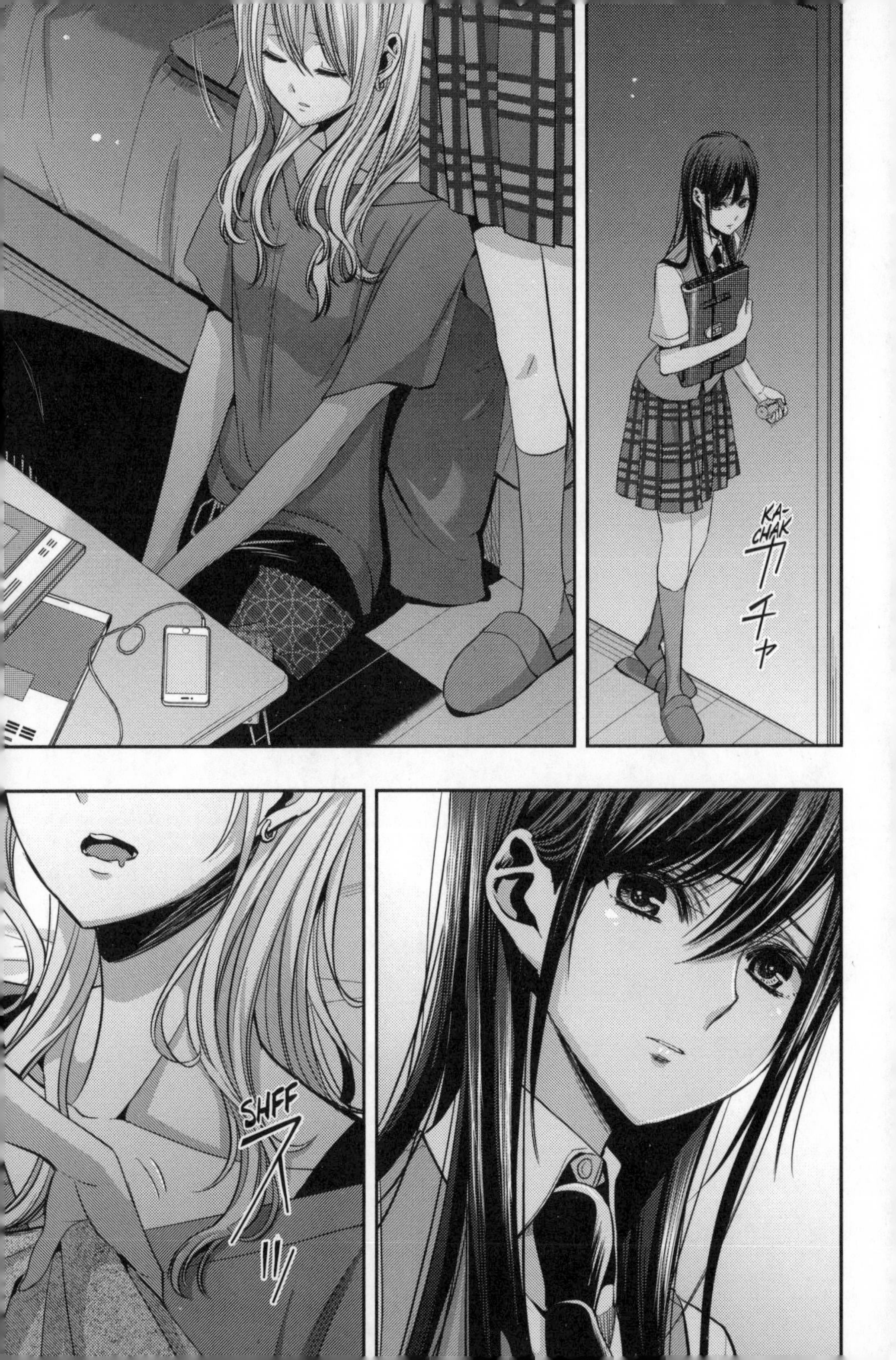
KA-CHAK
ガチャ
SHFF
スッ

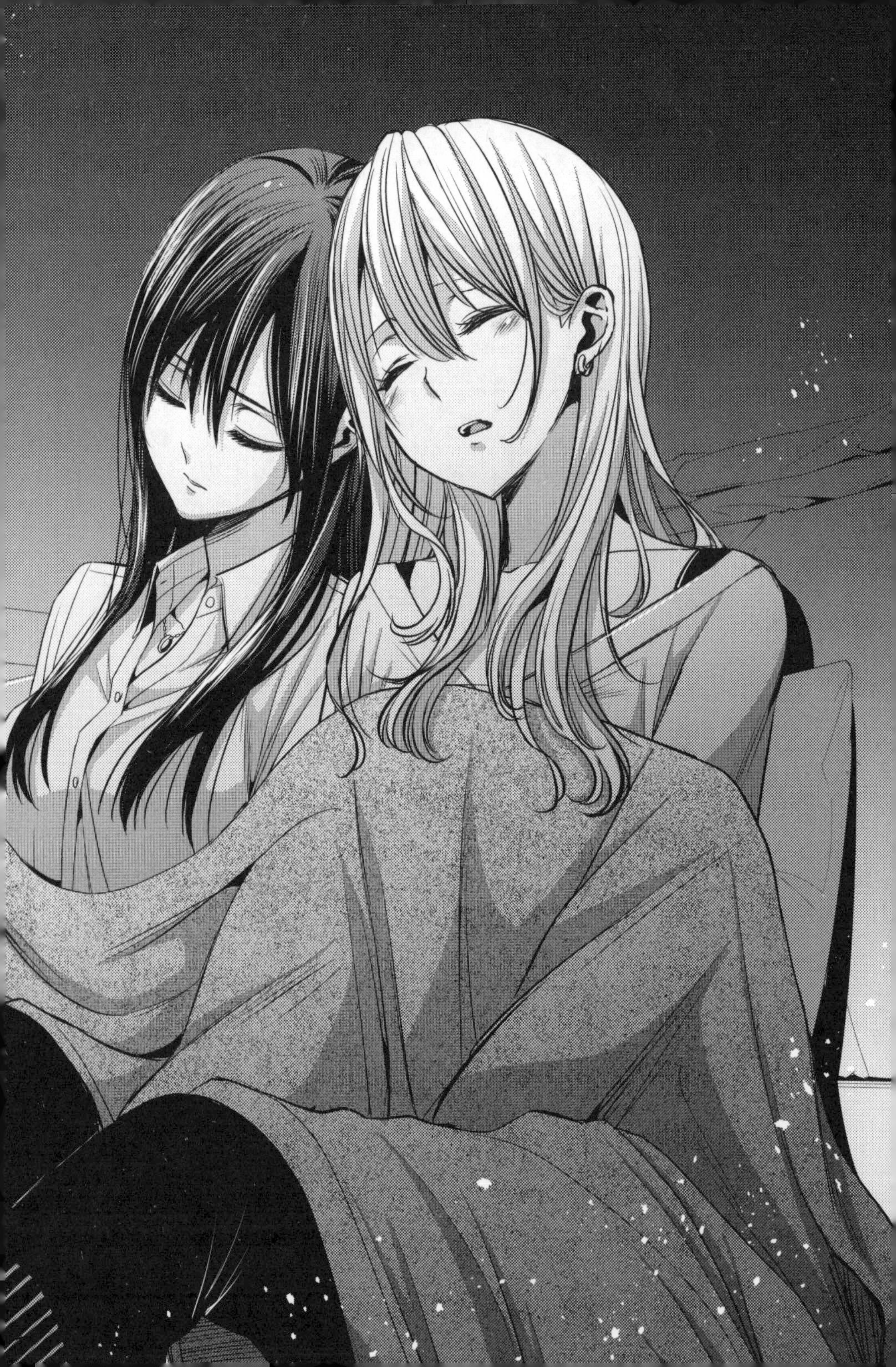

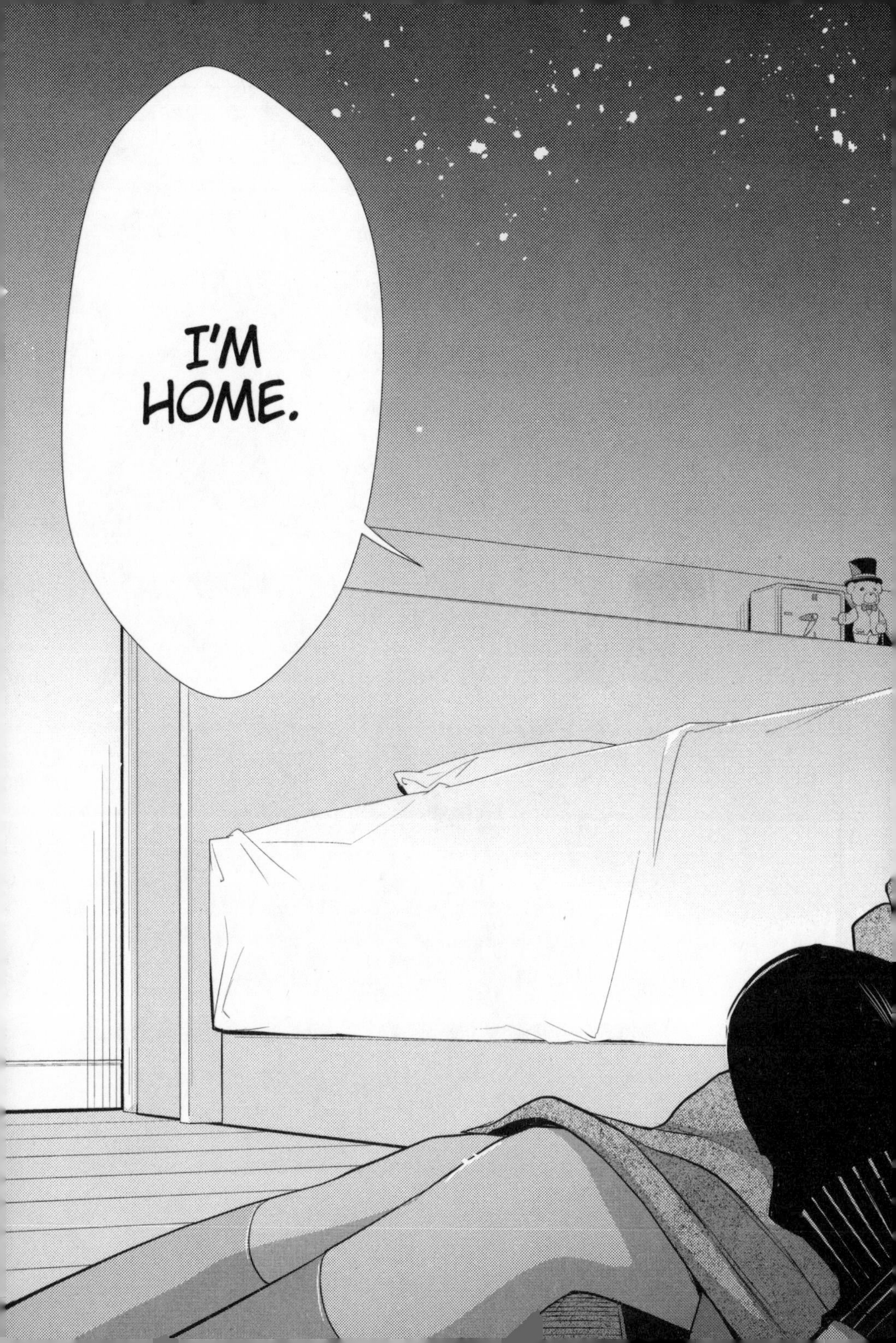
I'M HOME.

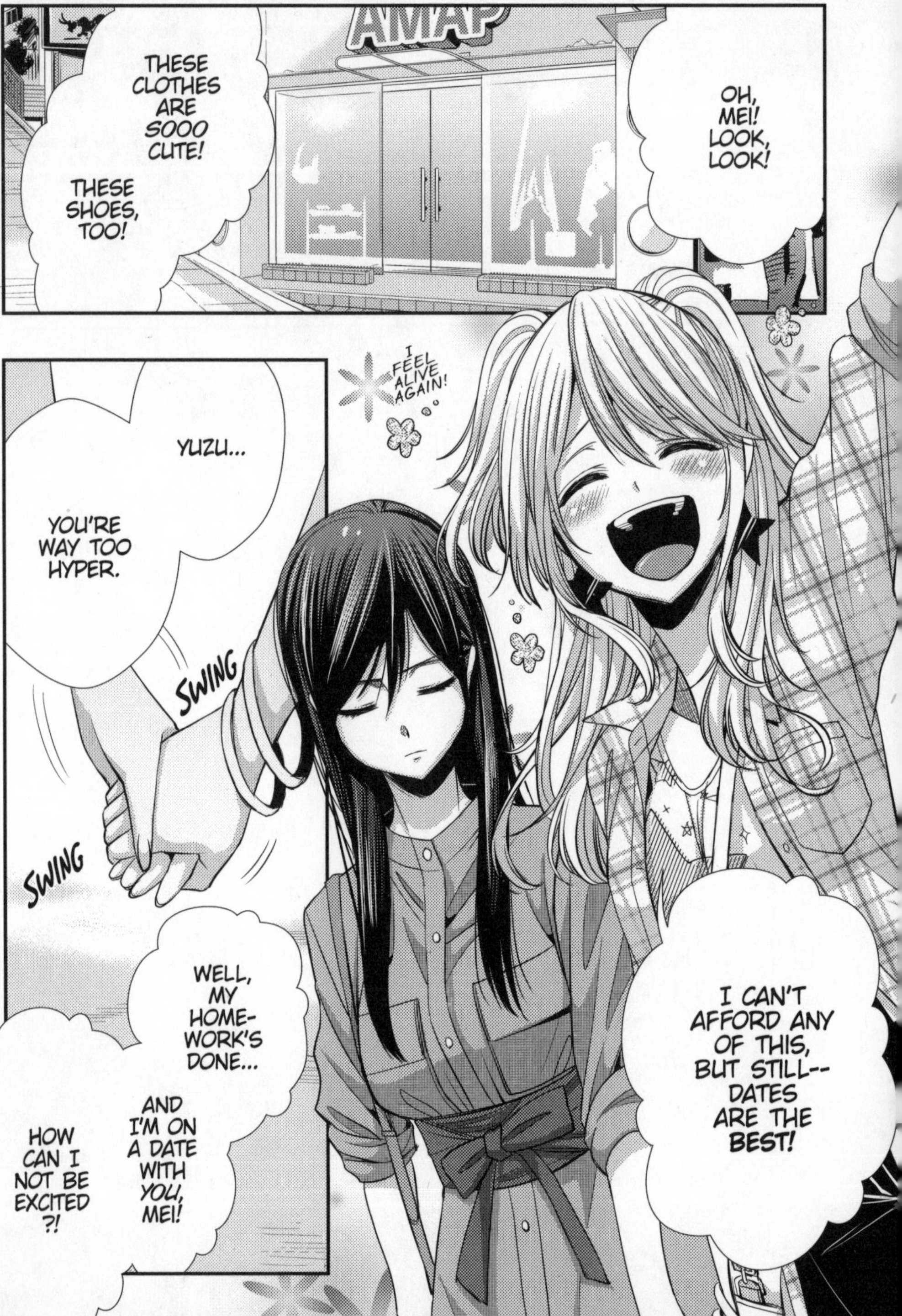
AMAP
OH, MEI! LOOK, LOOK!
THESE CLOTHES ARE SOOO CUTE!
THESE SHOES, TOO!
I FEEL ALIVE AGAIN!
YUZU...
YOU'RE WAY TOO HYPER.
SWING
SWING
I CAN'T AFFORD ANY OF THIS, BUT STILL-- DATES ARE THE BEST!
WELL, MY HOME-WORK'S DONE...
AND I'M ON A DATE WITH YOU, MEI!
HOW CAN I NOT BE EXCITED?!

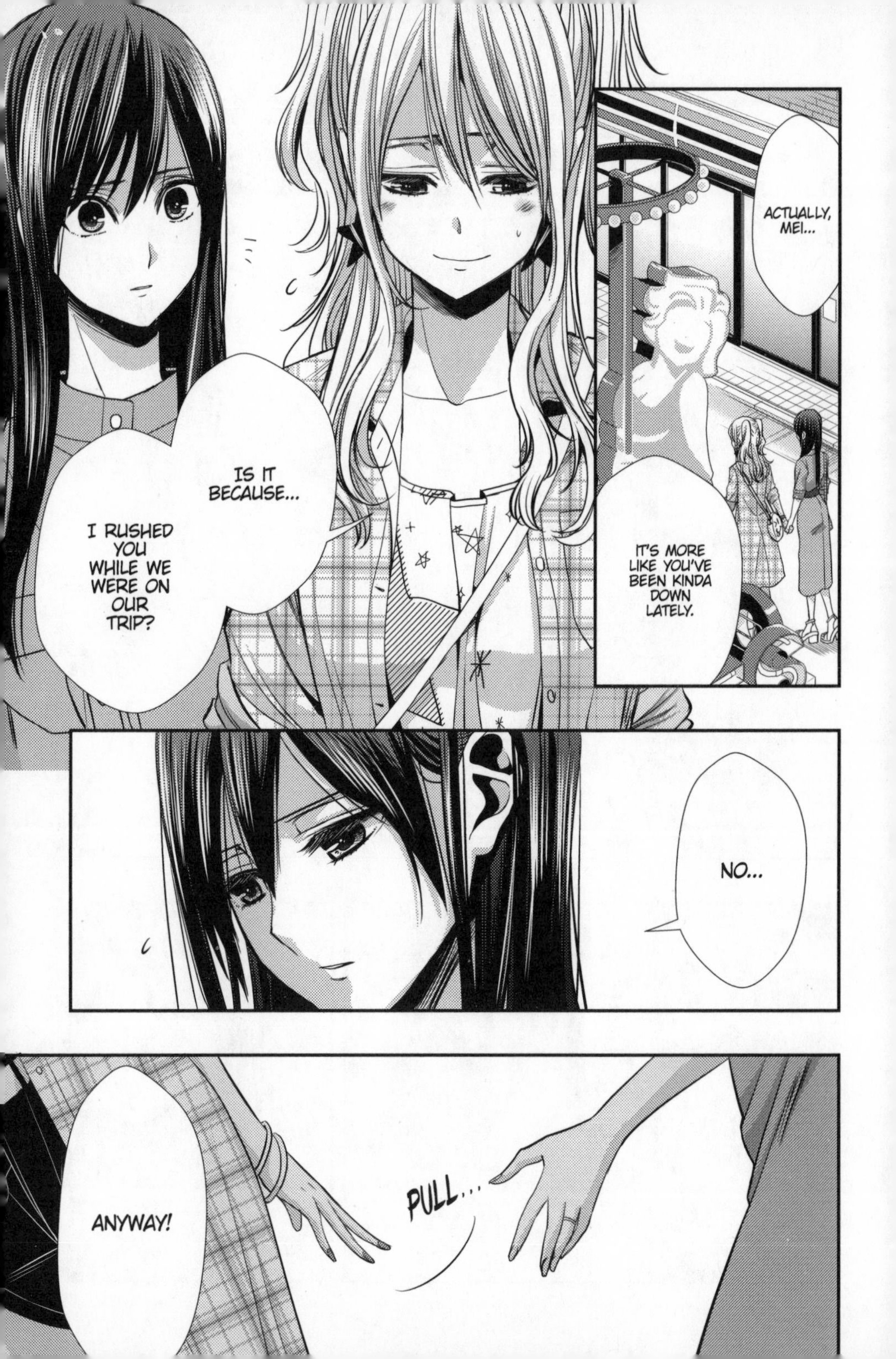
ACTUALLY, MEI...
IT'S MORE LIKE YOU'VE BEEN KINDA DOWN LATELY.
IS IT BECAUSE...
I RUSHED YOU WHILE WE WERE ON OUR TRIP?
NO...
PULL...
ANYWAY!

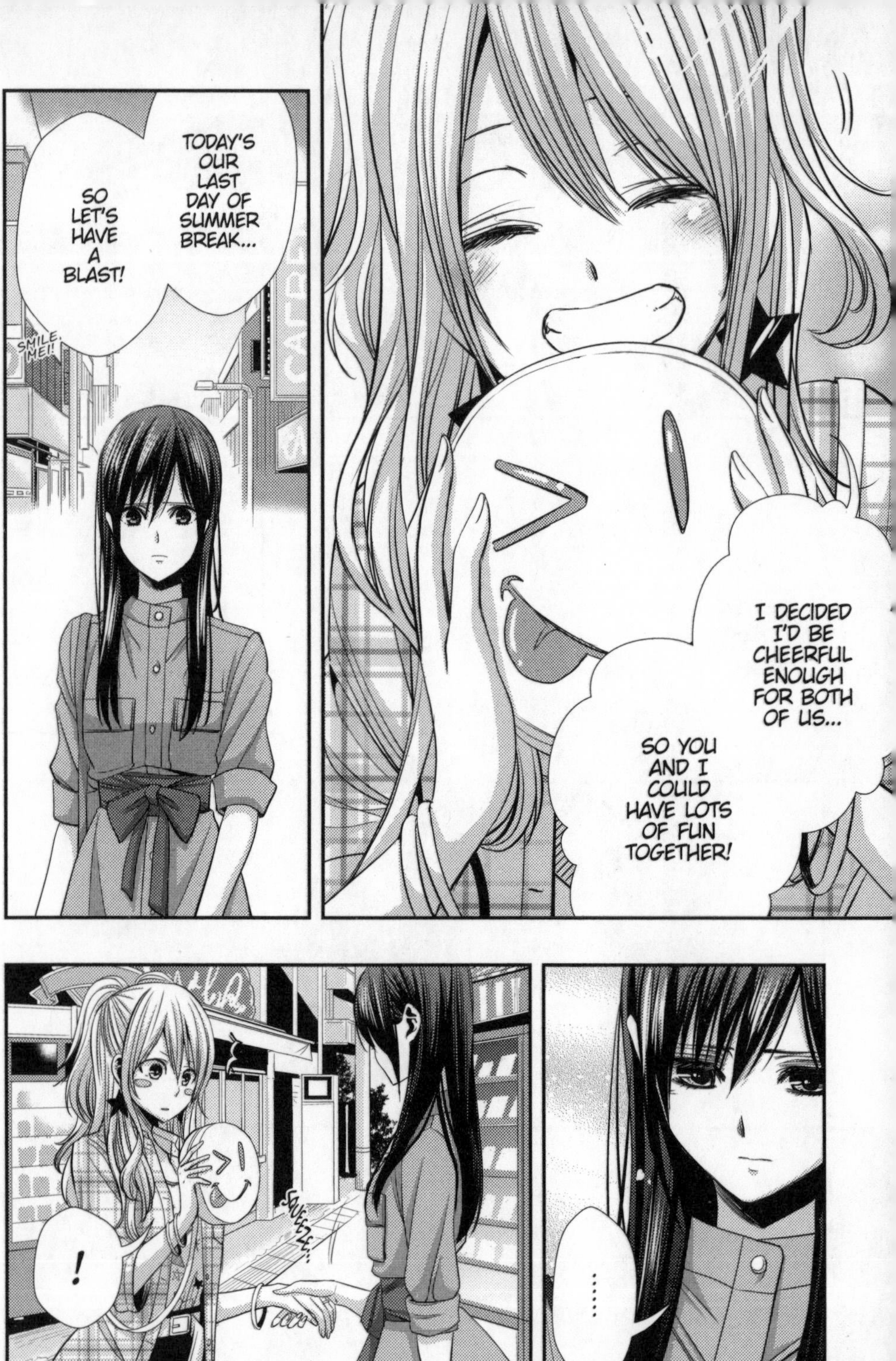
I DECIDED I'D BE CHEERFUL ENOUGH FOR BOTH OF US...
SO YOU AND I COULD HAVE LOTS OF FUN TOGETHER!
TODAY'S OUR LAST DAY OF SUMMER BREAK...
SO LET'S HAVE A BLAST!
SMILE, MEI!
.....
SQUEEZE...
!

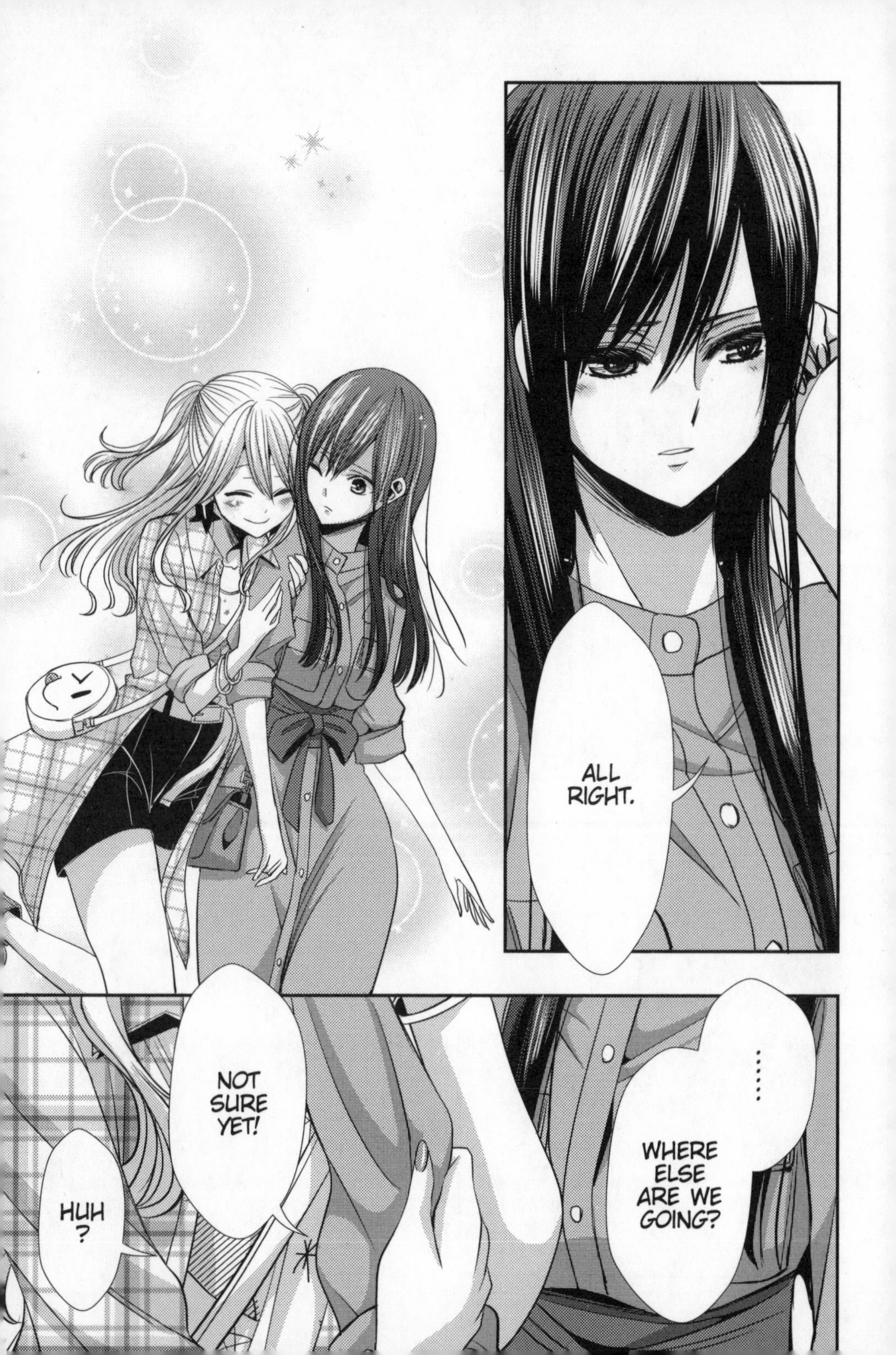
ALL RIGHT.
......
WHERE ELSE ARE WE GOING?
NOT SURE YET!
HUH?

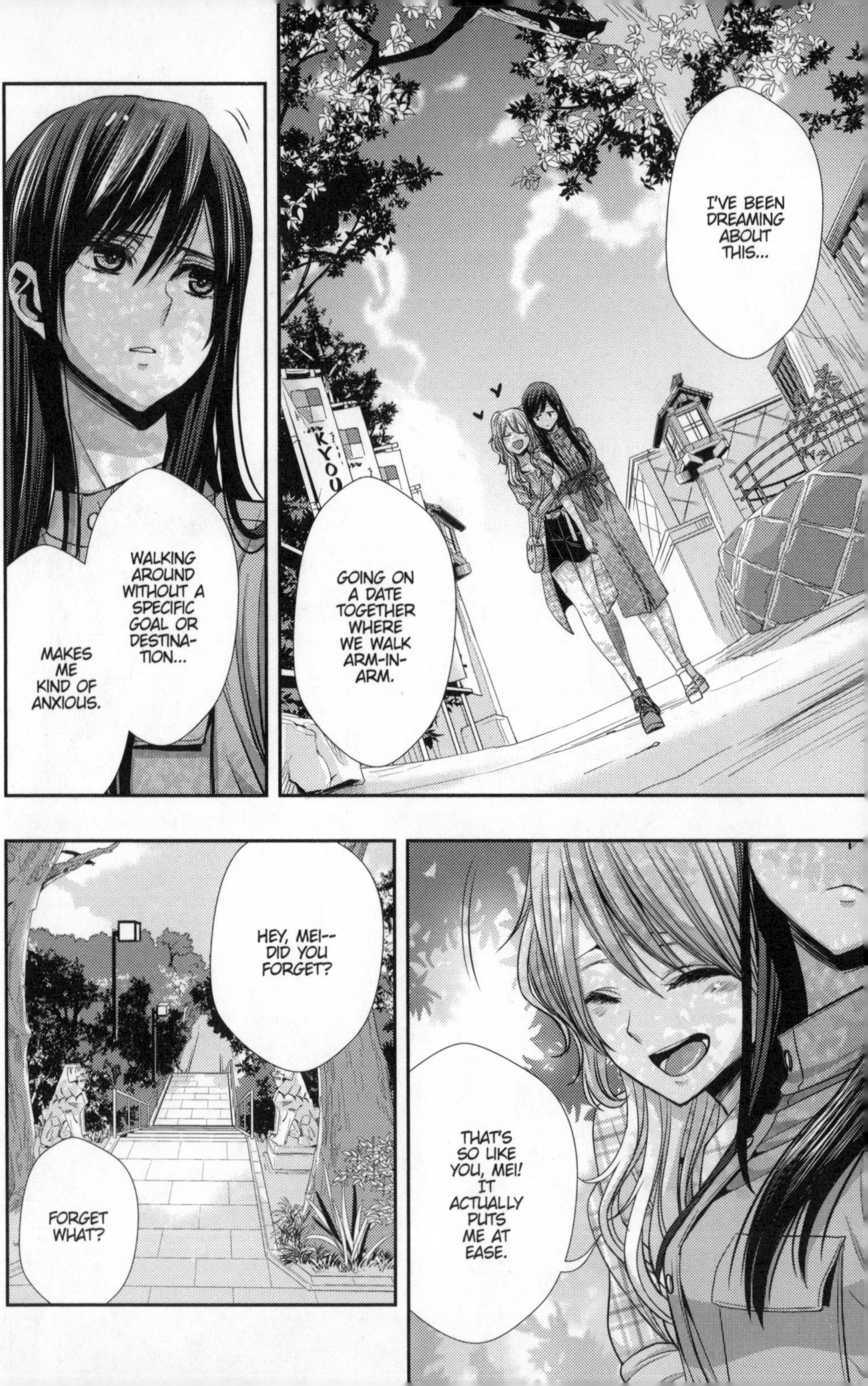
I'VE BEEN DREAMING ABOUT THIS...
GOING ON A DATE TOGETHER WHERE WE WALK ARM-IN-ARM.
WALKING AROUND WITHOUT A SPECIFIC GOAL OR DESTINATION...
MAKES ME KIND OF ANXIOUS.
THAT'S SO LIKE YOU, MEI! IT ACTUALLY PUTS ME AT EASE.
HEY, MEI-- DID YOU FORGET?
FORGET WHAT?

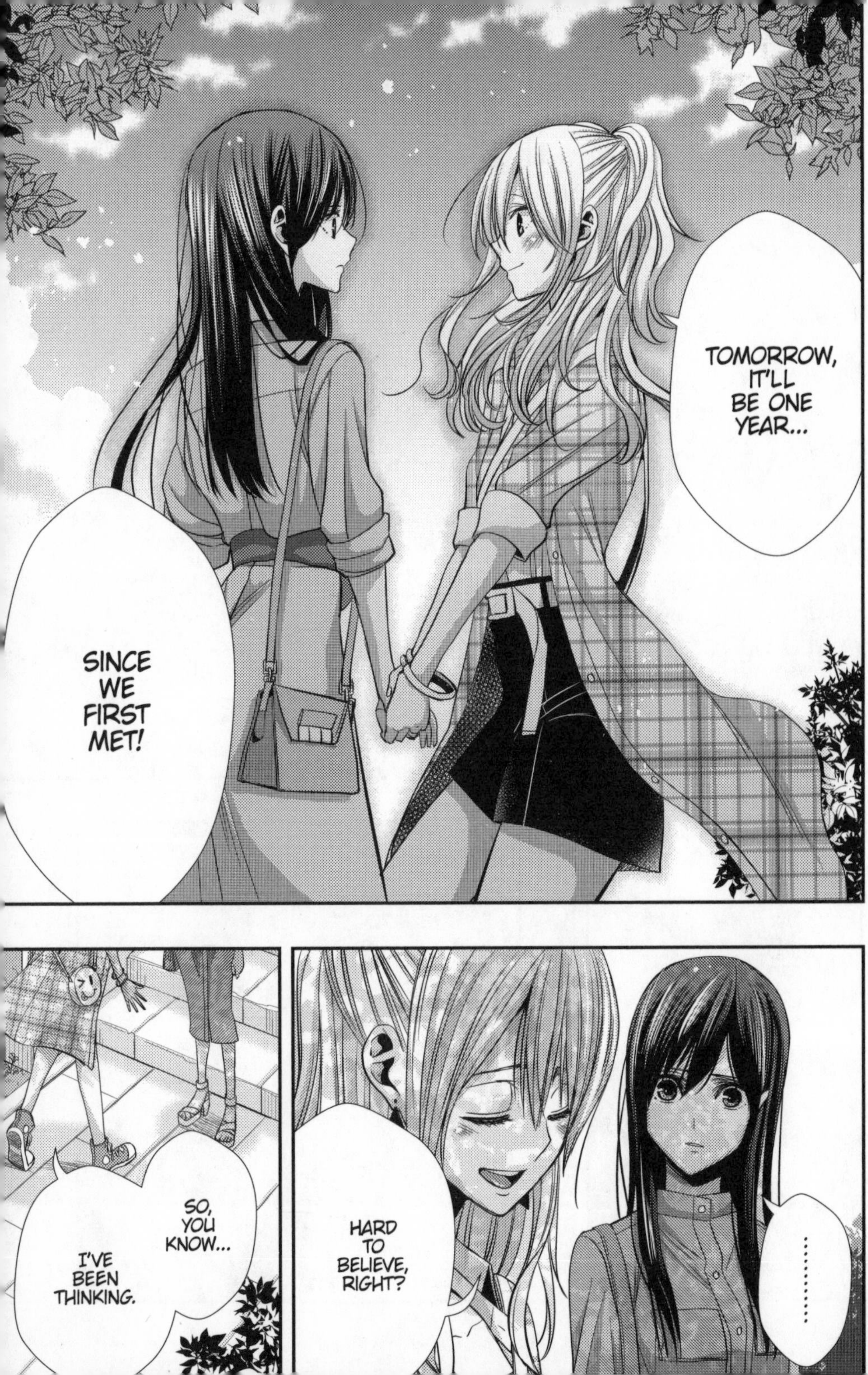
TOMORROW, IT'LL BE ONE YEAR...
SINCE WE FIRST MET!
HARD TO BELIEVE, RIGHT?
......
SO, YOU KNOW...
I'VE BEEN THINKING.

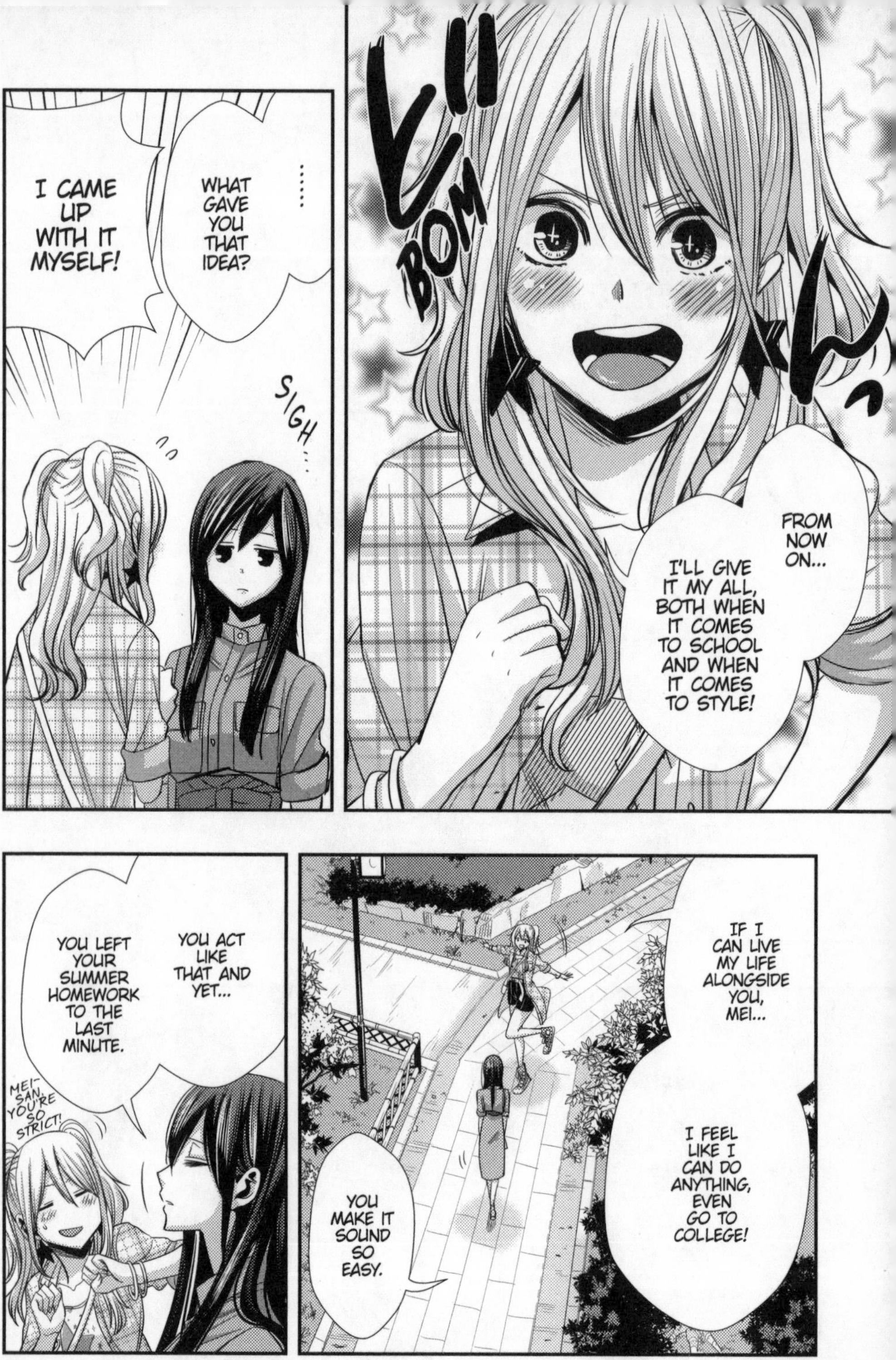
BOM
FROM NOW ON...
I'LL GIVE IT MY ALL, BOTH WHEN IT COMES TO SCHOOL AND WHEN IT COMES TO STYLE!
......
WHAT GAVE YOU THAT IDEA?
I CAME UP WITH IT MYSELF!
SIGH...
IF I CAN LIVE MY LIFE ALONGSIDE YOU, MEI...
I FEEL LIKE I CAN DO ANYTHING, EVEN GO TO COLLEGE!
YOU MAKE IT SOUND SO EASY.
YOU ACT LIKE THAT AND YET...
YOU LEFT YOUR SUMMER HOMEWORK TO THE LAST MINUTE.
MEI-SAN, YOU'RE SO STRICT!

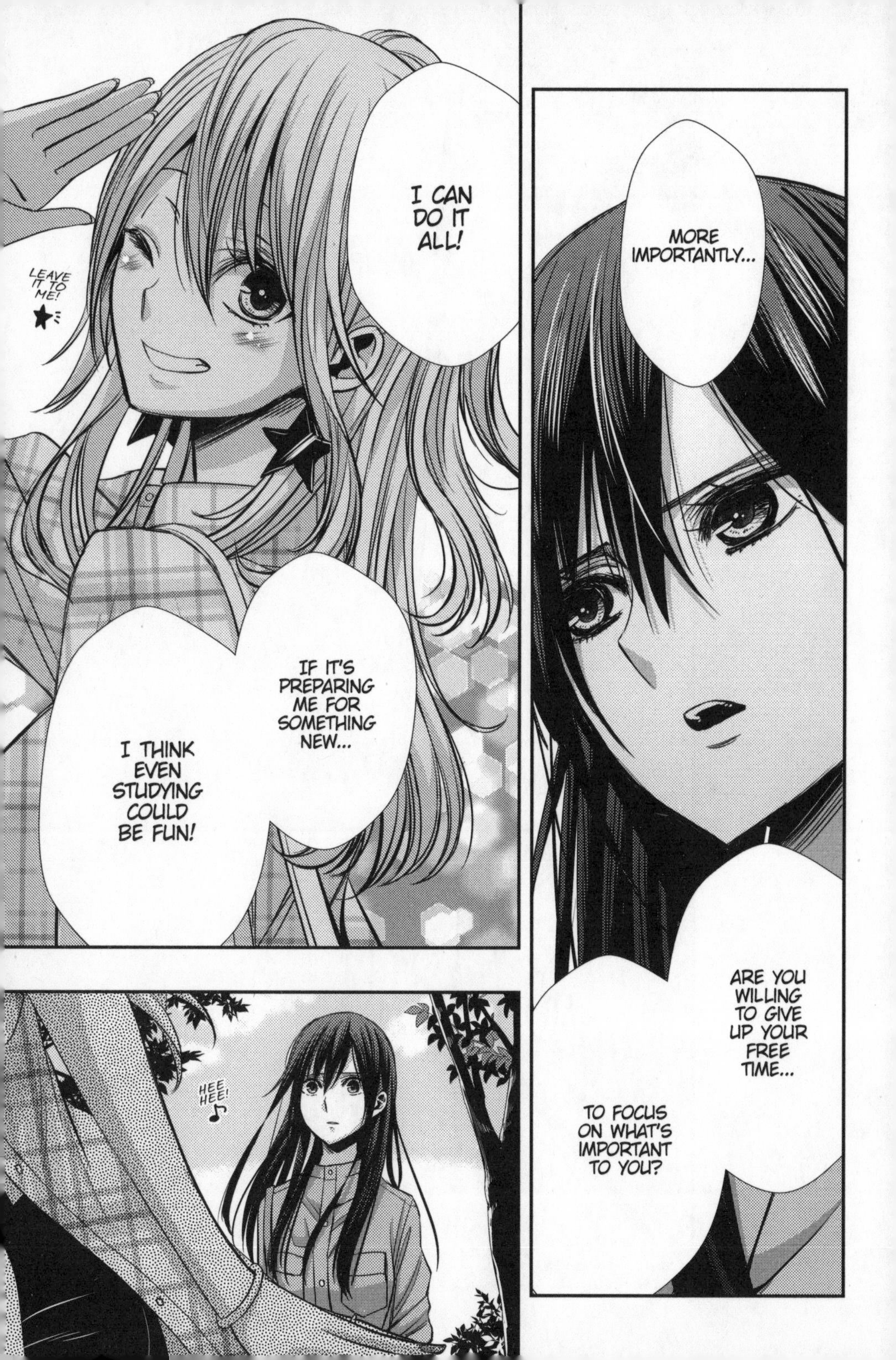
MORE IMPORTANTLY...
ARE YOU WILLING TO GIVE UP YOUR FREE TIME...
TO FOCUS ON WHAT'S IMPORTANT TO YOU?
I CAN DO IT ALL!
LEAVE IT TO ME!
IF IT'S PREPARING ME FOR SOMETHING NEW...
I THINK EVEN STUDYING COULD BE FUN!
HEE HEE!

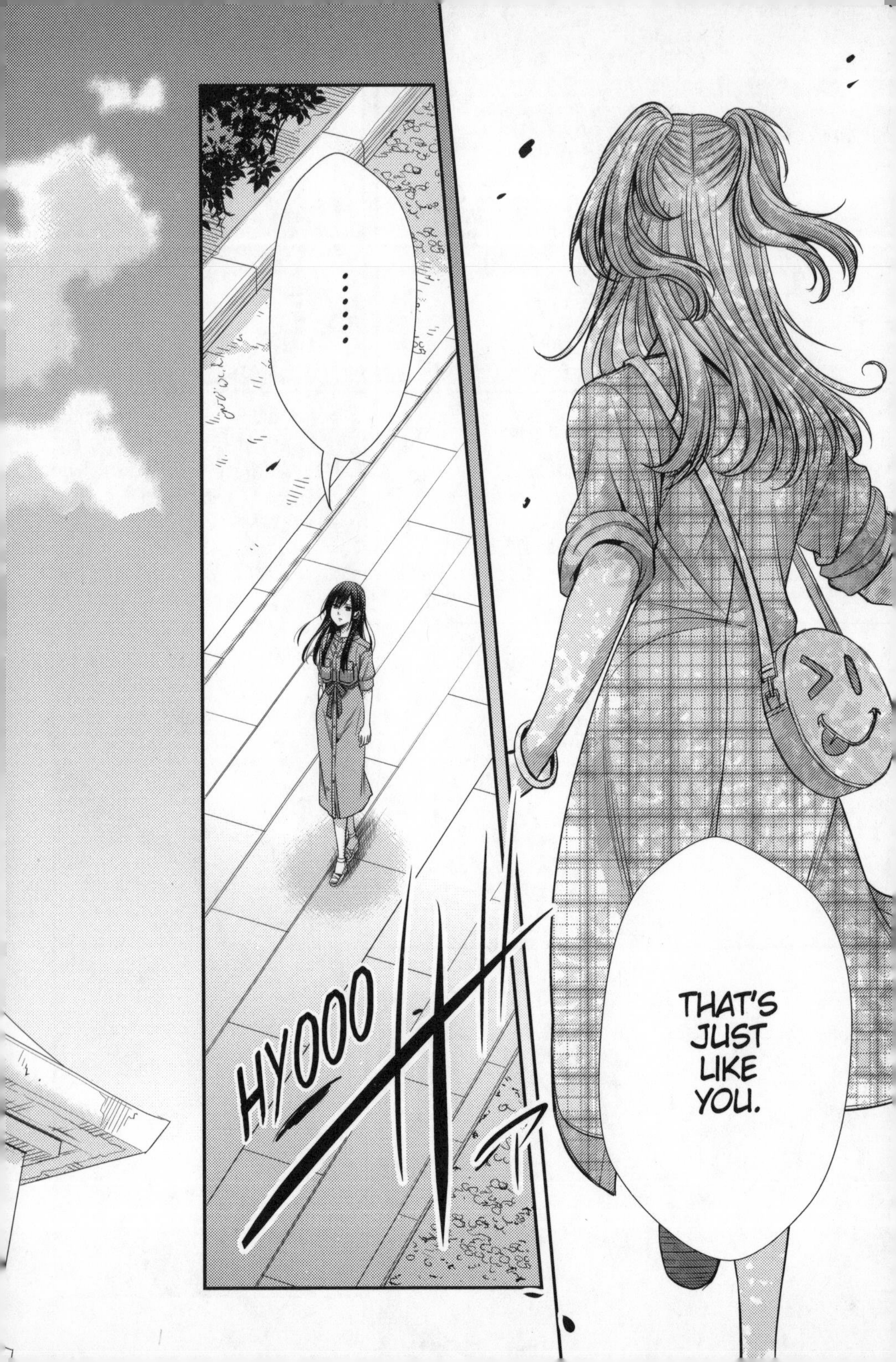
THAT'S JUST LIKE YOU.
......
HYOOO

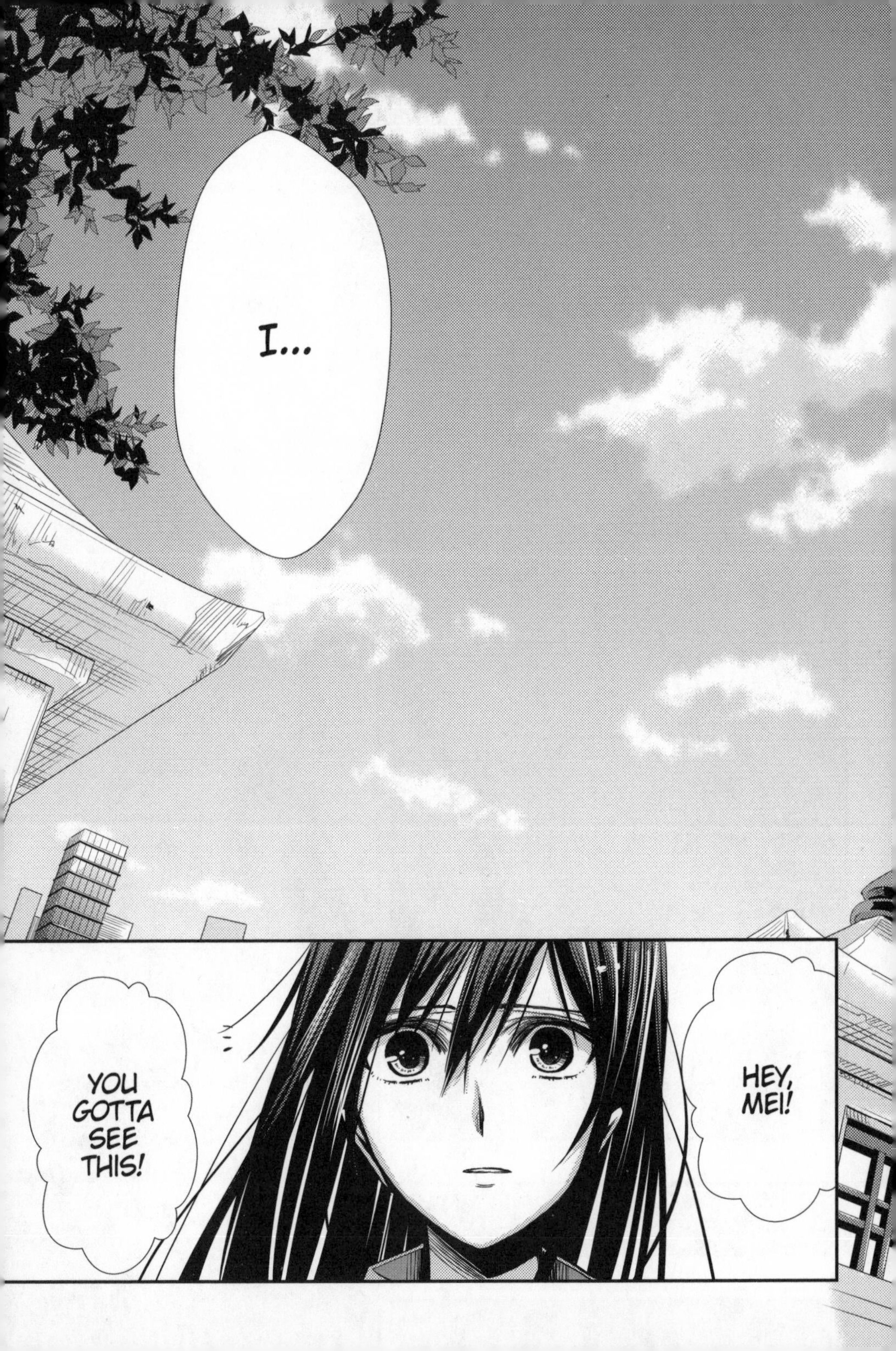
I...
HEY, MEI!
YOU GOTTA SEE THIS!

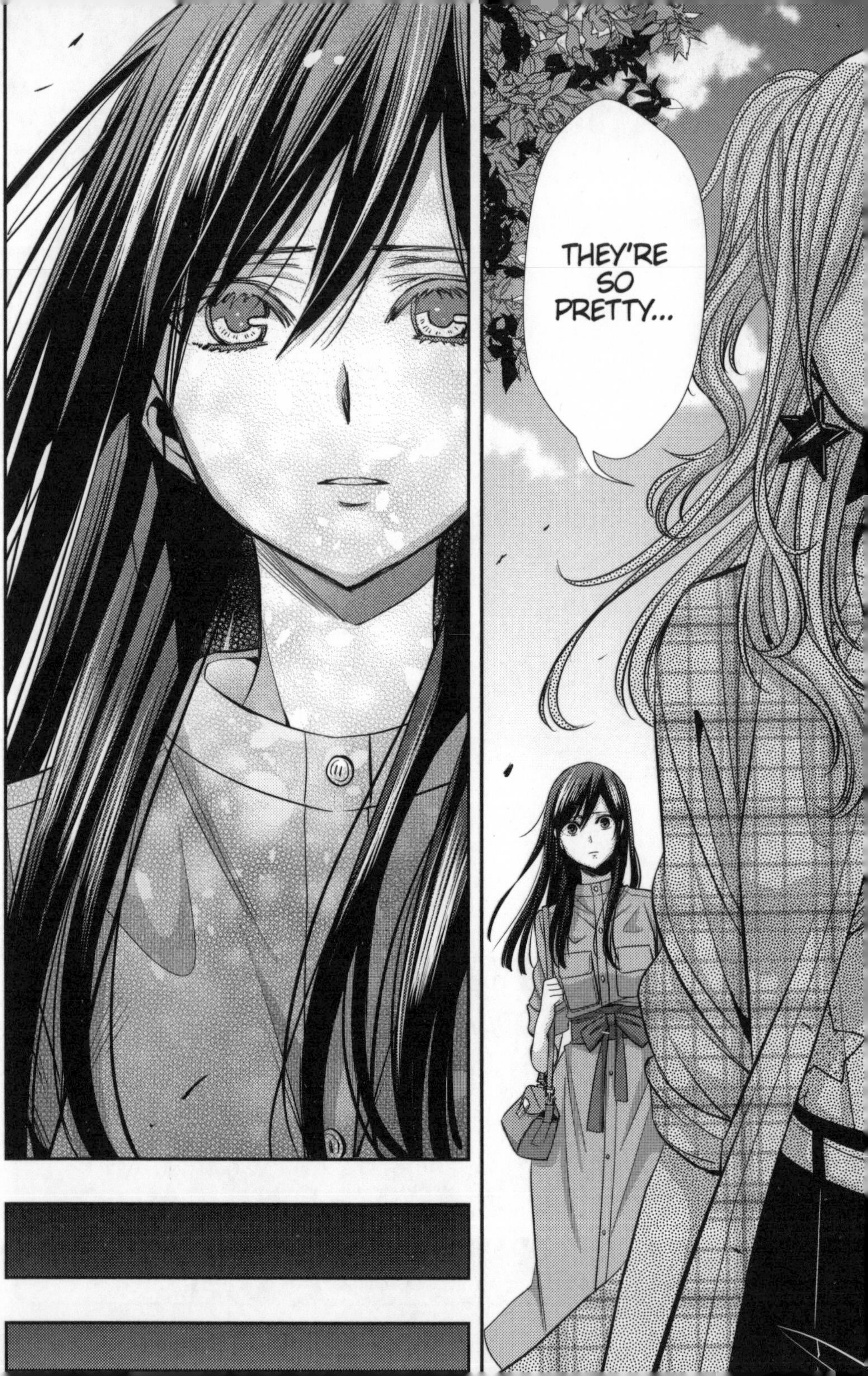
THEY'RE SO PRETTY...

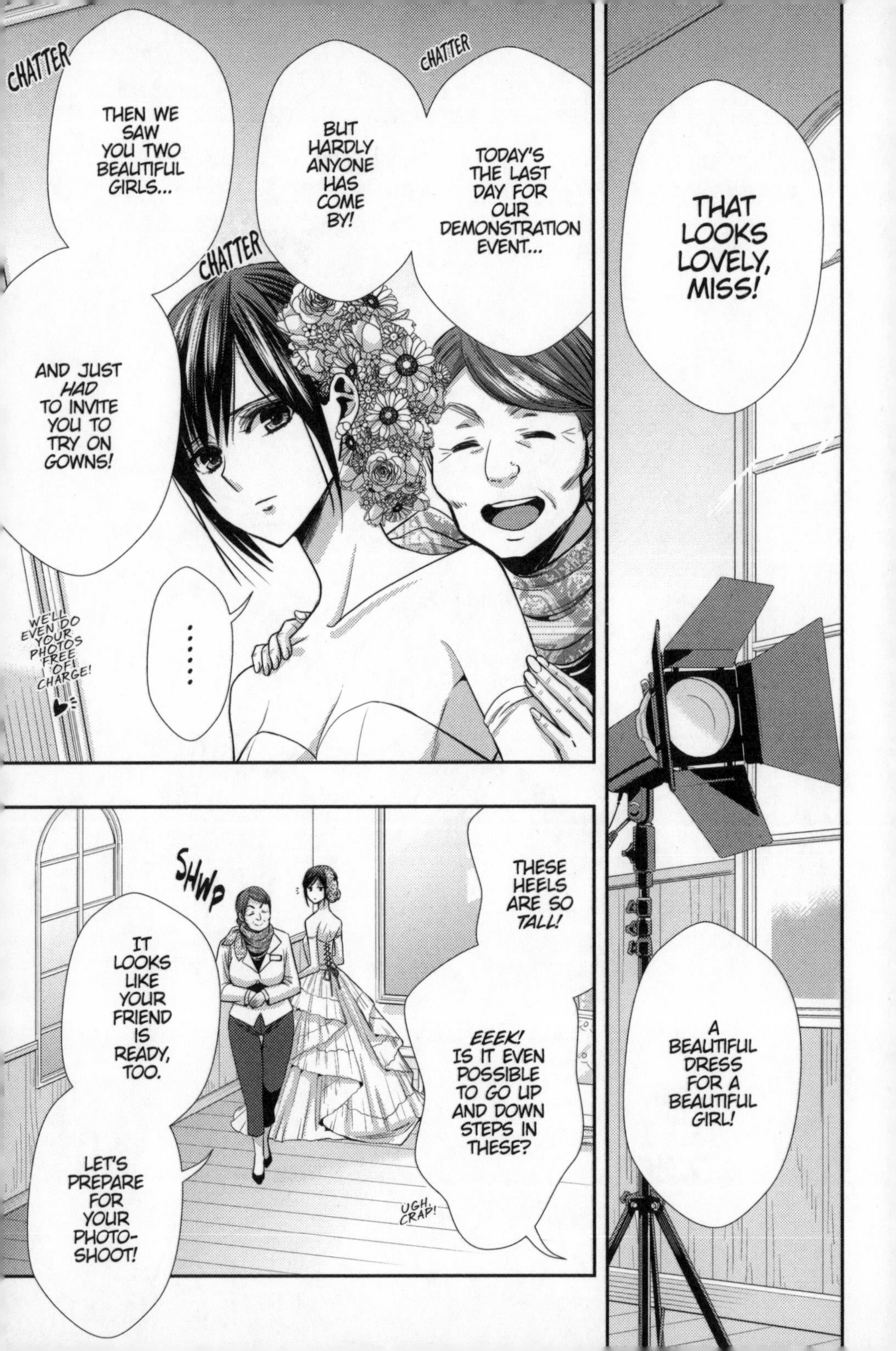
THAT LOOKS LOVELY, MISS!
A BEAUTIFUL DRESS FOR A BEAUTIFUL GIRL!
CHATTER
TODAY'S THE LAST DAY FOR OUR DEMONSTRATION EVENT...
BUT HARDLY ANYONE HAS COME BY!
CHATTER
THEN WE SAW YOU TWO BEAUTIFUL GIRLS...
CHATTER
AND JUST *HAD* TO INVITE YOU TO TRY ON GOWNS!
WE'LL EVEN DO YOUR PHOTOS FREE OF CHARGE!
......
THESE HEELS ARE SO *TALL!*
EEEK! IS IT EVEN POSSIBLE TO GO UP AND DOWN STEPS IN THESE?
UGH, CRAP!
SHWP
IT LOOKS LIKE YOUR FRIEND IS READY, TOO.
LET'S PREPARE FOR YOUR PHOTO-SHOOT!

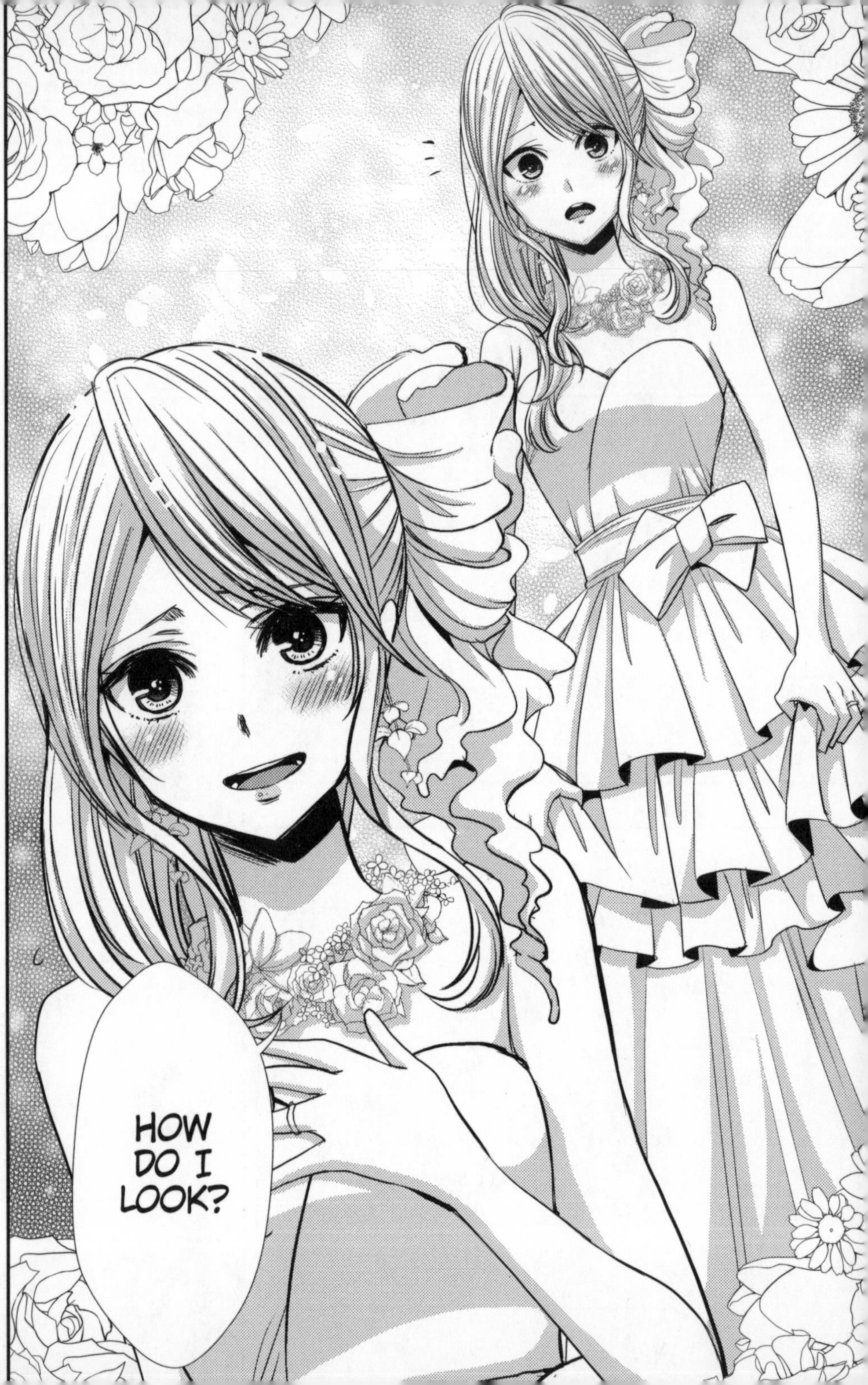
HOW DO I LOOK?

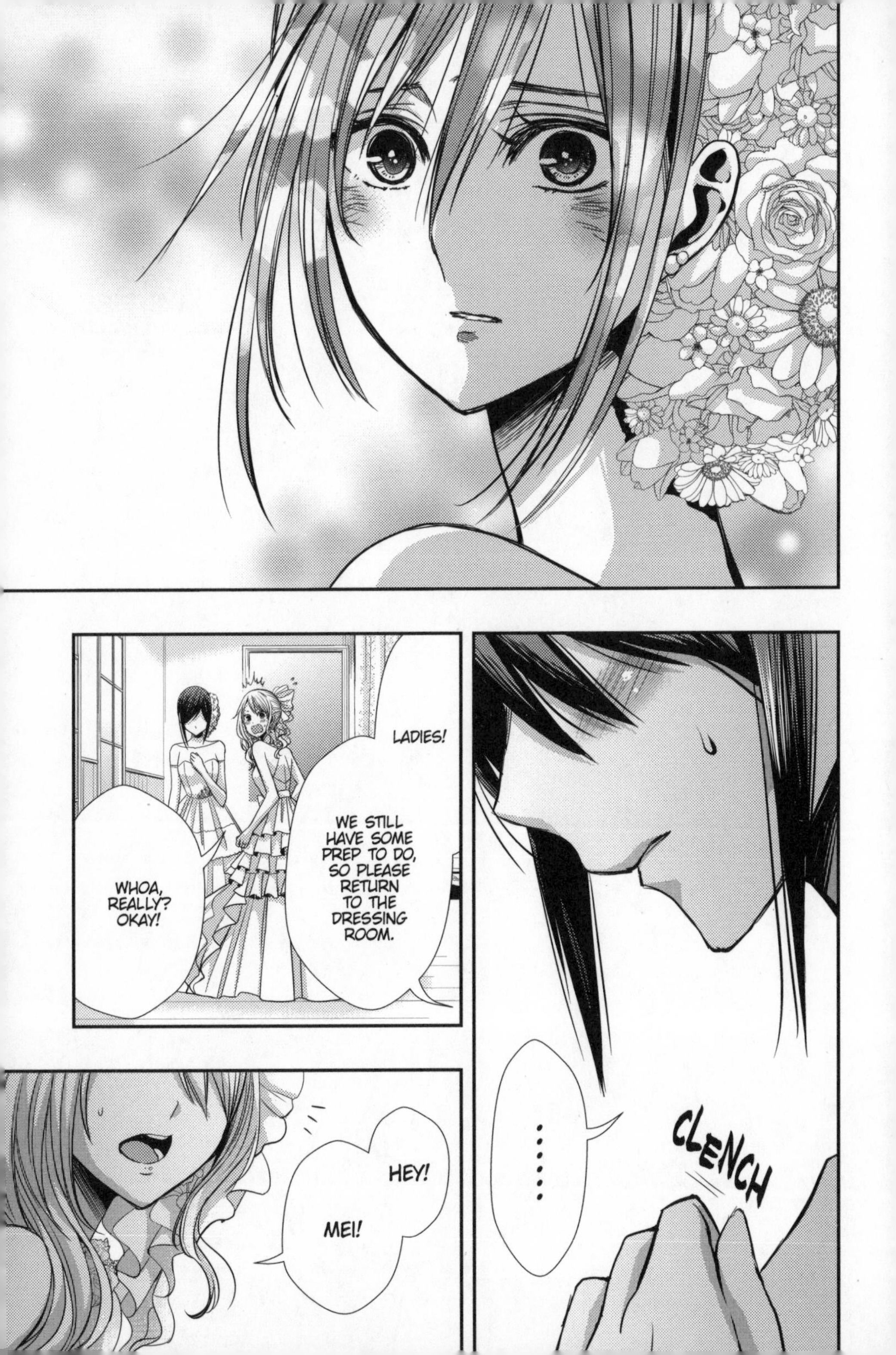
......
CLENCH
LADIES!
WE STILL HAVE SOME PREP TO DO, SO PLEASE RETURN TO THE DRESSING ROOM.
WHOA, REALLY? OKAY!
HEY!
MEI!

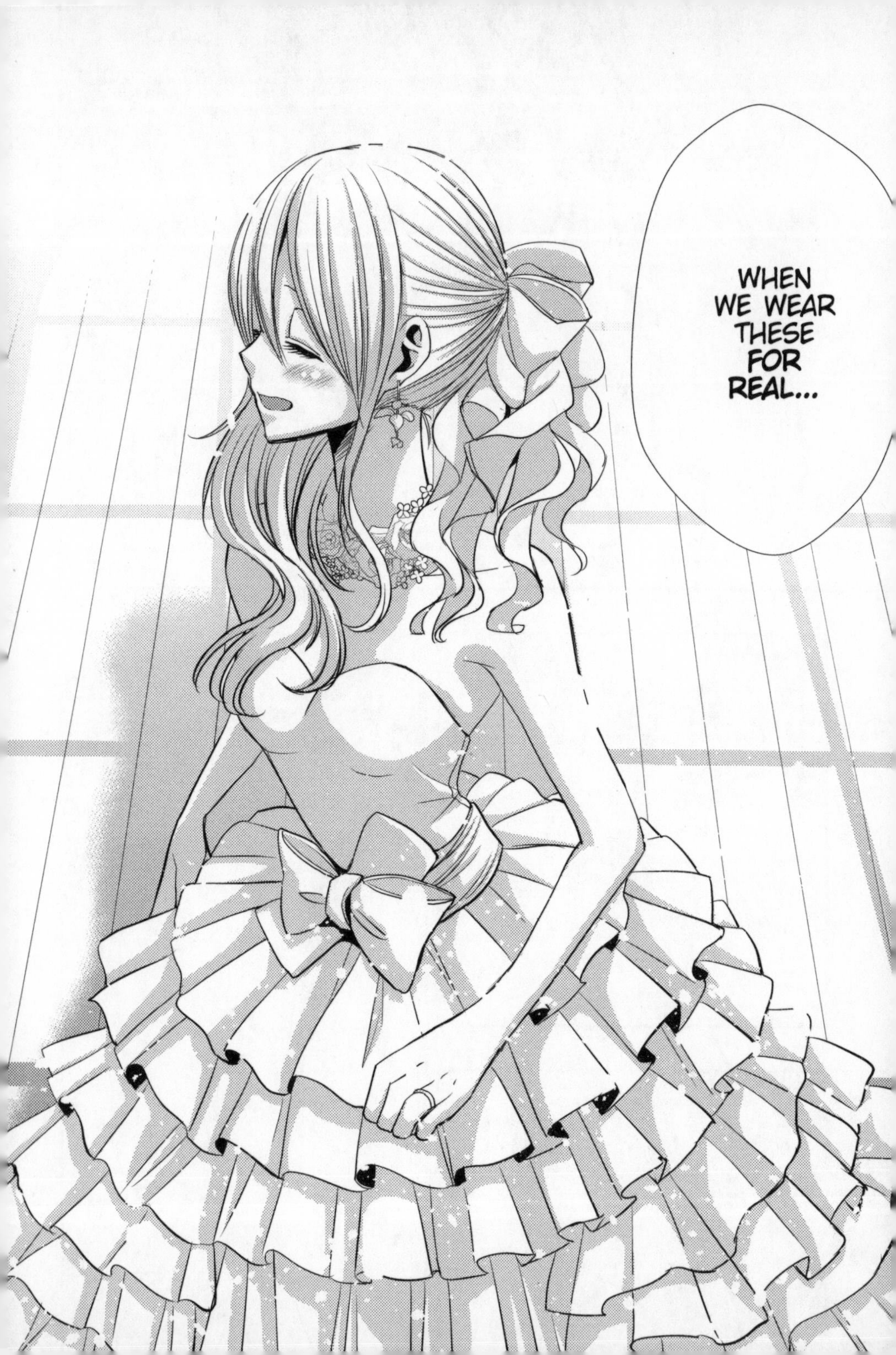
WHEN WE WEAR THESE FOR REAL...

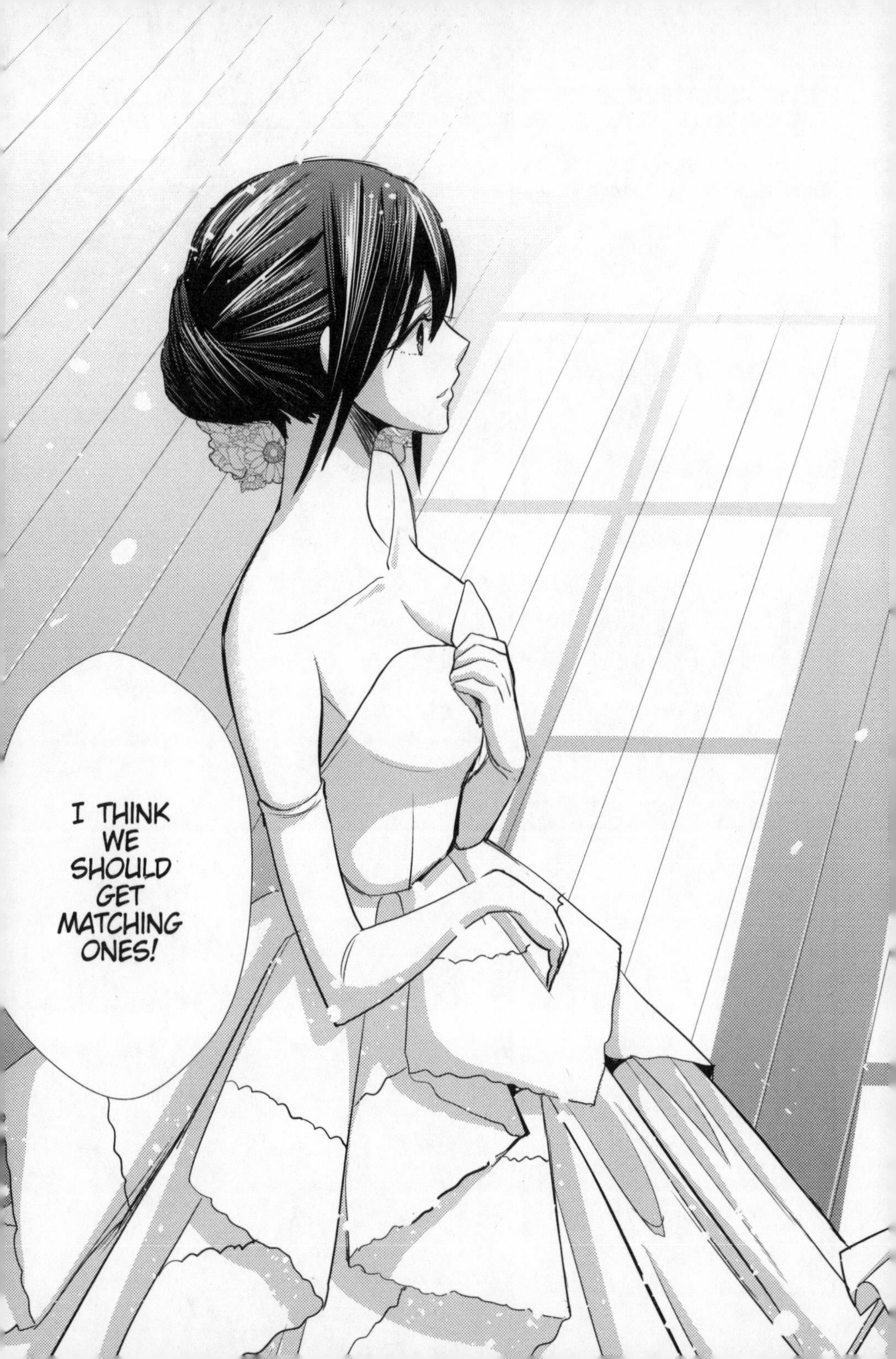
I THINK WE SHOULD GET MATCHING ONES!

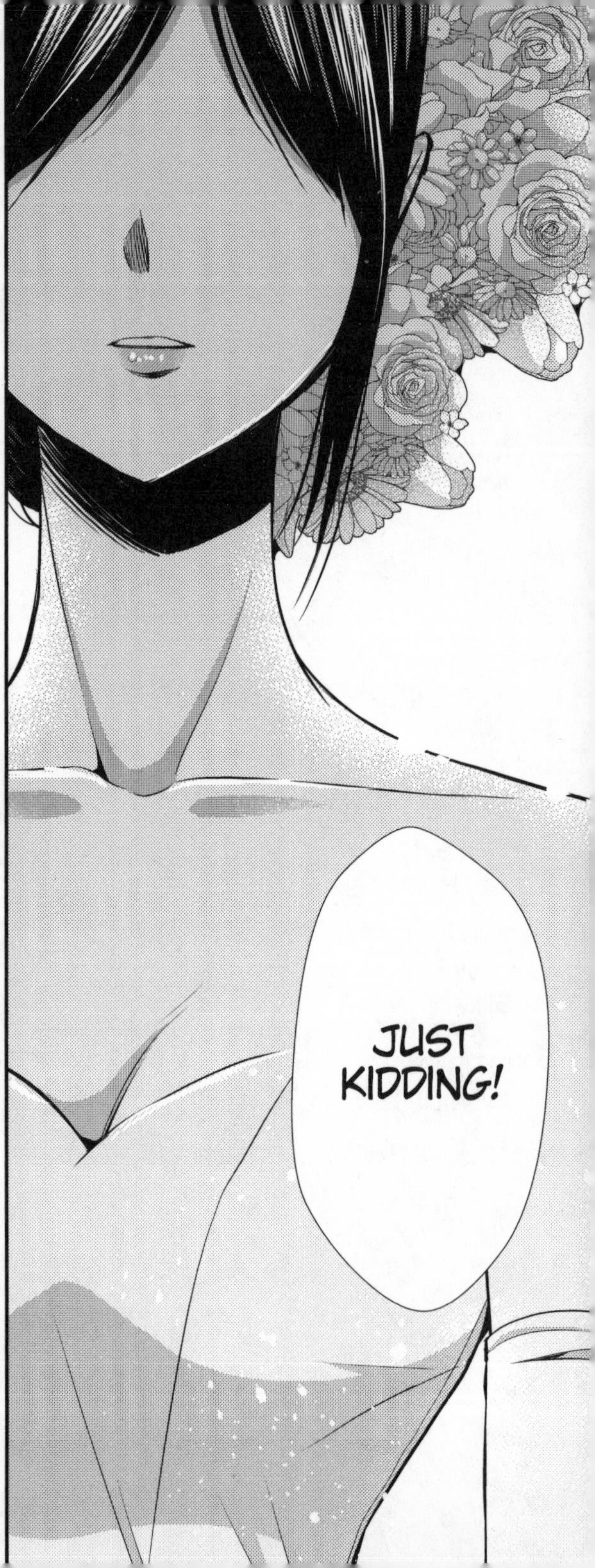
JUST KIDDING!
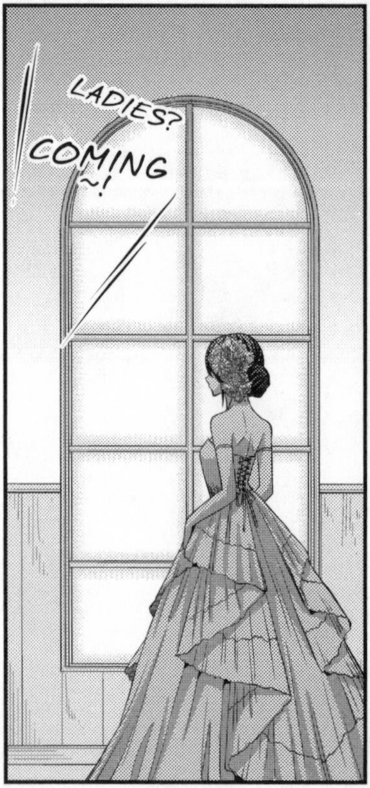
LADIES? COMING ~!
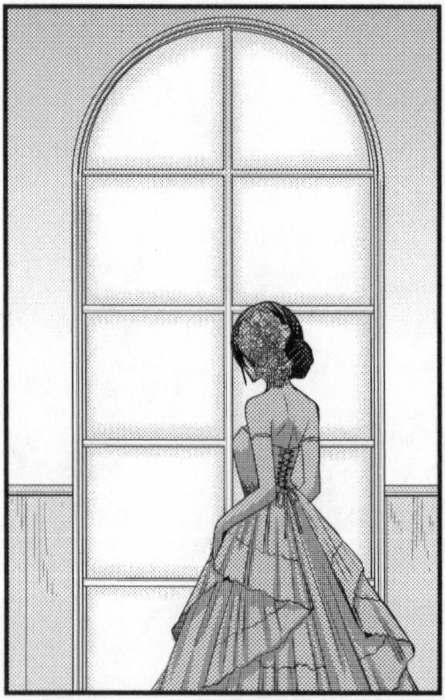

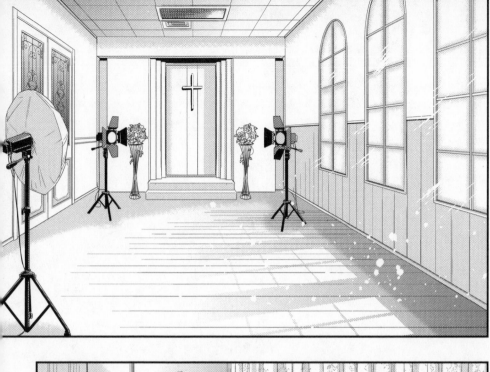

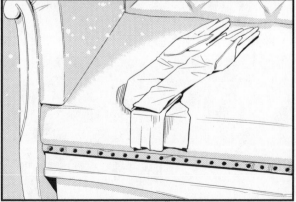

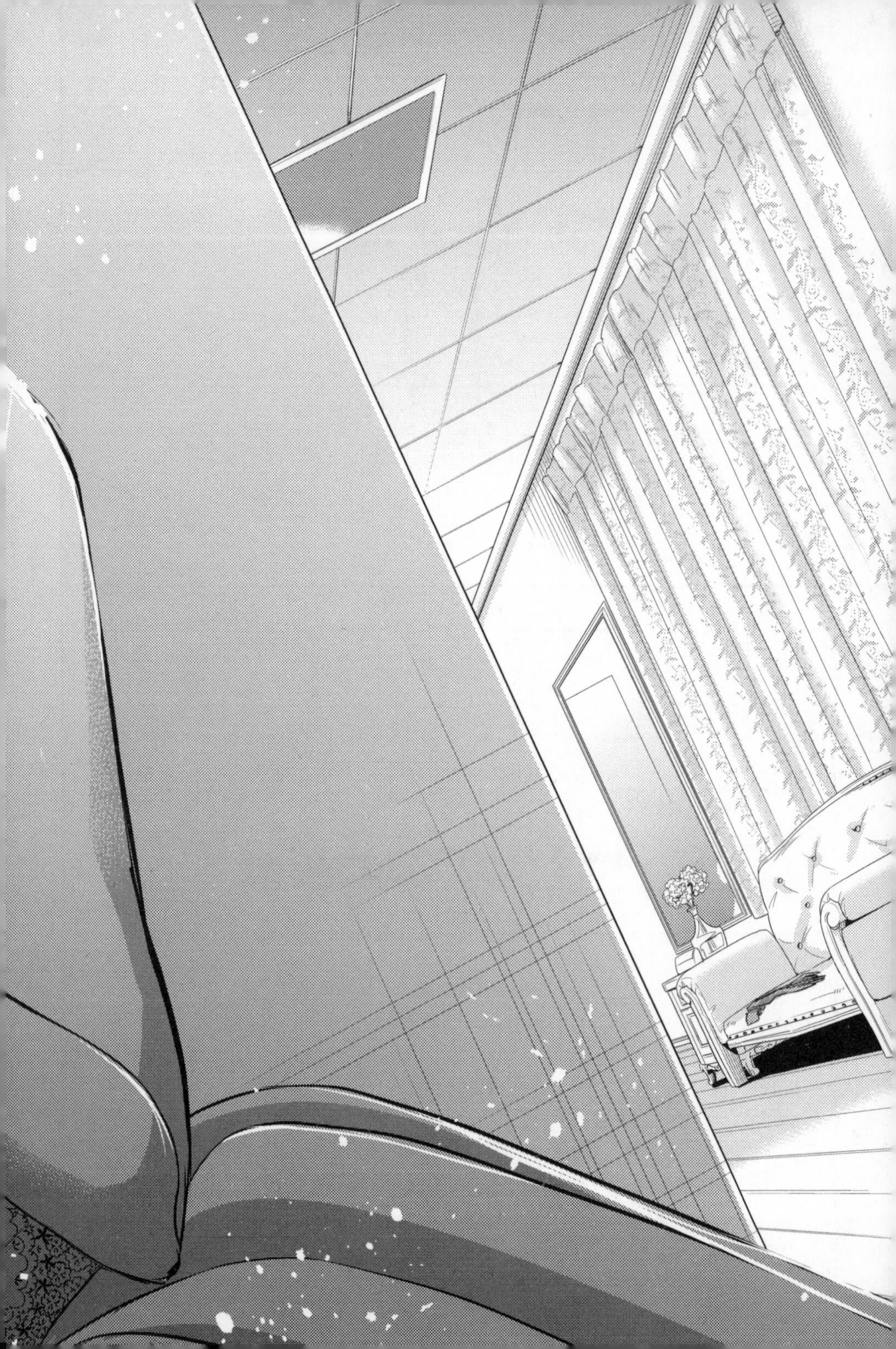

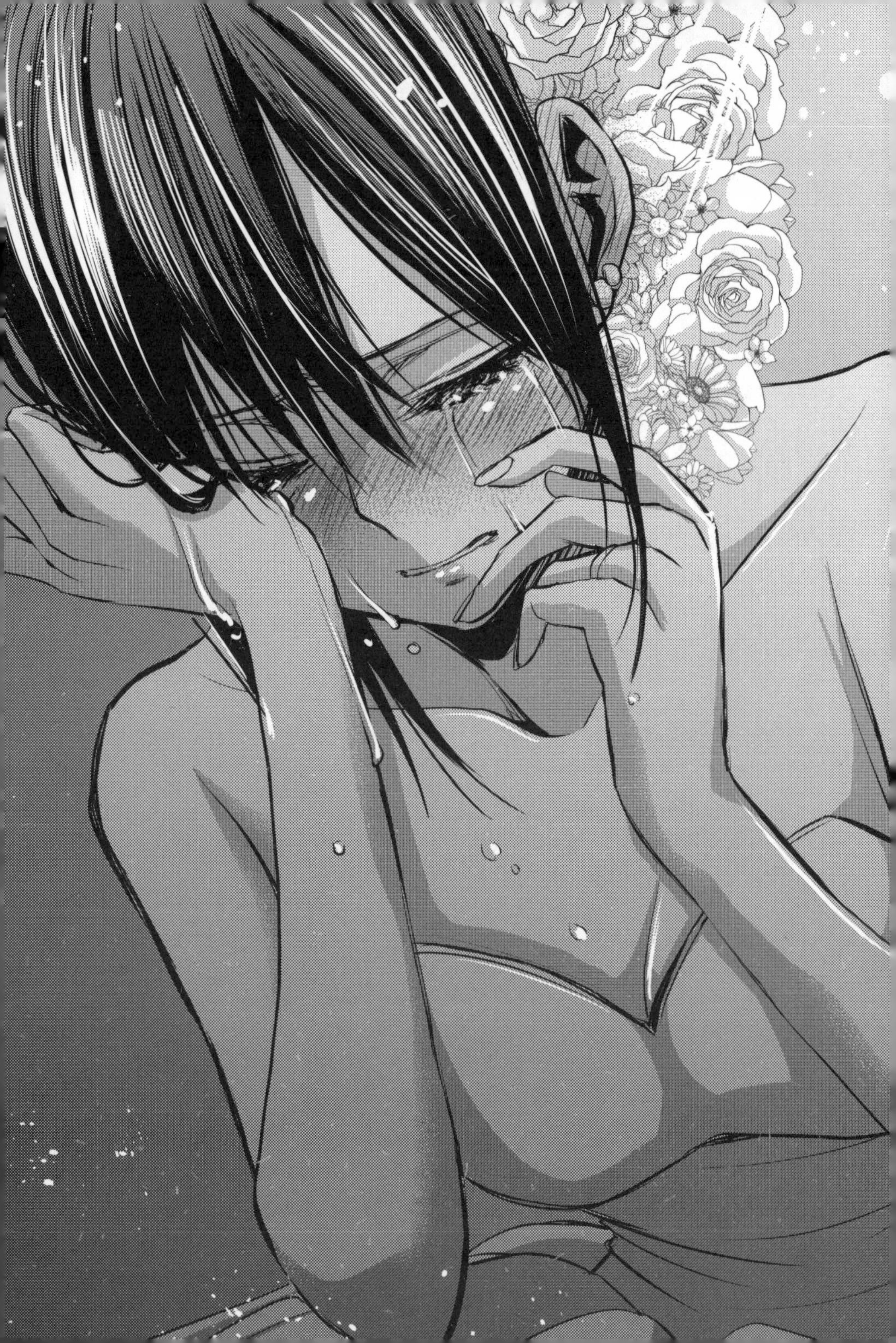

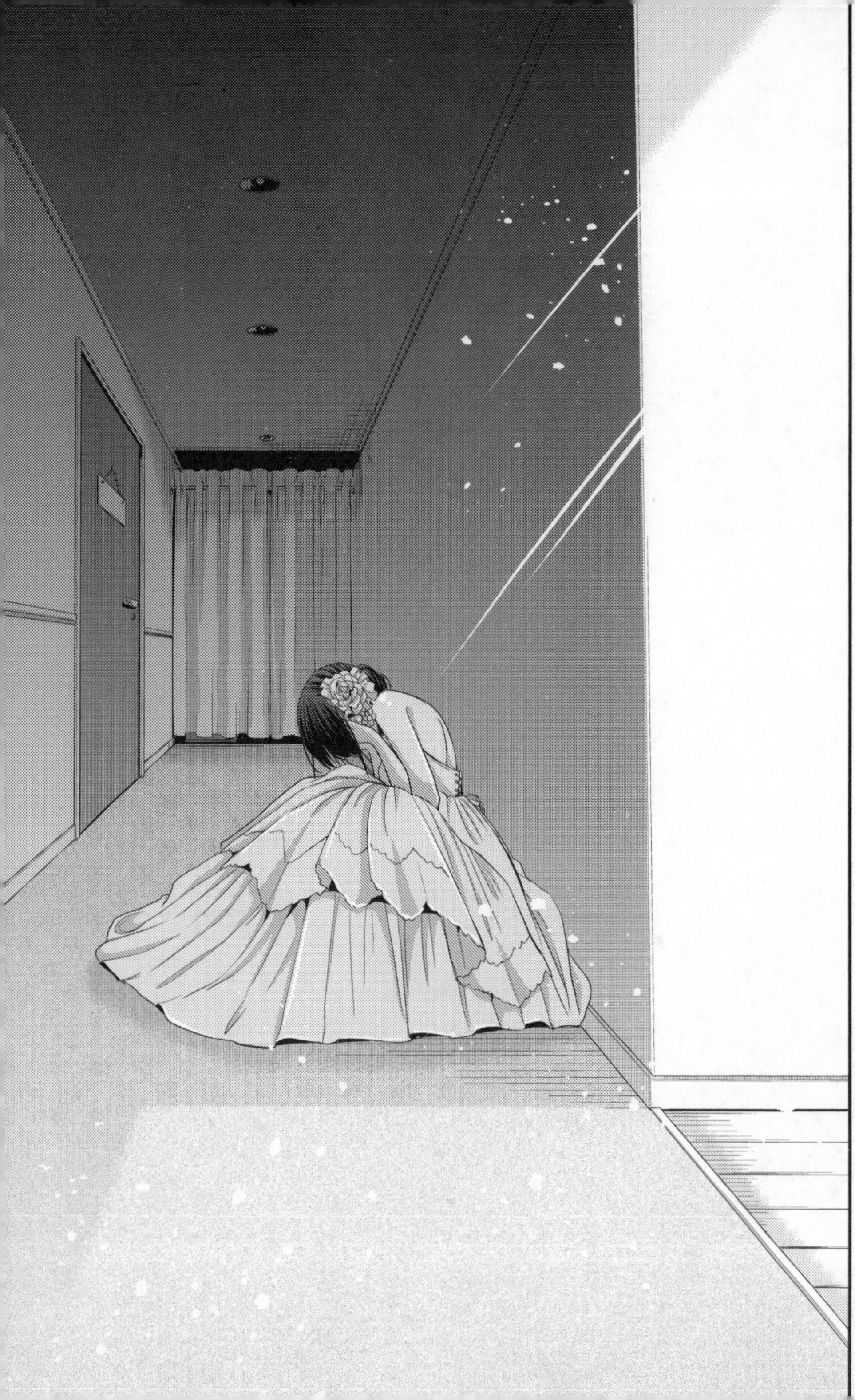

36. Whereabouts of love

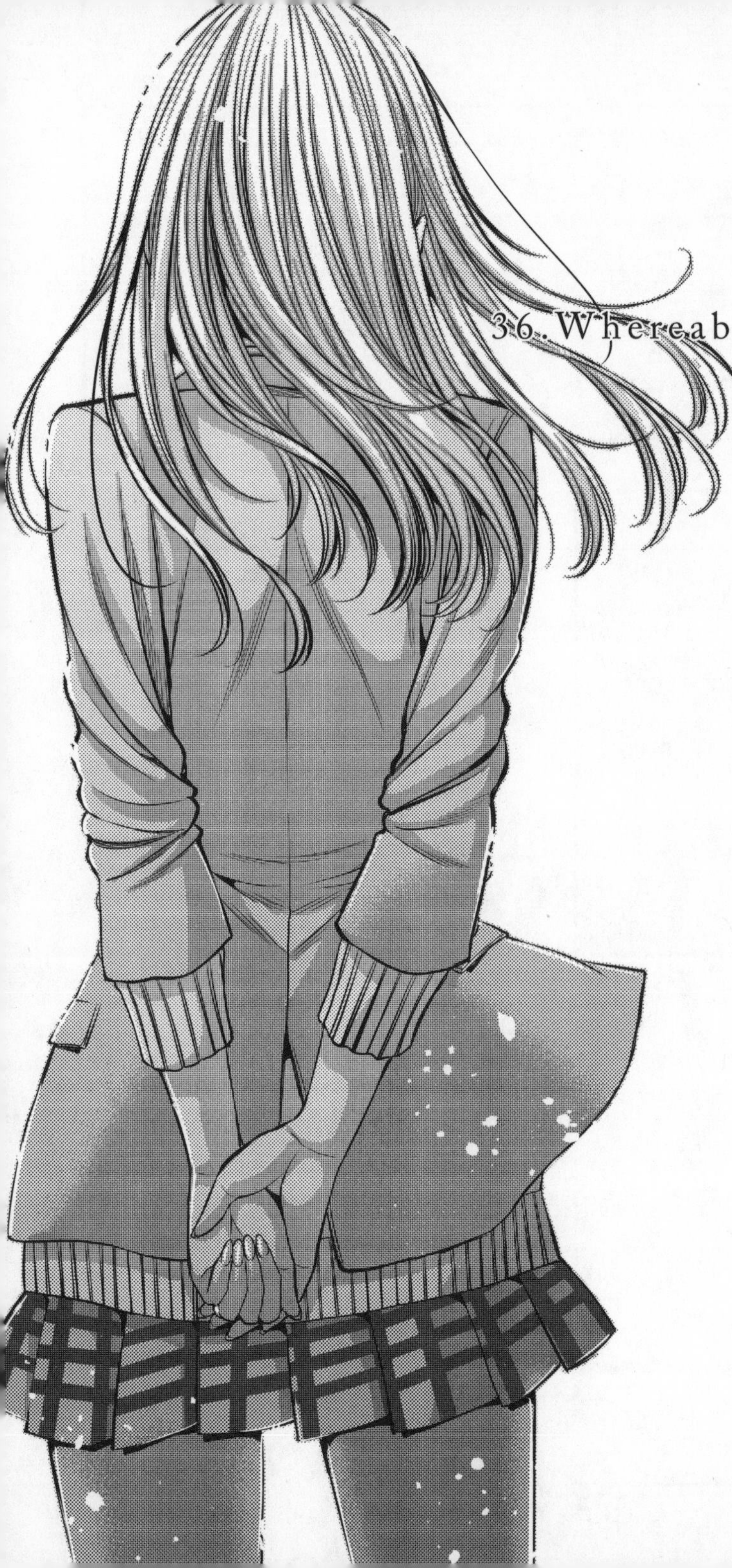

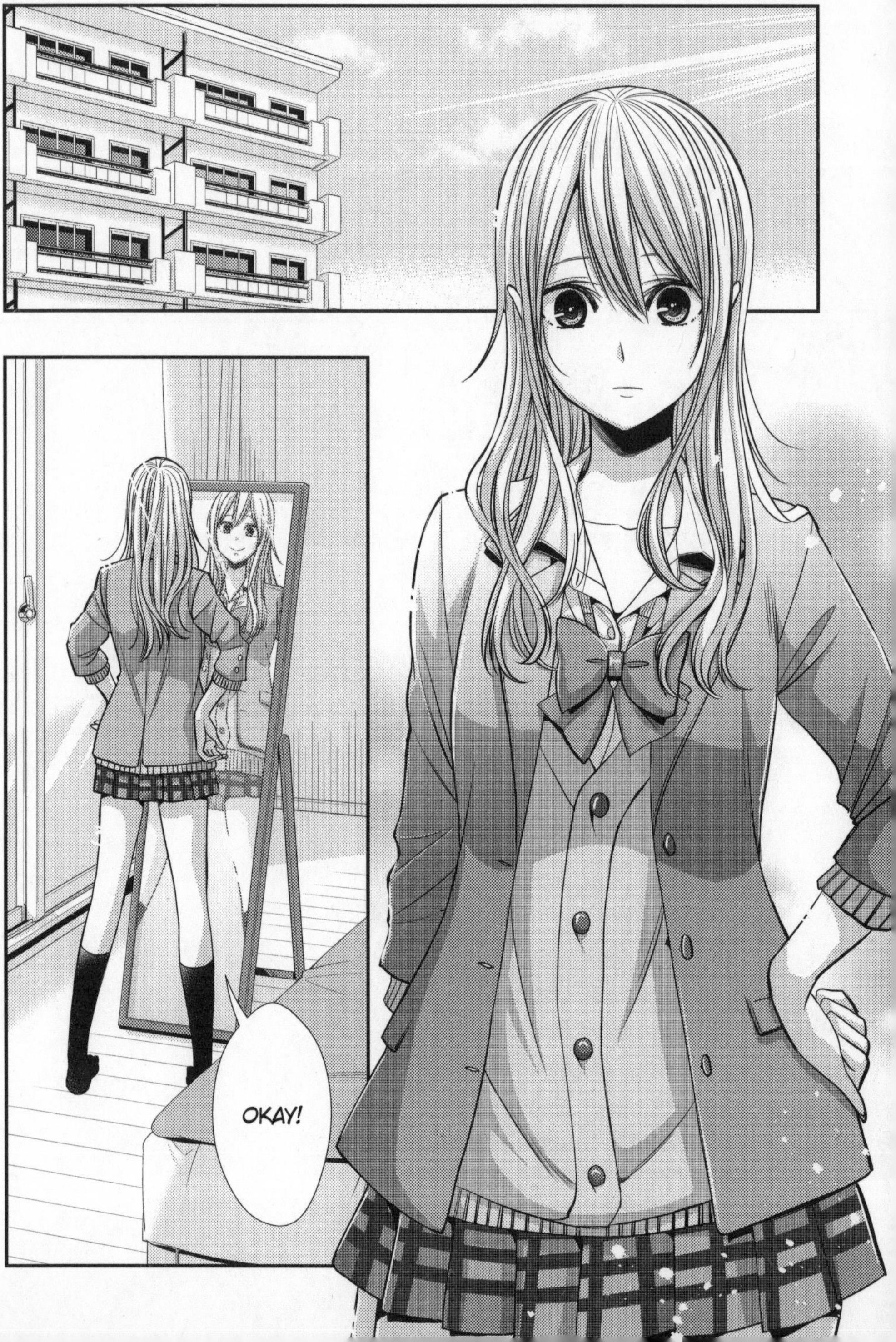
OKAY!

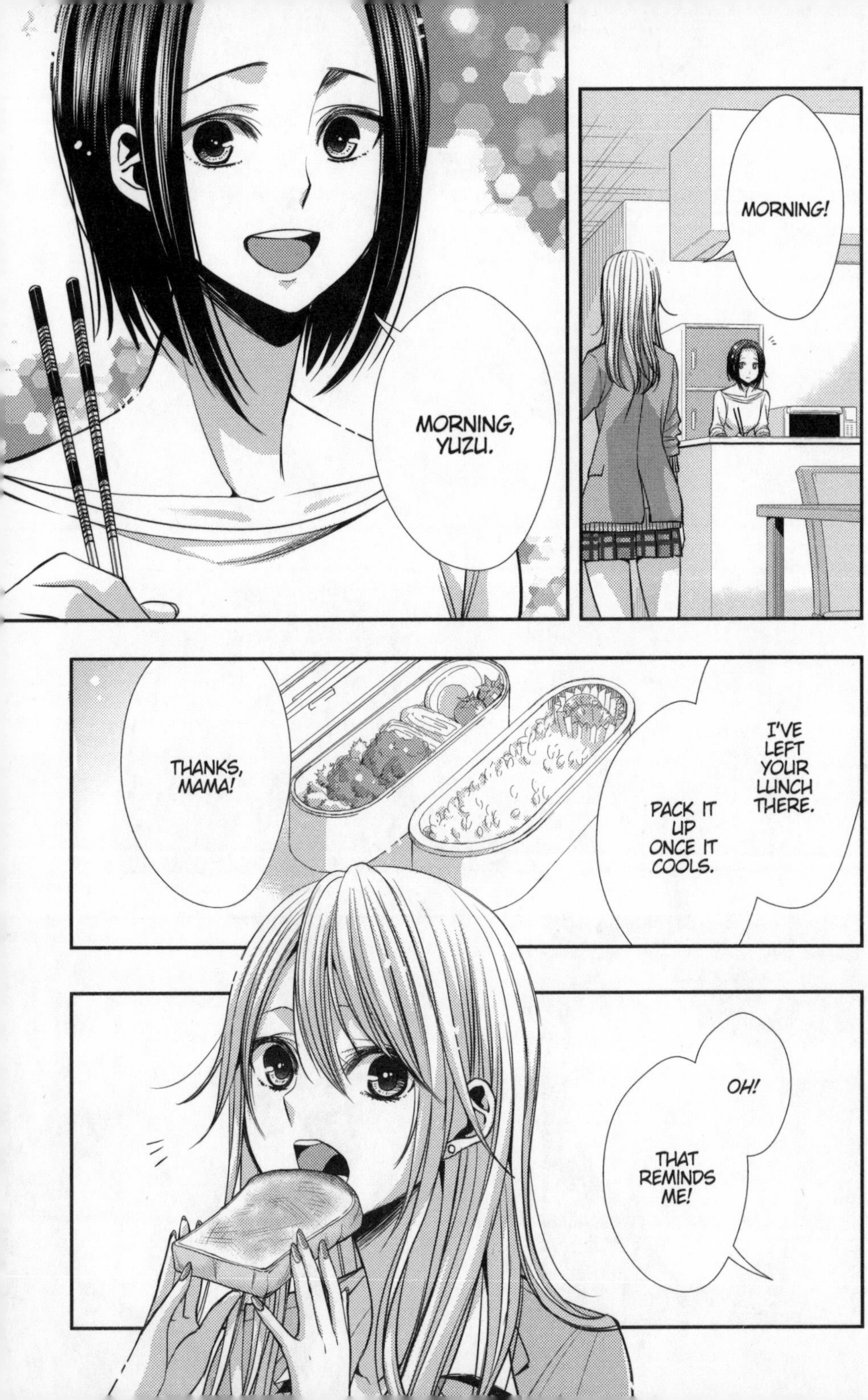
MORNING!
MORNING, YUZU.
I'VE LEFT YOUR LUNCH THERE.
PACK IT UP ONCE IT COOLS.
THANKS, MAMA!
OH!
THAT REMINDS ME!

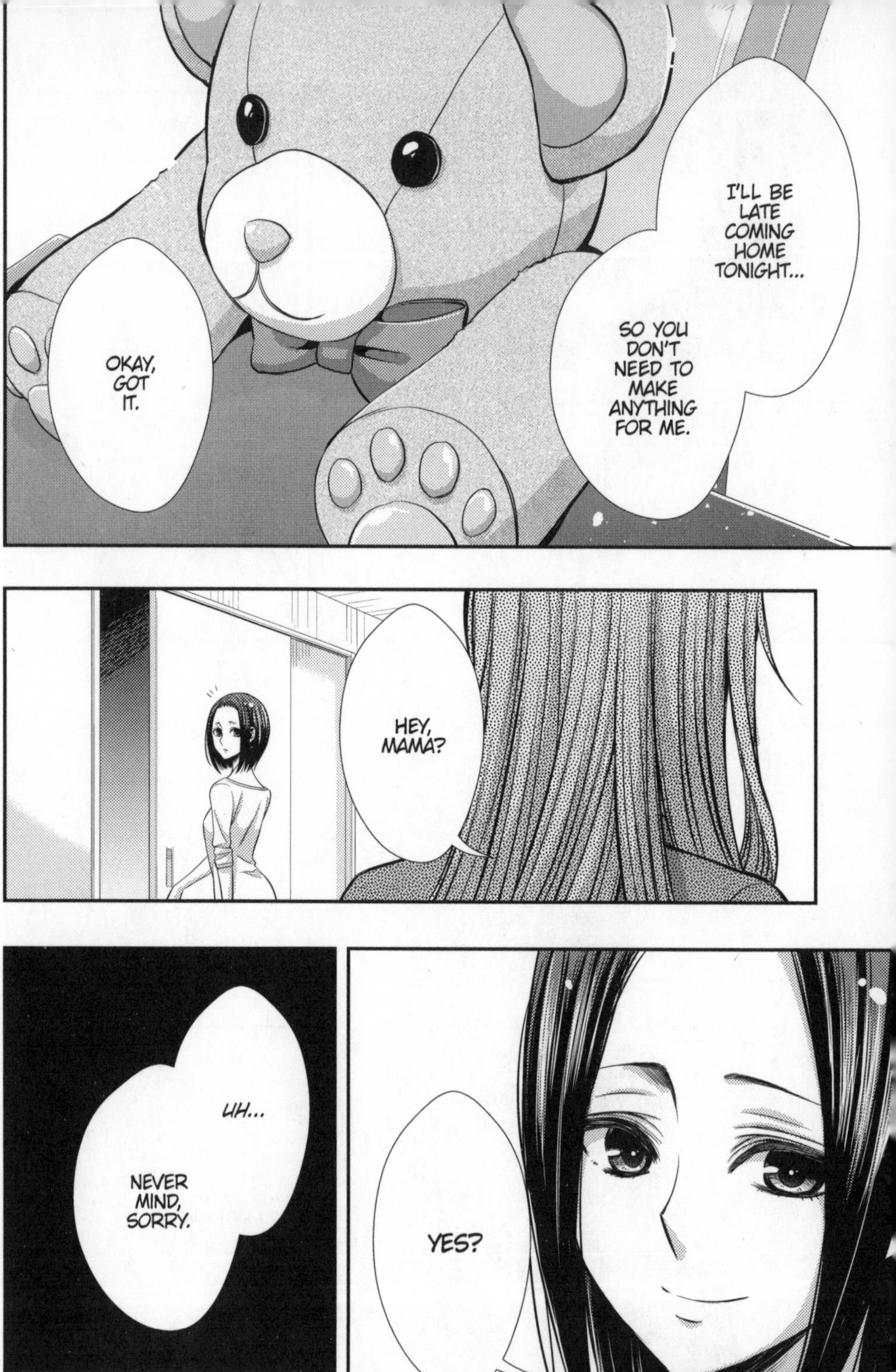
I'LL BE LATE COMING HOME TONIGHT...
SO YOU DON'T NEED TO MAKE ANYTHING FOR ME.
OKAY, GOT IT.
HEY, MAMA?
YES?
UH...
NEVER MIND, SORRY.

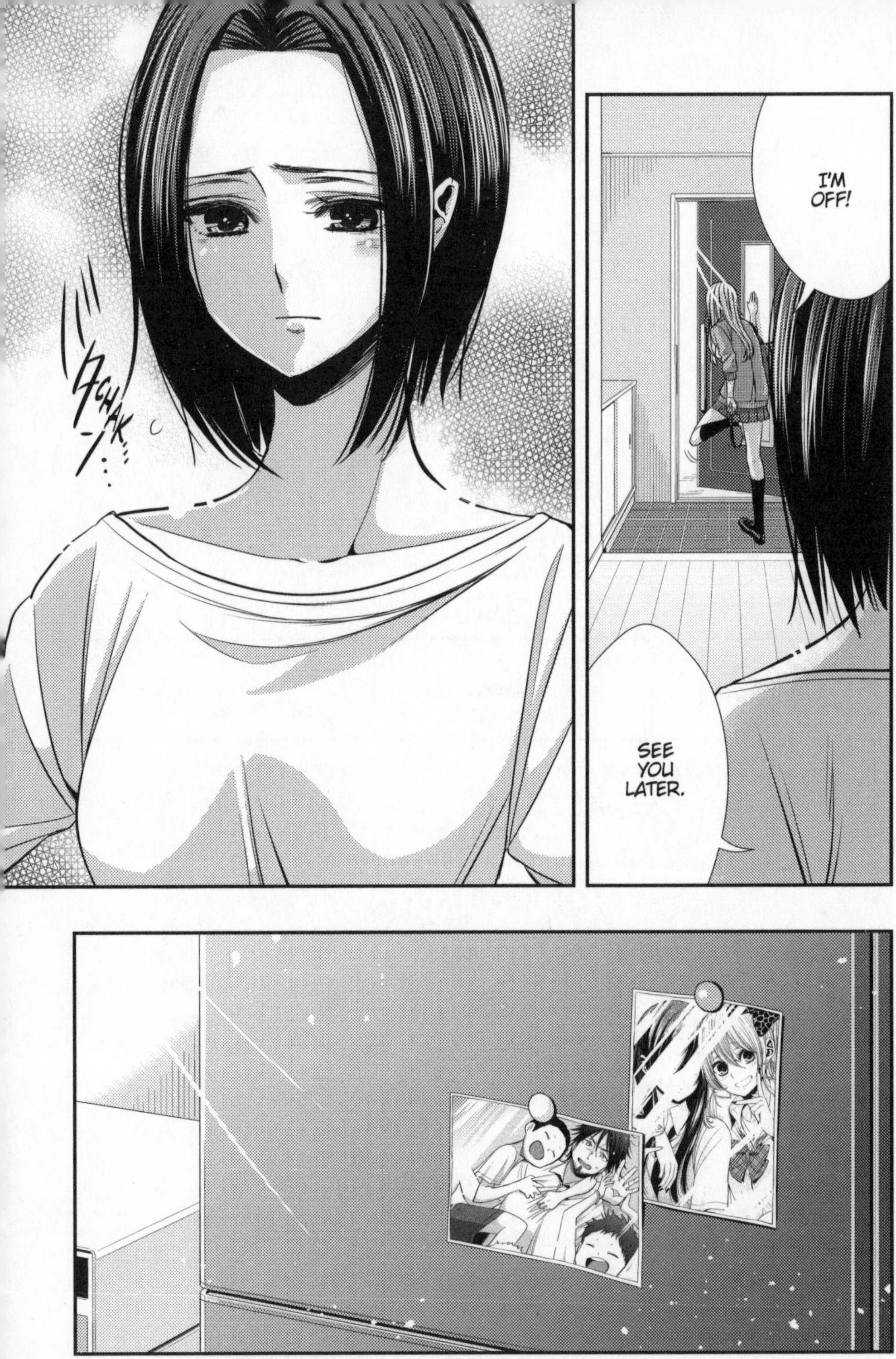
I'M OFF!
SEE YOU LATER.
CHAK

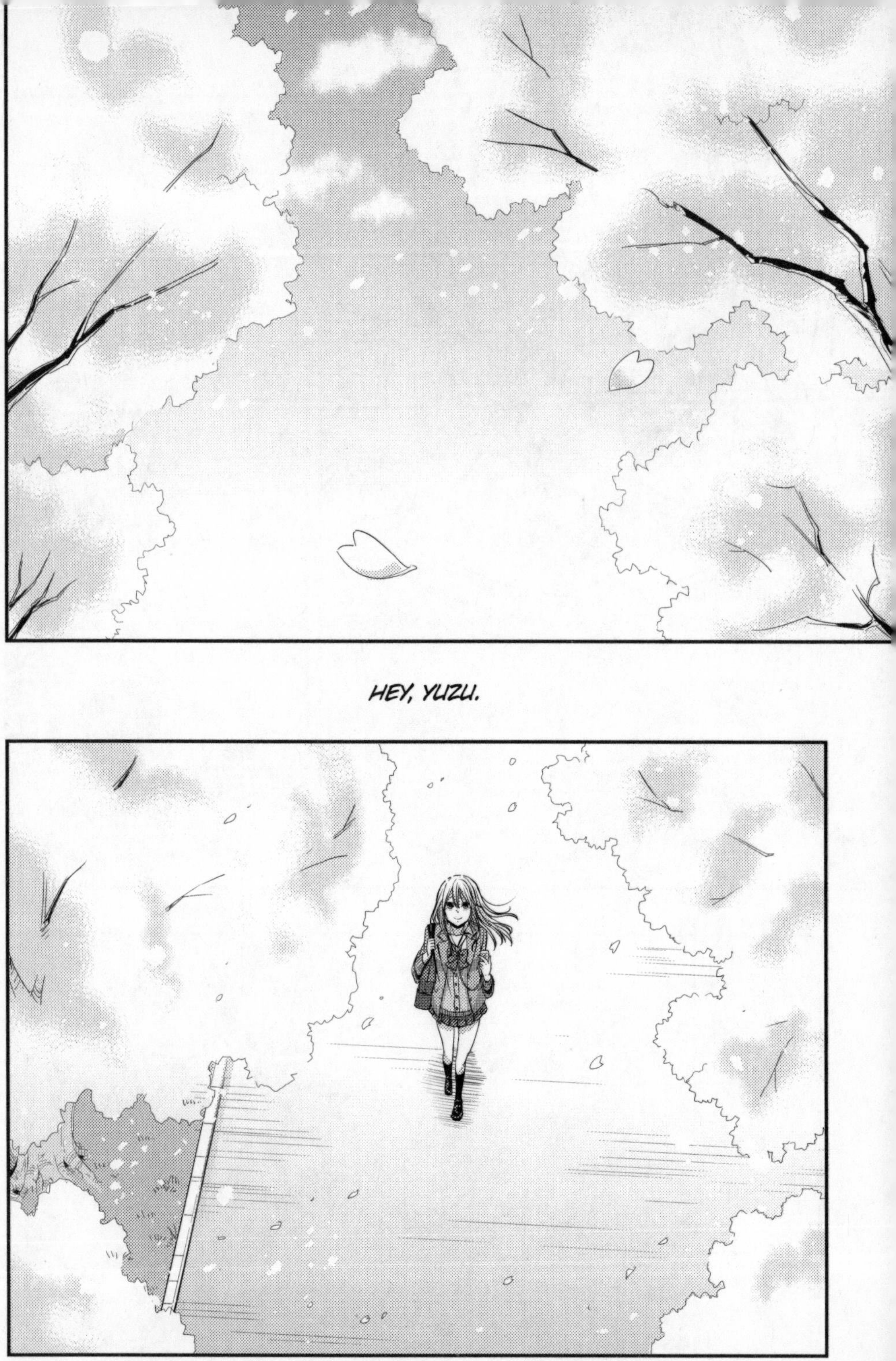
HEY, YUZU.

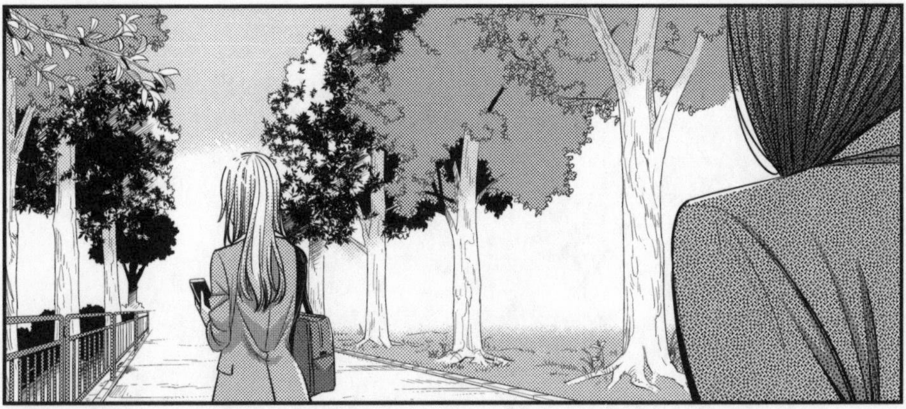

DO YOU REMEMBER WHAT HAPPENED THE FIRST NIGHT WE BECAME SISTERS?

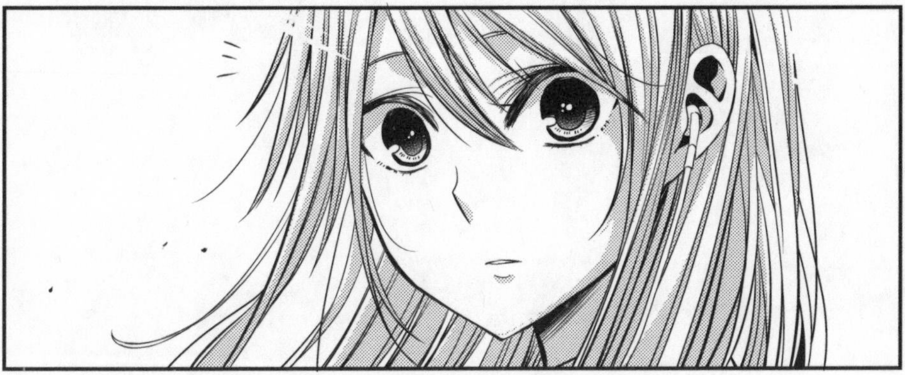

WHEN I SHOULD HAVE BEEN ACCEPTING YOU AS MY BIG SISTER...

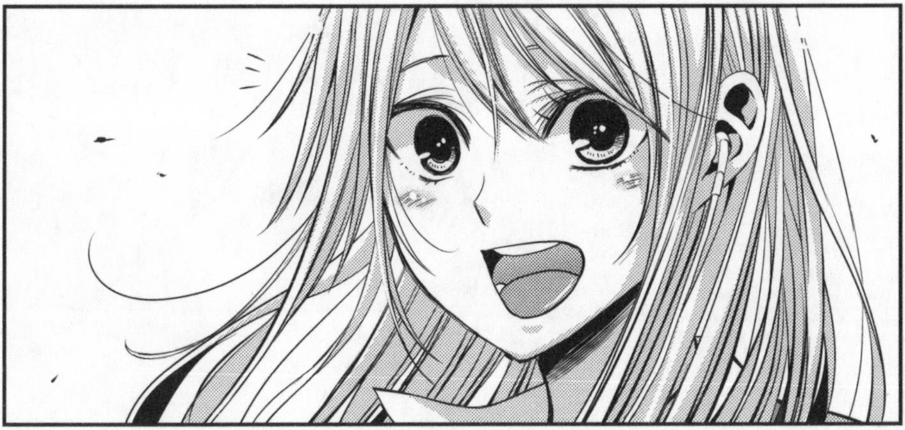

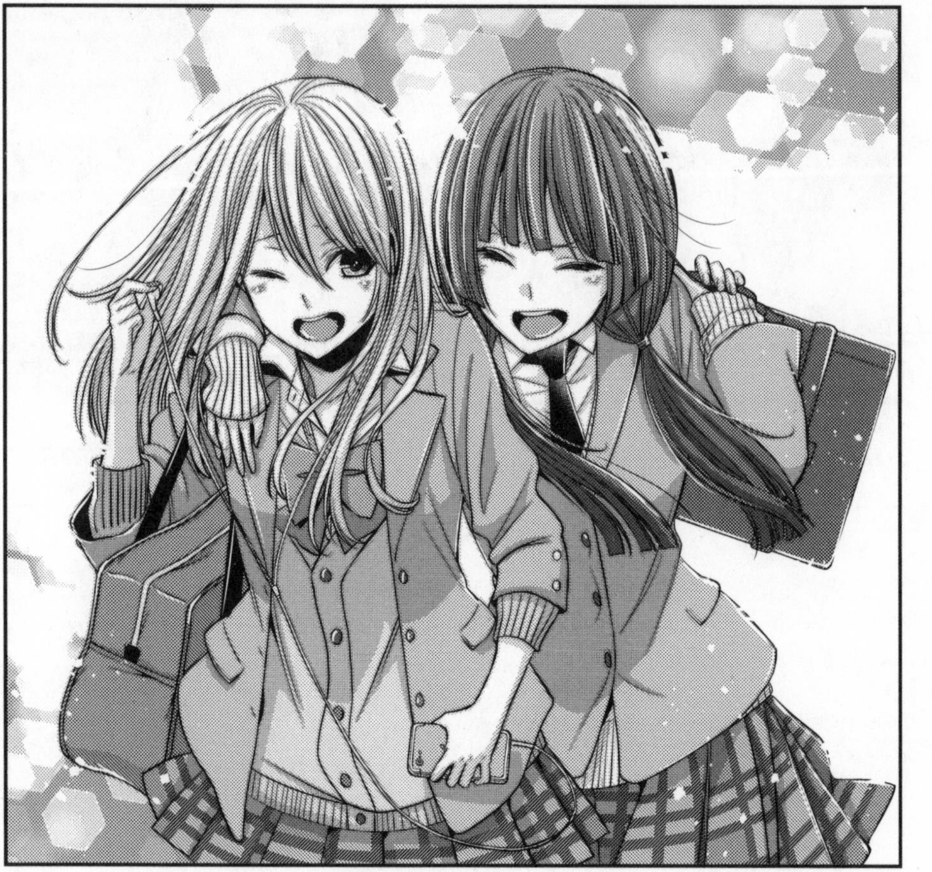

I KISSED YOU INSTEAD.

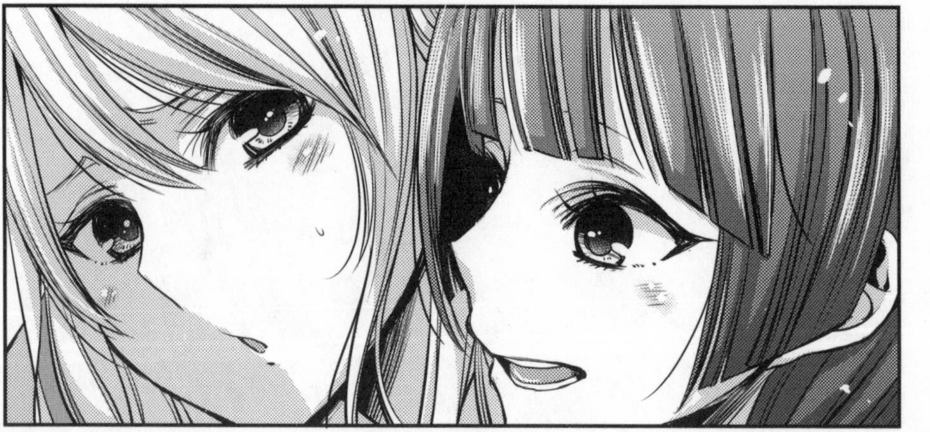

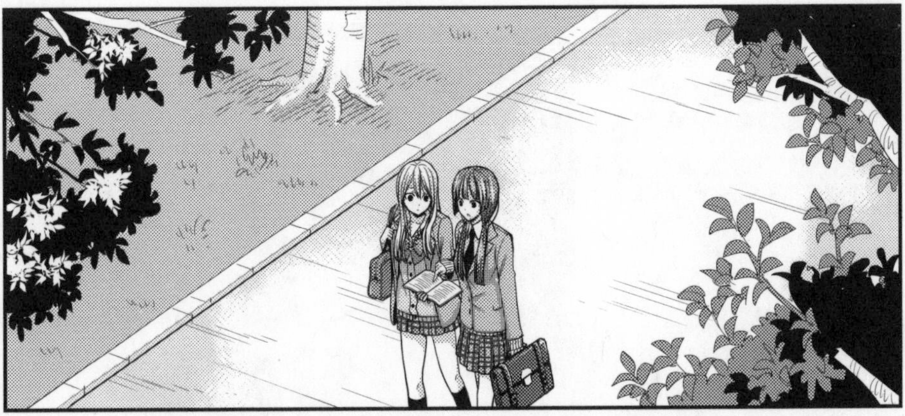

BACK THEN, I THOUGHT THE ONLY THING I HAD TO LIVE FOR WAS LOOKING AFTER MY FATHER'S SCHOOL...

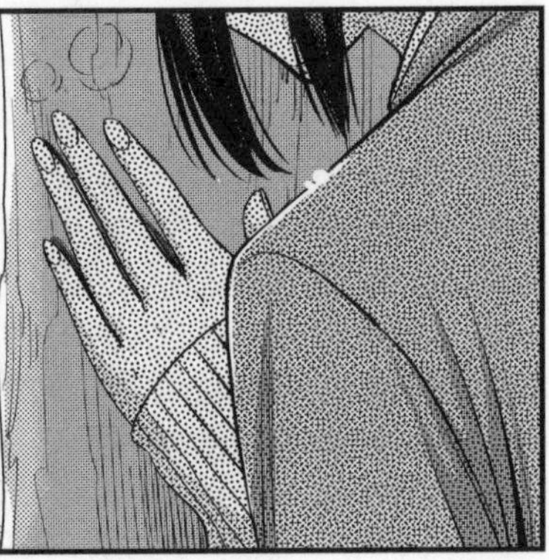

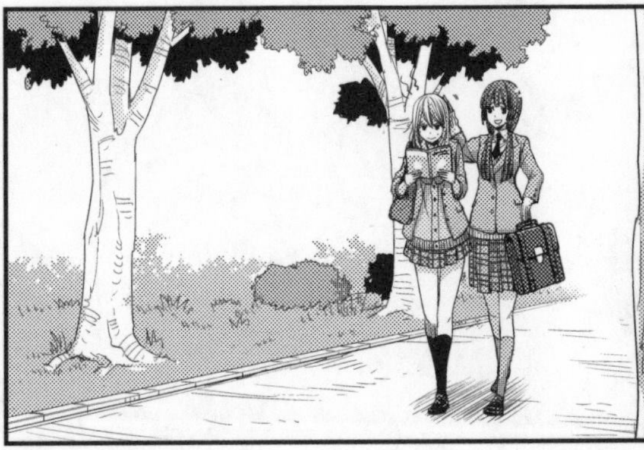

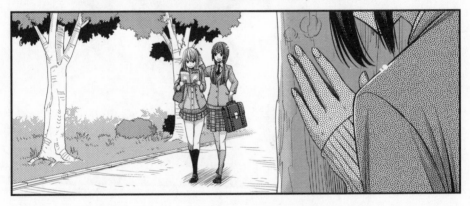

FOR THE SAKE OF THE AIHARA FAMILY...AND MYSELF.

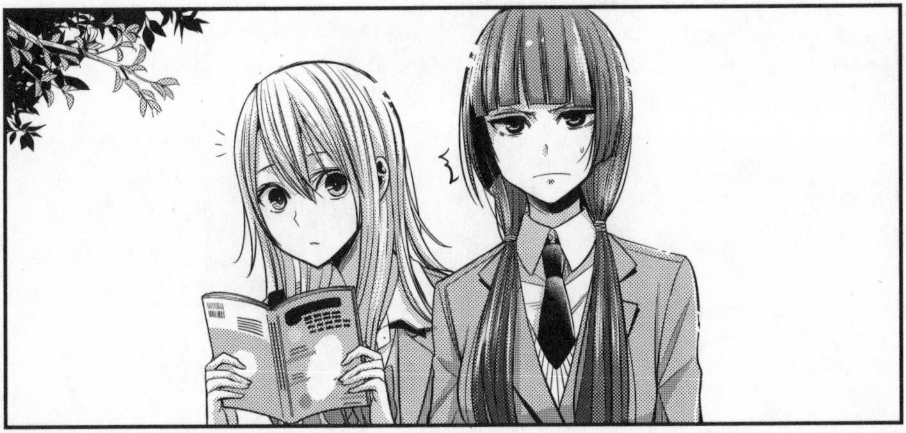

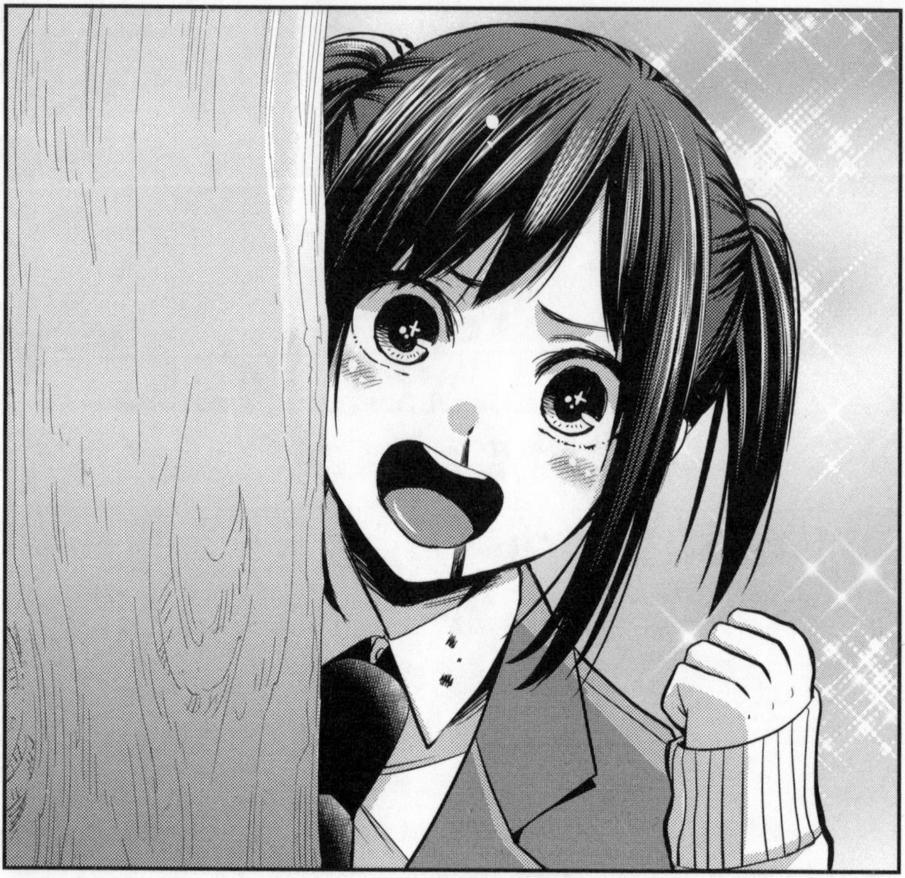

BUT THERE YOU WERE, SO WILD AND FREE, TALKING ON AND ON ABOUT ***LOVE.***

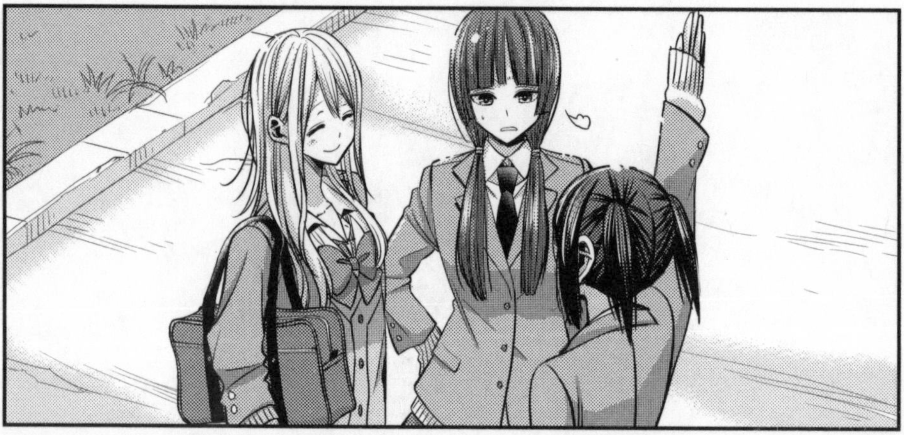

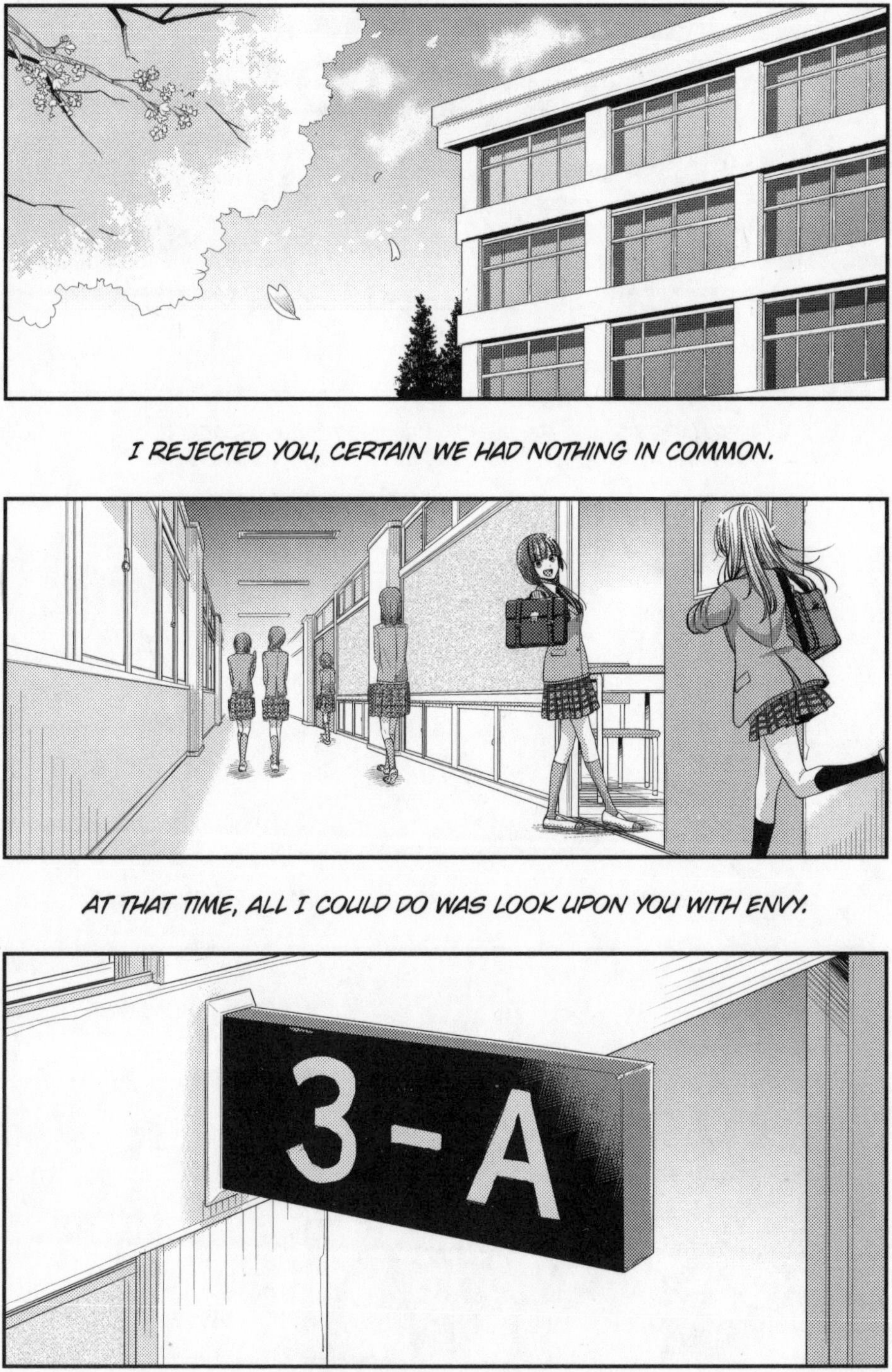
I REJECTED YOU, CERTAIN WE HAD NOTHING IN COMMON.
AT THAT TIME, ALL I COULD DO WAS LOOK UPON YOU WITH ENVY.
3-A

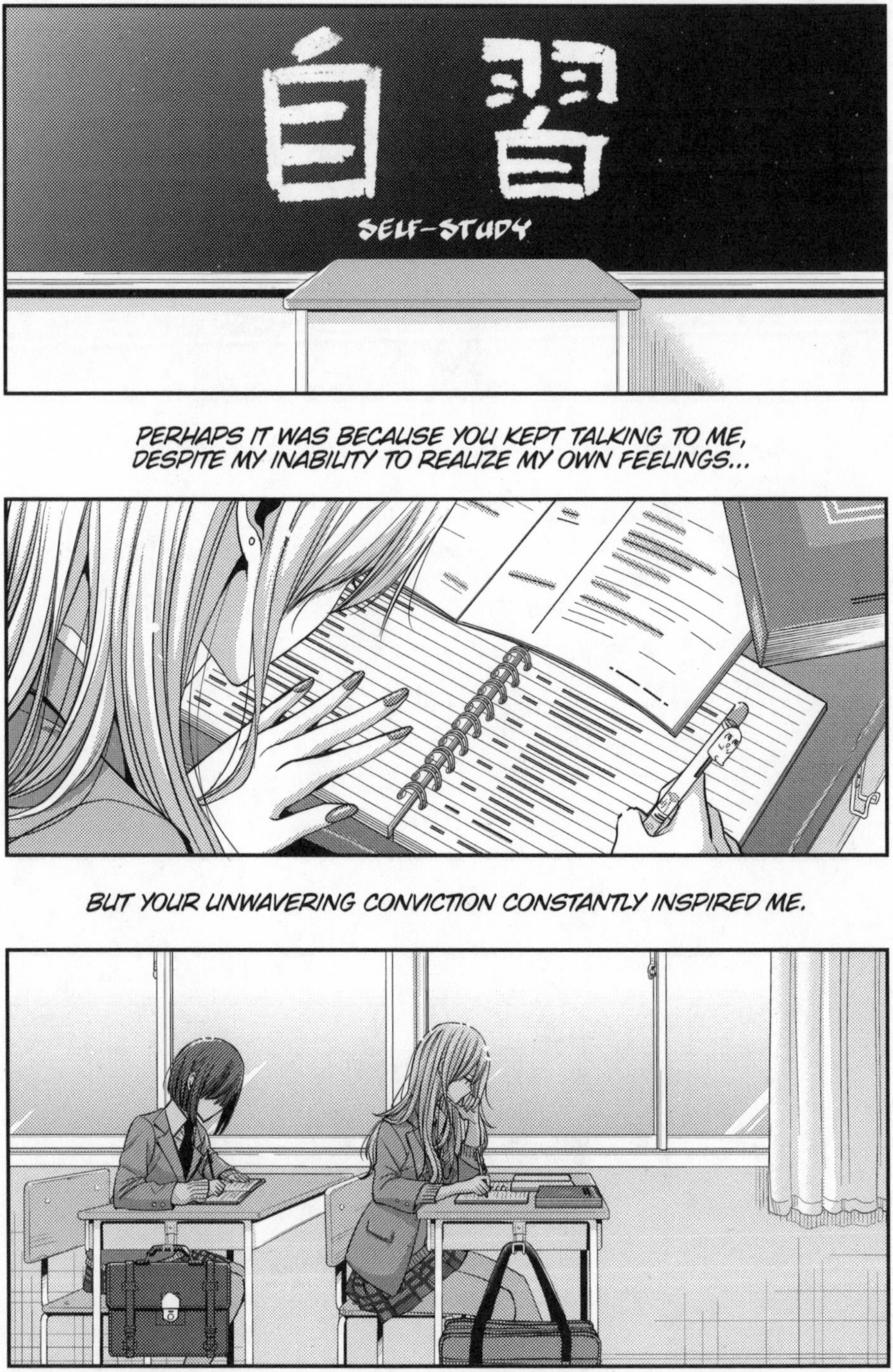
自習
SELF-STUDY
PERHAPS IT WAS BECAUSE YOU KEPT TALKING TO ME, DESPITE MY INABILITY TO REALIZE MY OWN FEELINGS...
BUT YOUR UNWAVERING CONVICTION CONSTANTLY INSPIRED ME.

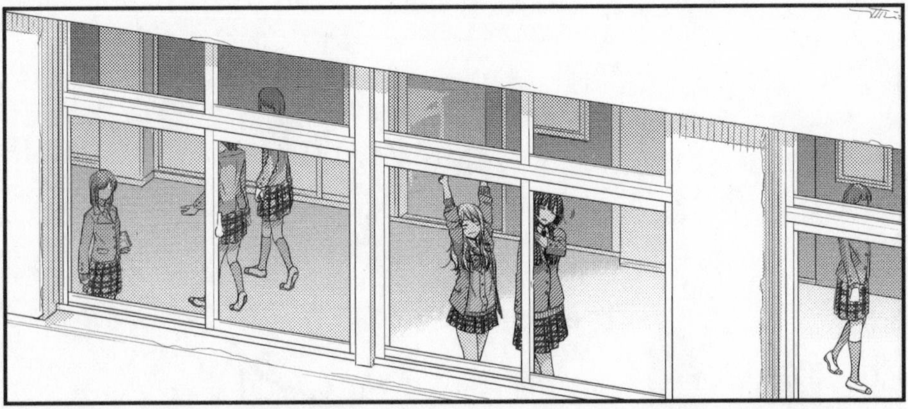

AND BECAUSE OF THAT, I WAS ABLE TO TELL MY FATHER THE THINGS I HAD LOCKED AWAY INSIDE...

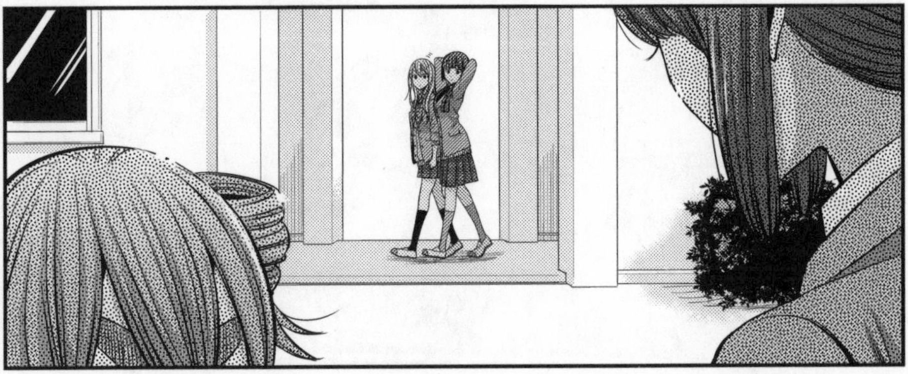

AND TO SEE THE IMPORTANCE OF FACING MY TRUE FEELINGS.

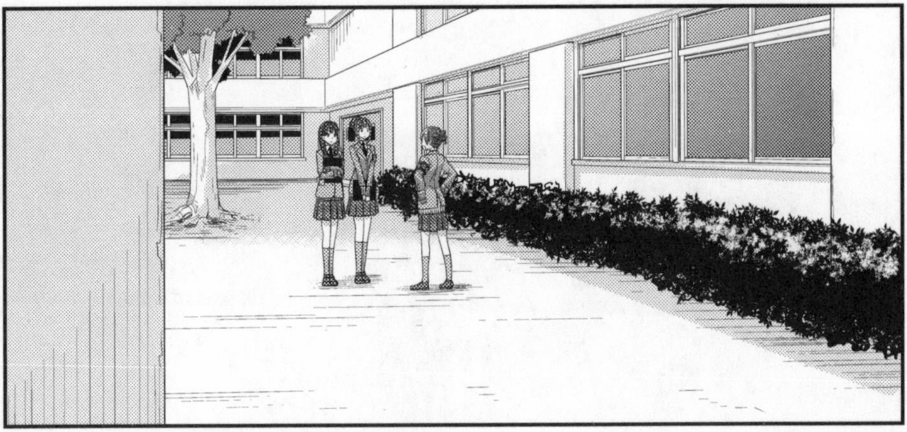

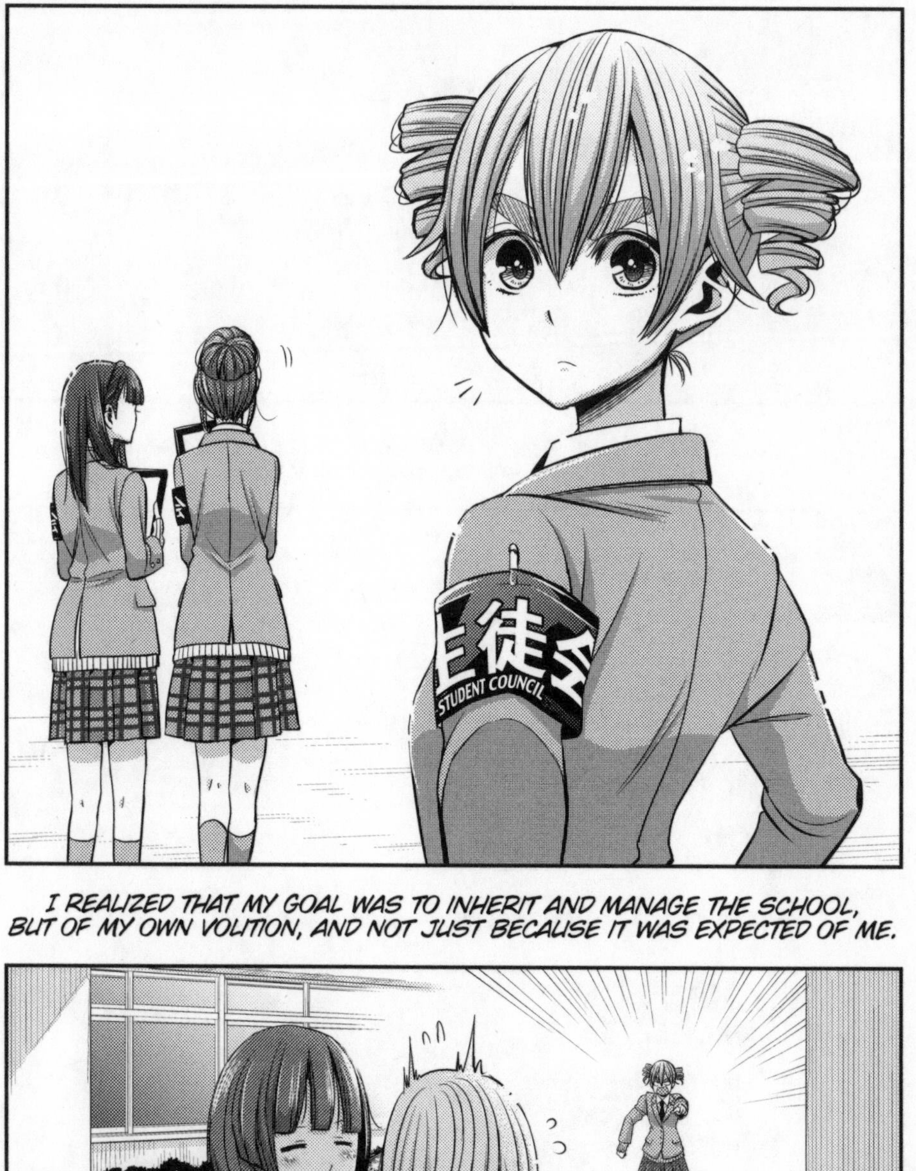
STUDENT COUNCIL

I REALIZED THAT MY GOAL WAS TO INHERIT AND MANAGE THE SCHOOL, BUT OF MY OWN VOLITION, AND NOT JUST BECAUSE IT WAS EXPECTED OF ME.

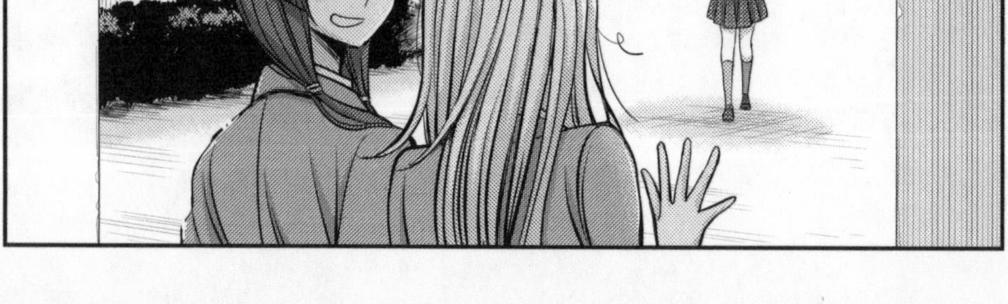

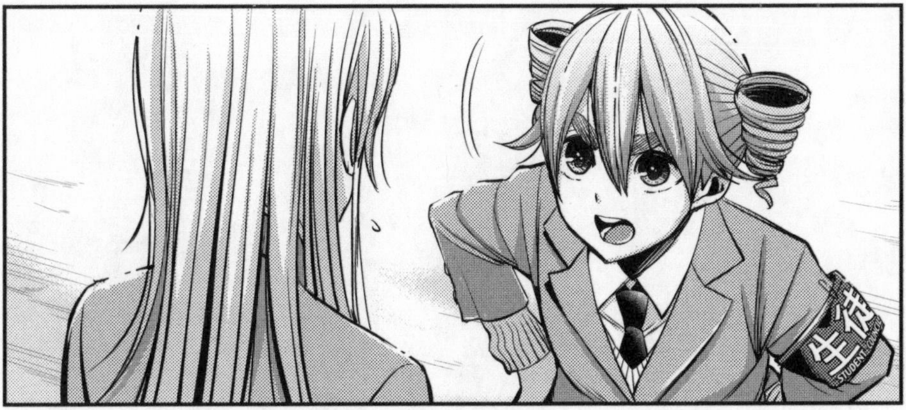
生徒

HOWEVER...

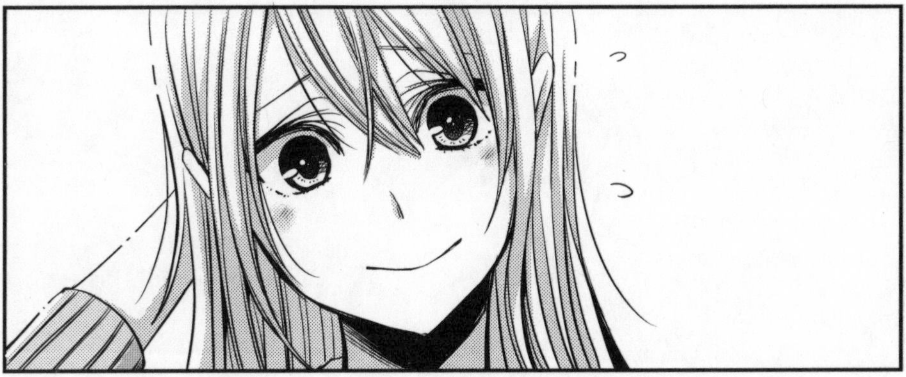

AT THE SAME TIME, I BECAME AWARE OF **SOMETHING ELSE.**

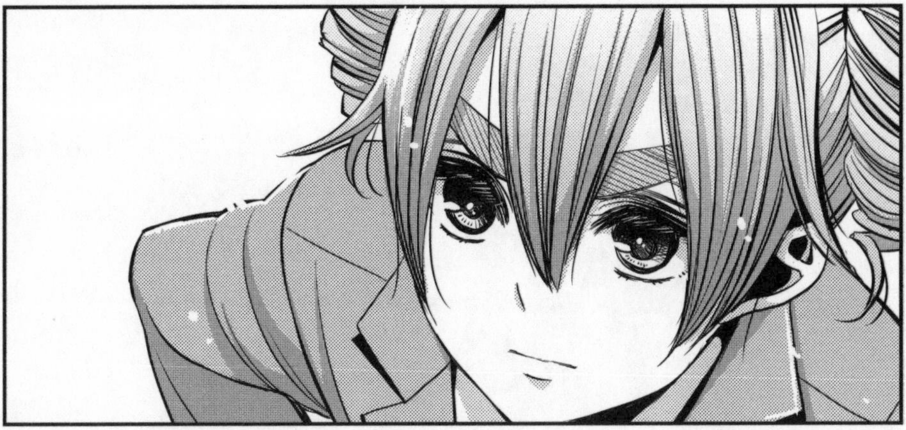

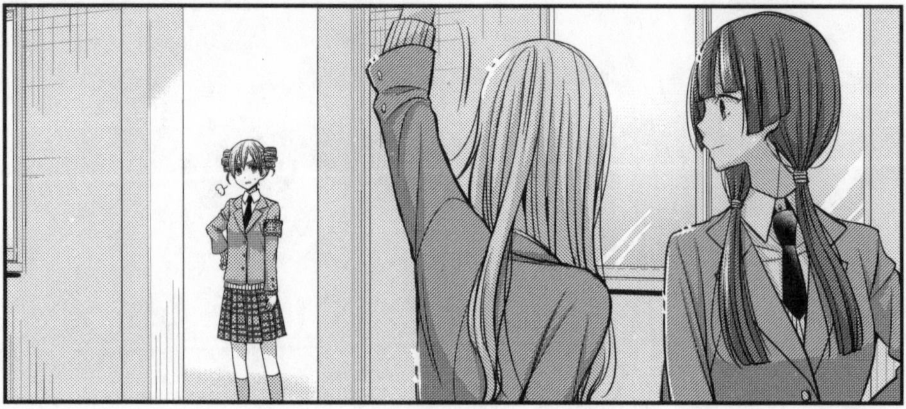

YOUR WARMTH.

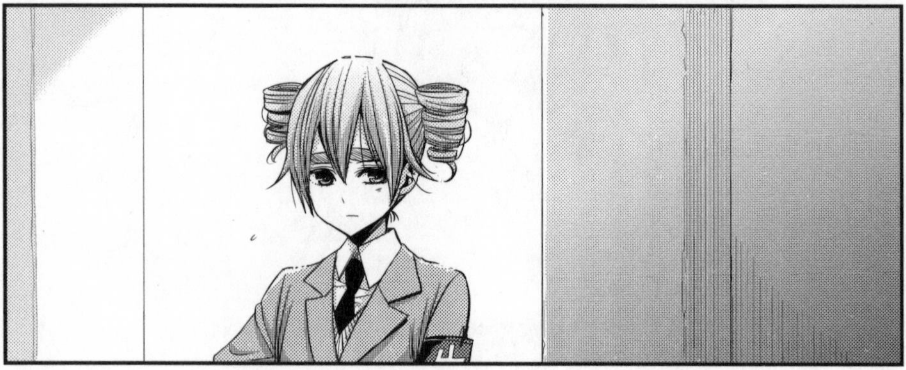

YET EVEN AS I ALLOWED IT TO COVER MY HEART...

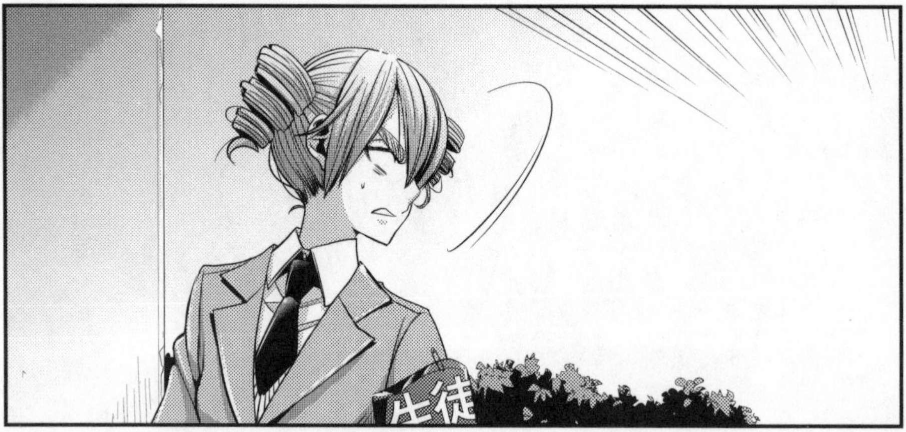
生徒

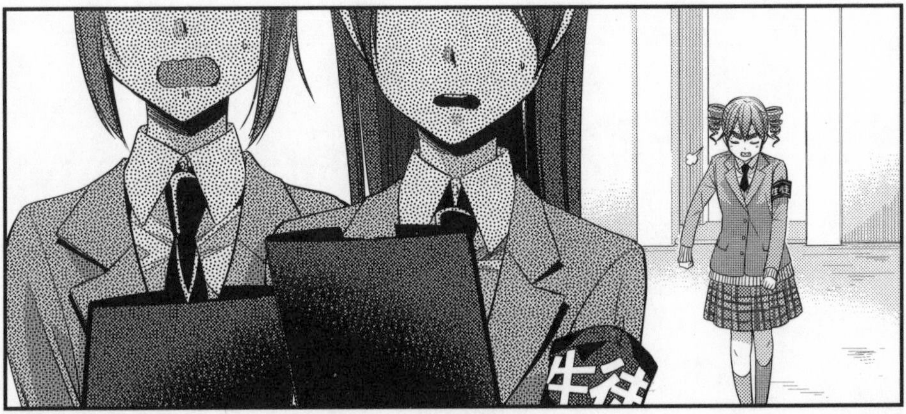

A SENSE OF FEAR GREW WITHIN ME...

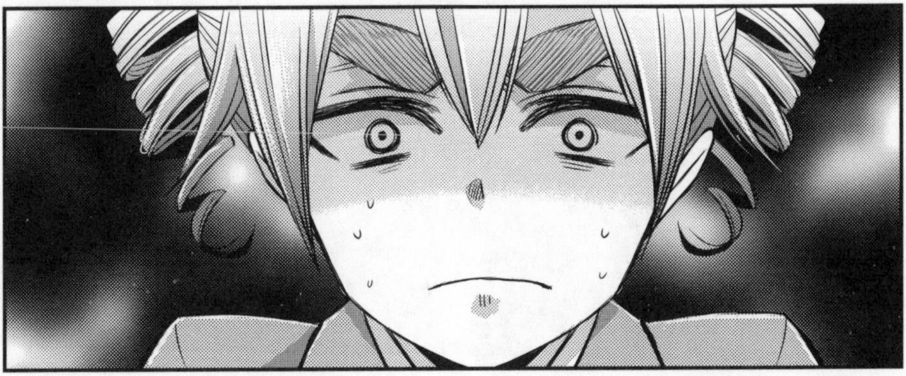

JUST AS I WAS BEGINNING TO PURSUE MY OWN GOALS.

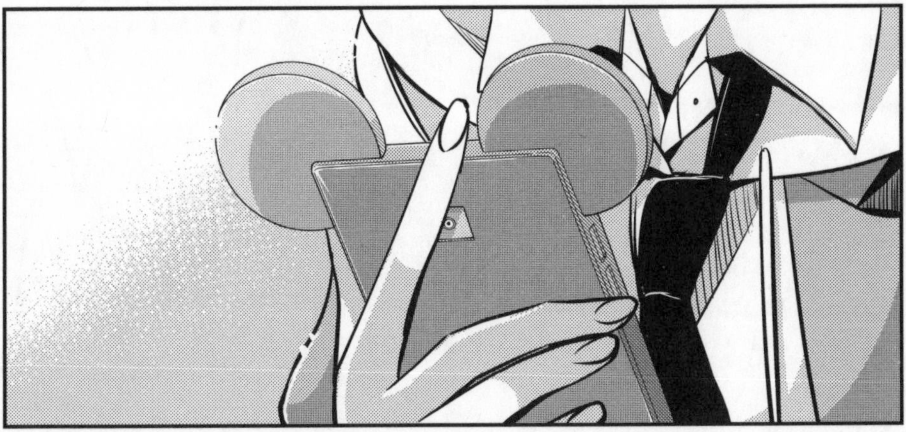

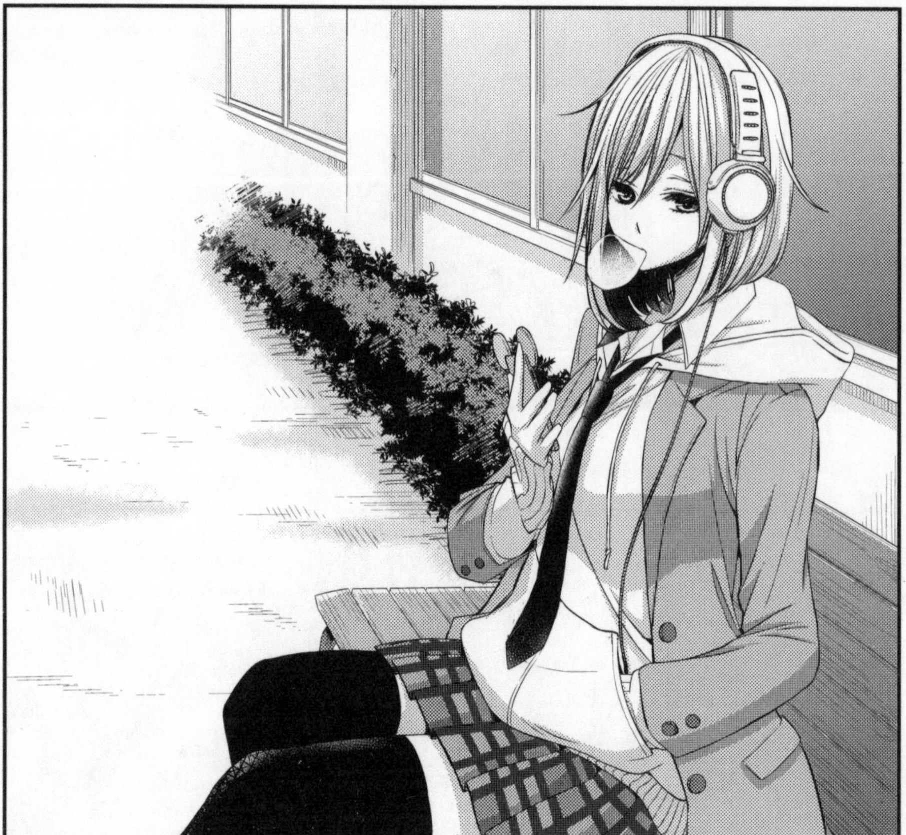

I TRIED ONCE MORE TO HIDE THE FEELINGS BUDDING WITHIN ME.

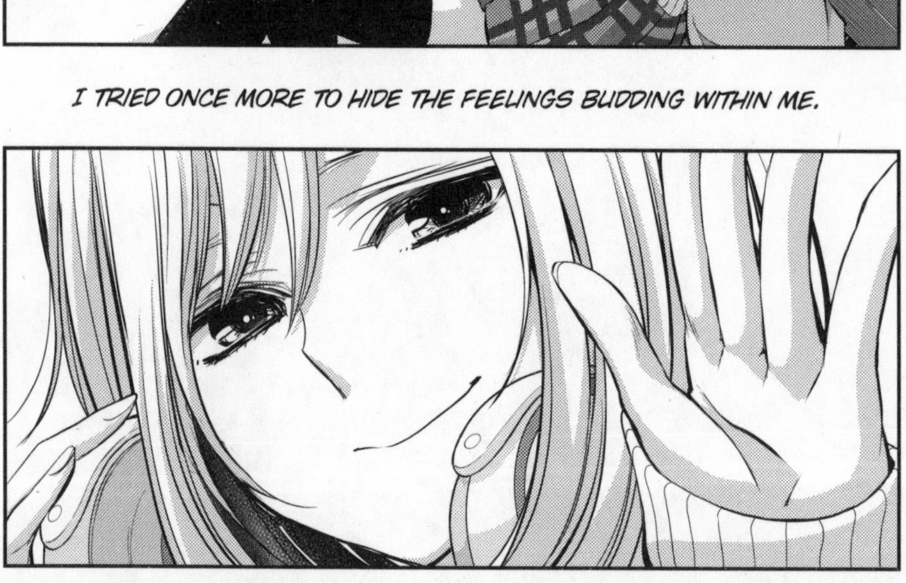

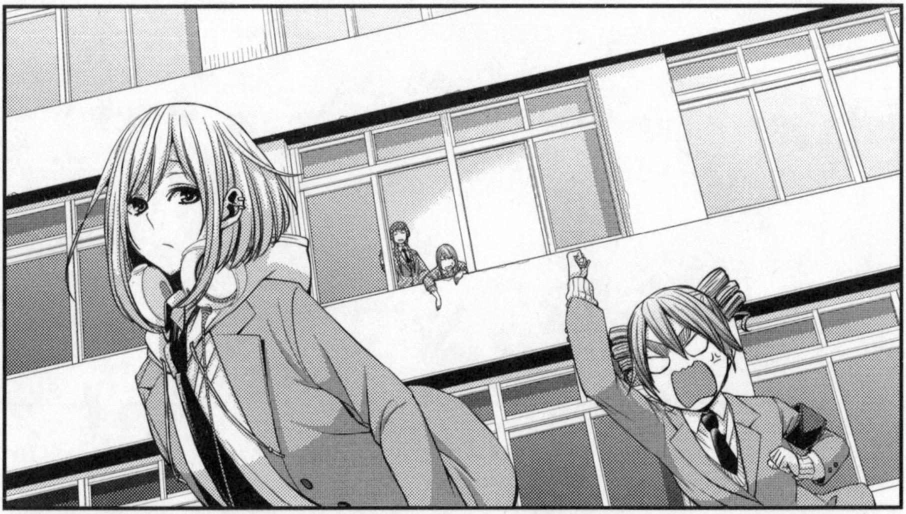

BUT NOW THAT I KNOW HOW IMPORTANT IT IS TO EMBRACE MY FEELINGS...

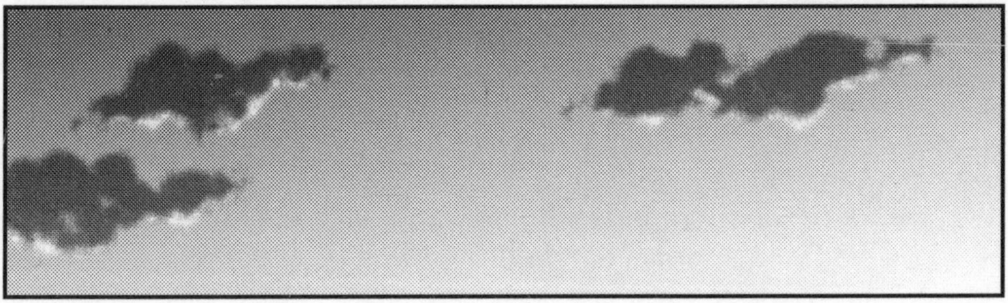

I CAN'T GO BACK TO THE WAY I WAS BEFORE I MET YOU.

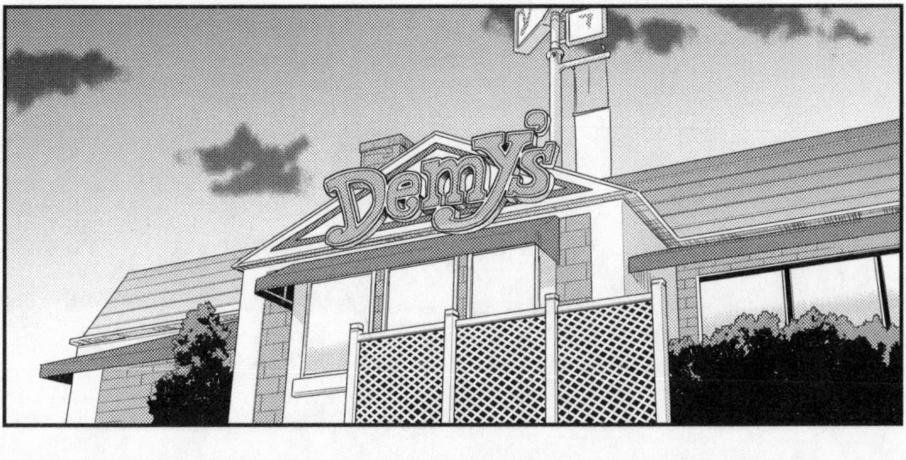

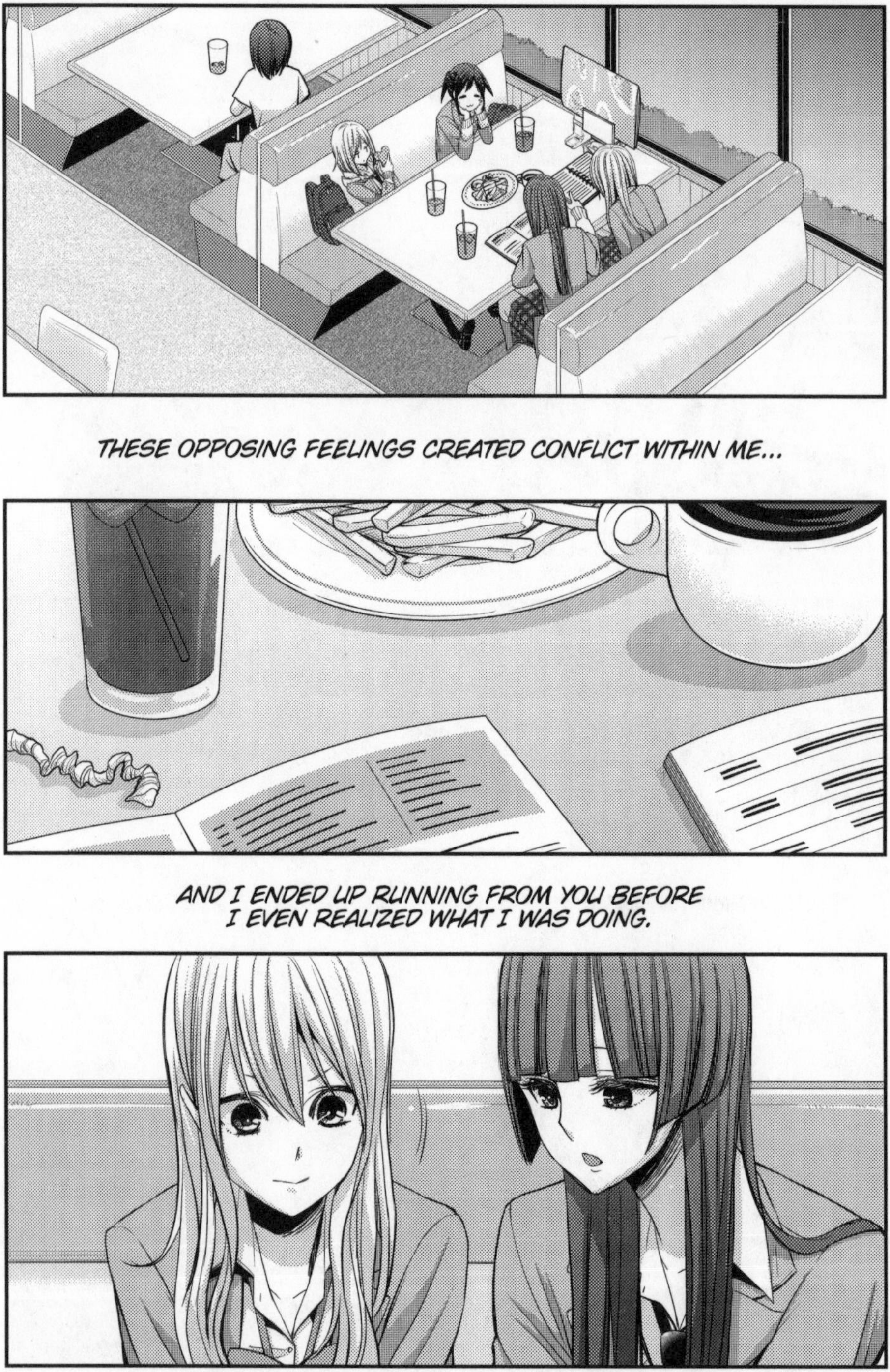
THESE OPPOSING FEELINGS CREATED CONFLICT WITHIN ME...
AND I ENDED UP RUNNING FROM YOU BEFORE I EVEN REALIZED WHAT I WAS DOING.

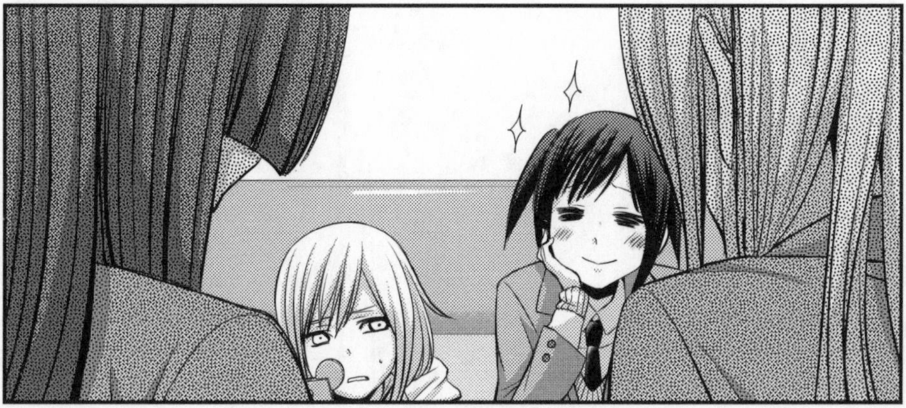

STILL, YOU PURSUED ME...

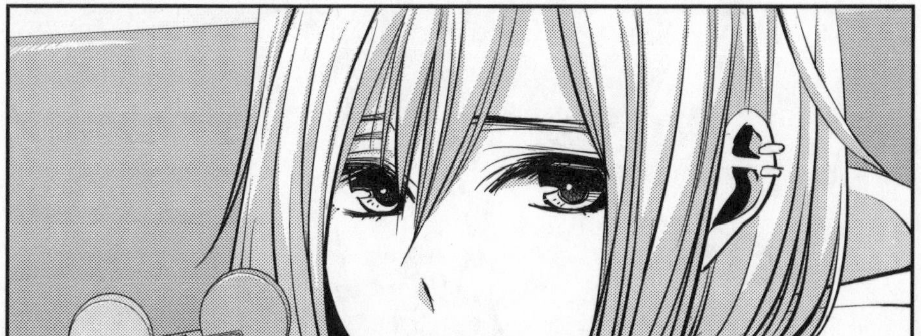

AND WHEN YOU CONFESSED YOUR FEELINGS TO ME,
BLUNTLY AND WITHOUT ANY HIDDEN MOTIVE...

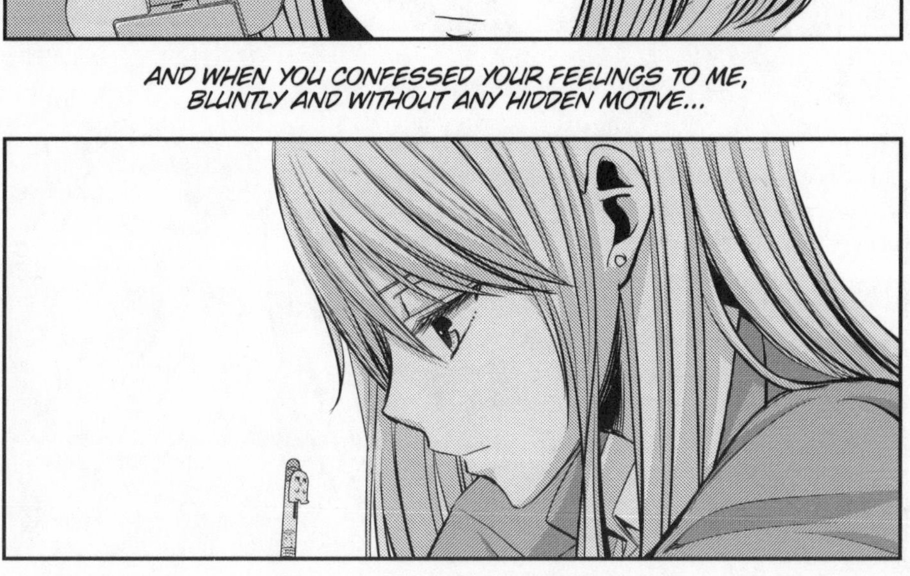

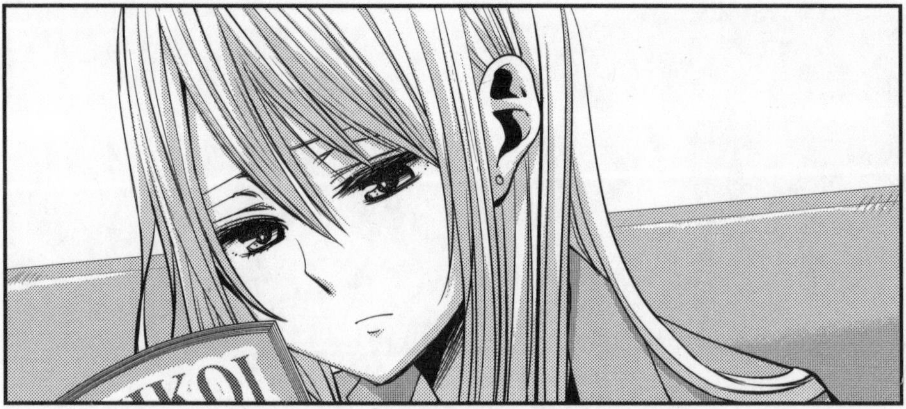

IT MADE ME FEEL AS IF I COULD CONFIDE MY OWN GENUINE FEELINGS TO YOU.

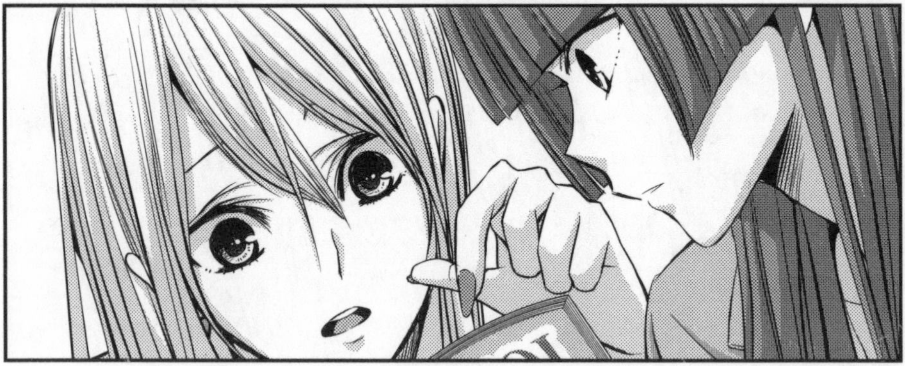

WHEN I THINK BACK ON THAT KISS...

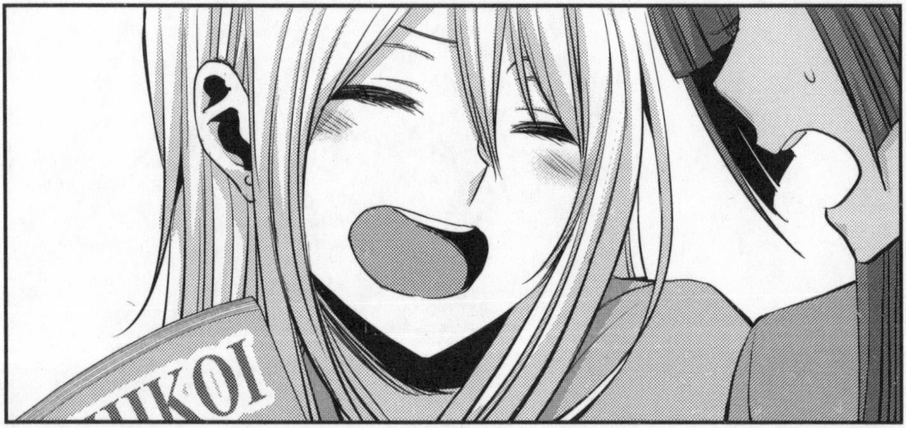

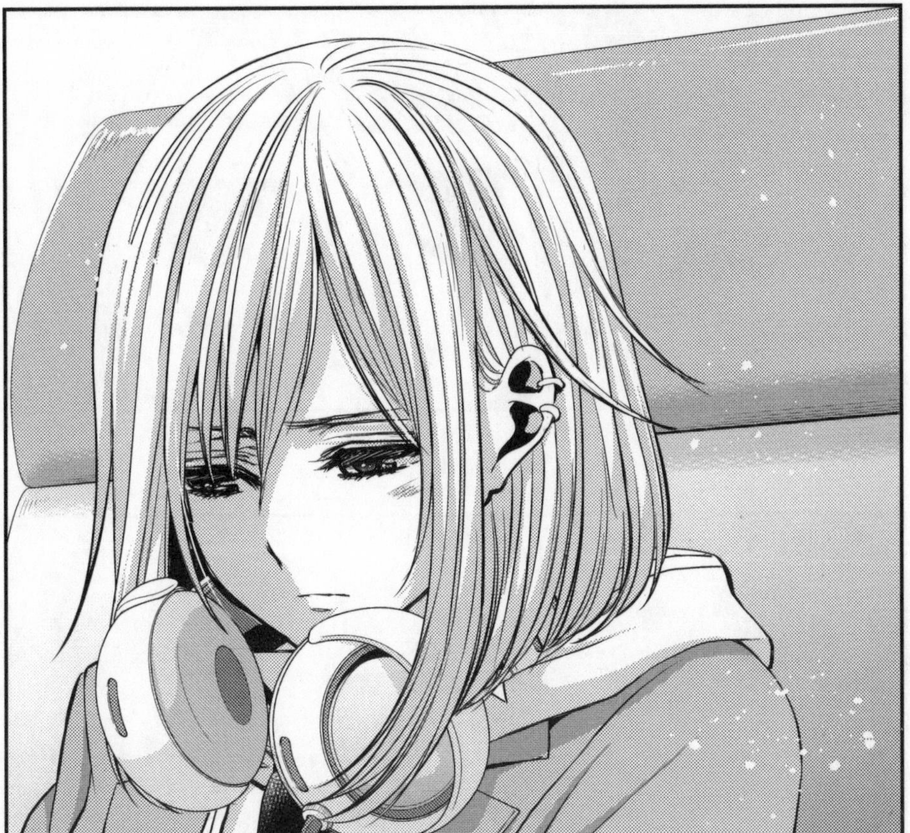

IT FILLS ME WITH GENUINE HAPPINESS.

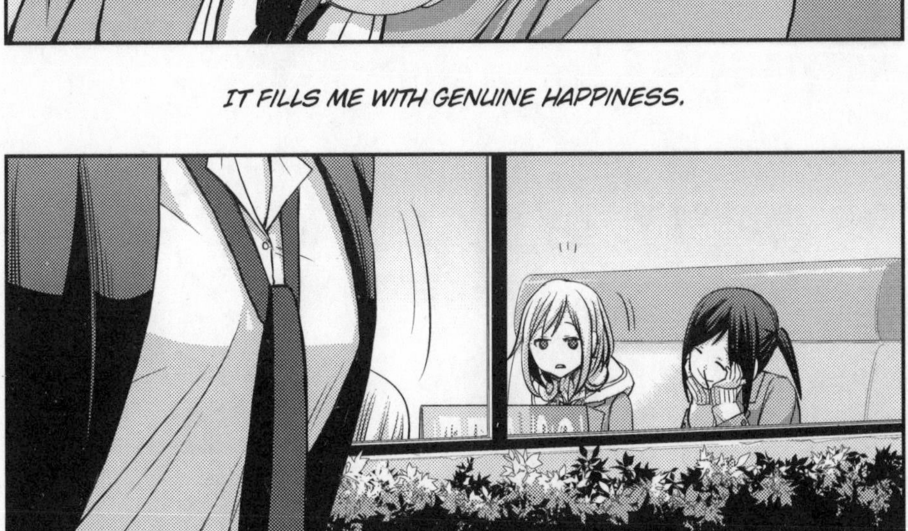

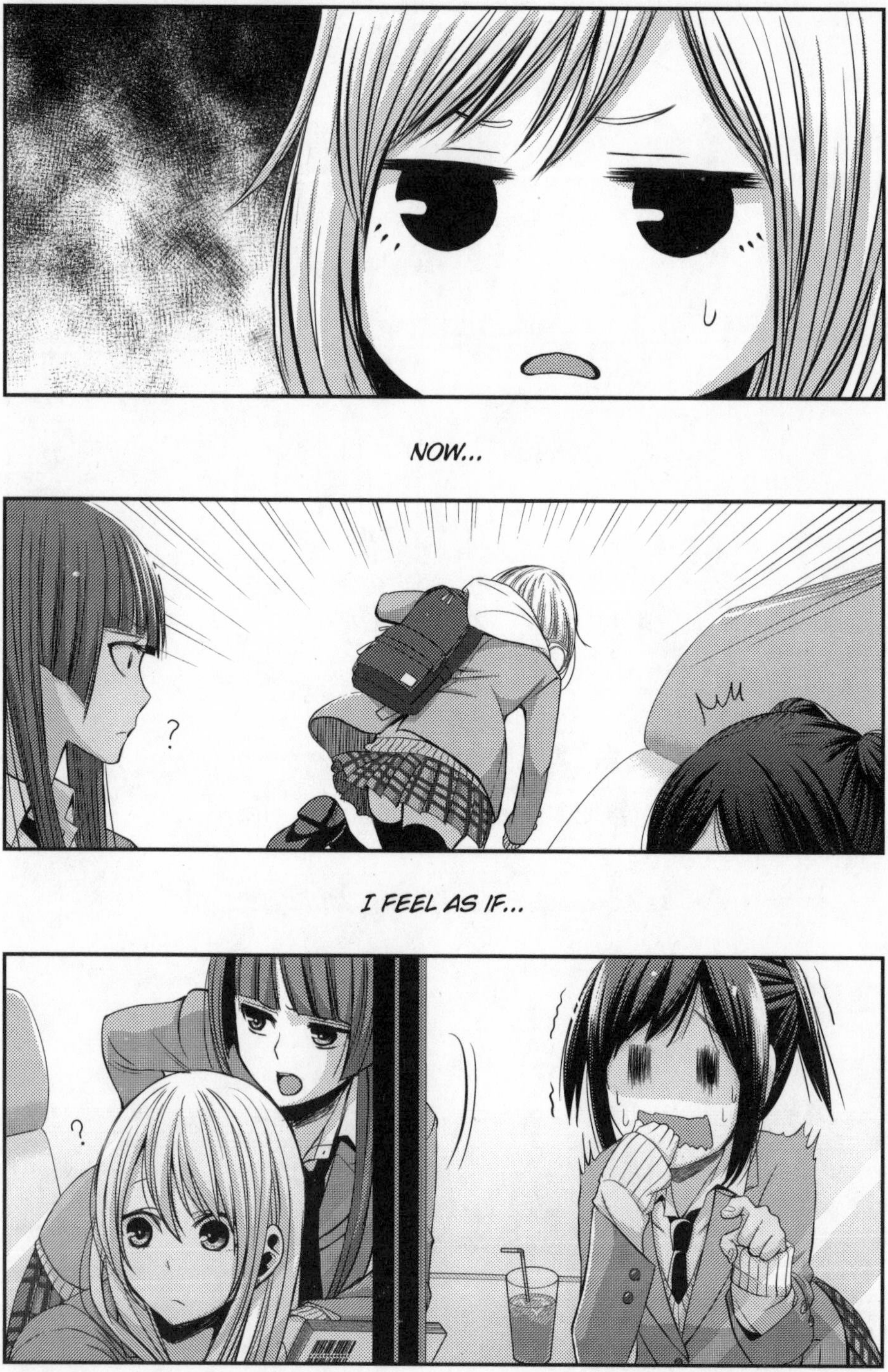
NOW...
I FEEL AS IF...

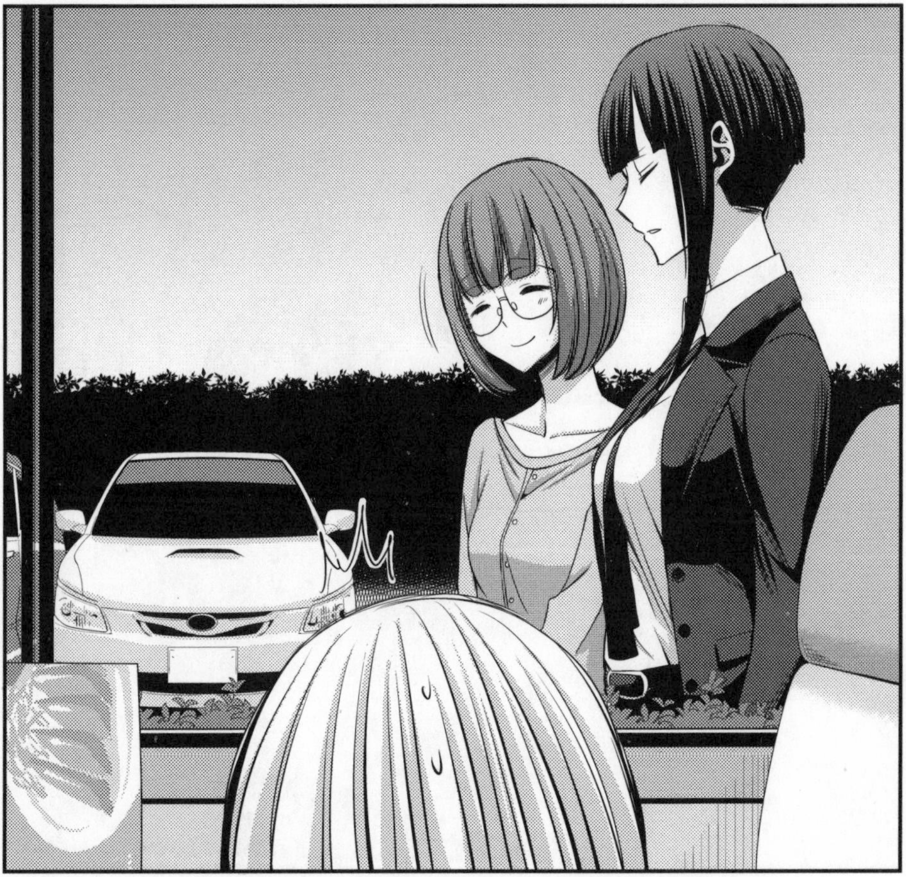

I WANT TO BE THE PERSON YOU BELIEVE ME TO BE,
FOR HOWEVER LONG WE HAVE LEFT TOGETHER.

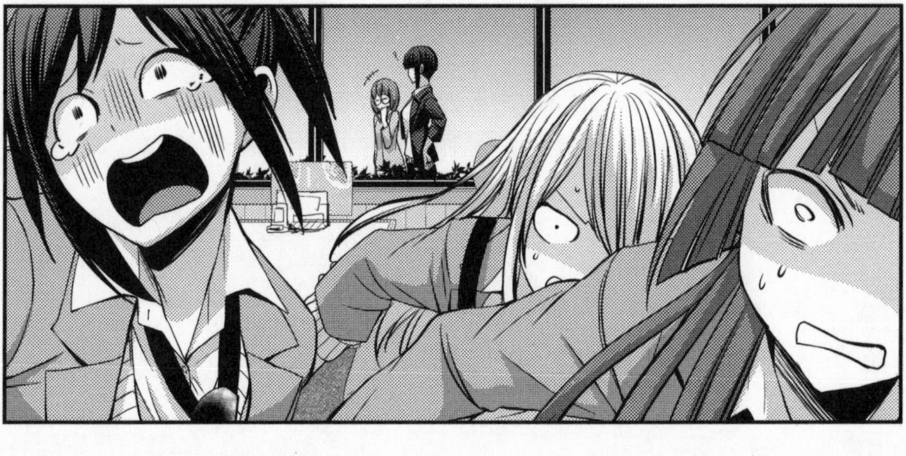

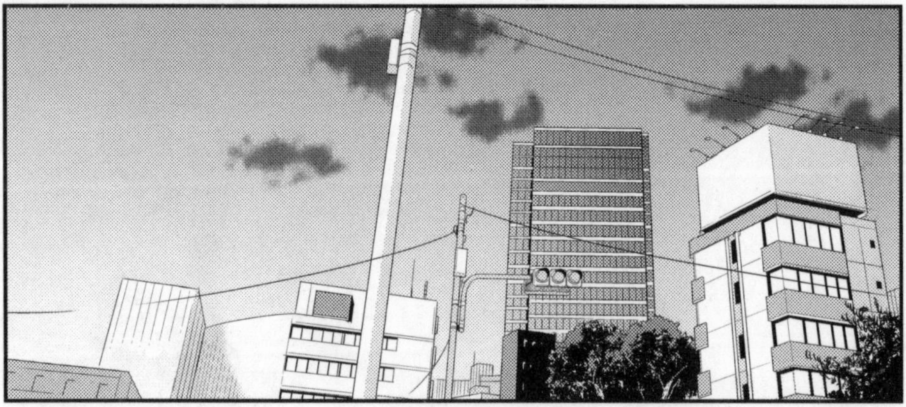

THROUGH THE CHALLENGES WE'VE FACED TOGETHER...

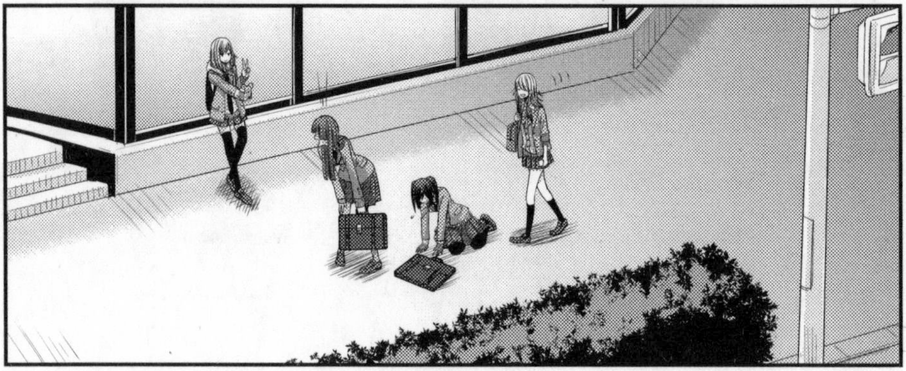

AS WELL AS THROUGH READING THIS NOTEBOOK...

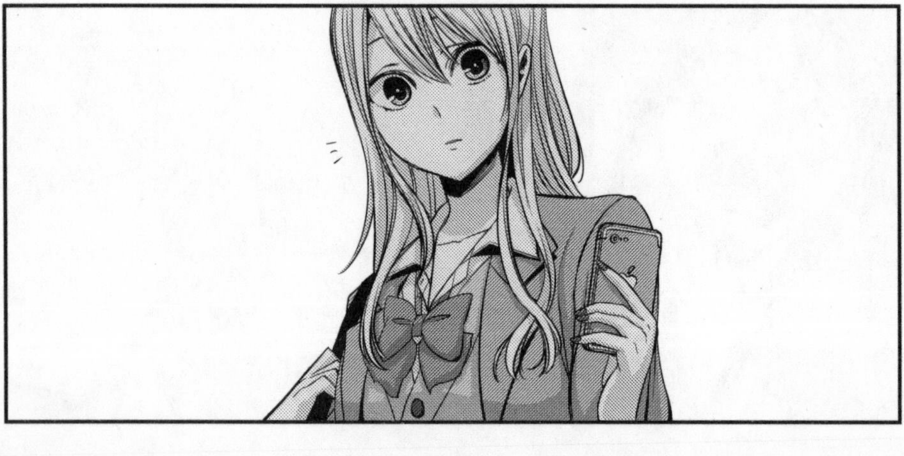

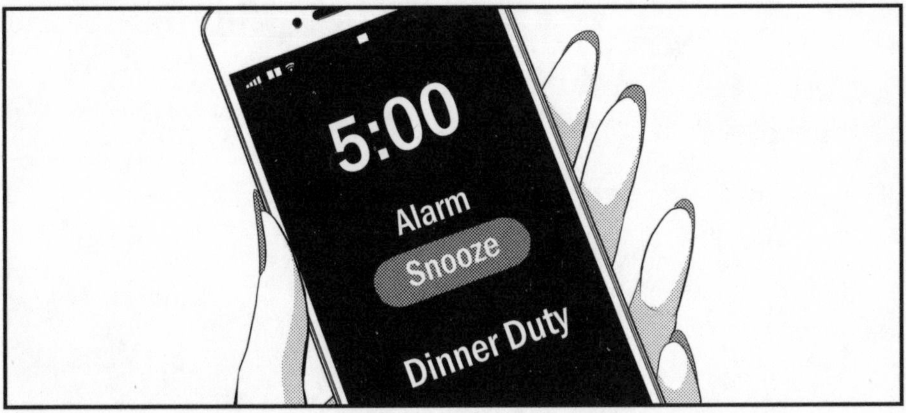
5:00
Alarm
Snooze
Dinner Duty

I'VE LEARNED ABOUT YOU AND YOUR DESIRES.

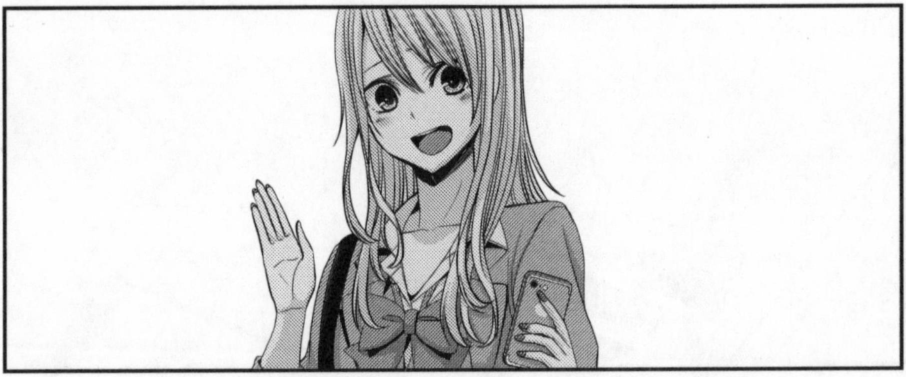

THE RING YOU GAVE ME WILL ALWAYS BE MY MOST PRECIOUS TREASURE, TO WHICH NO OTHER GIFT WILL EVER COMPARE.

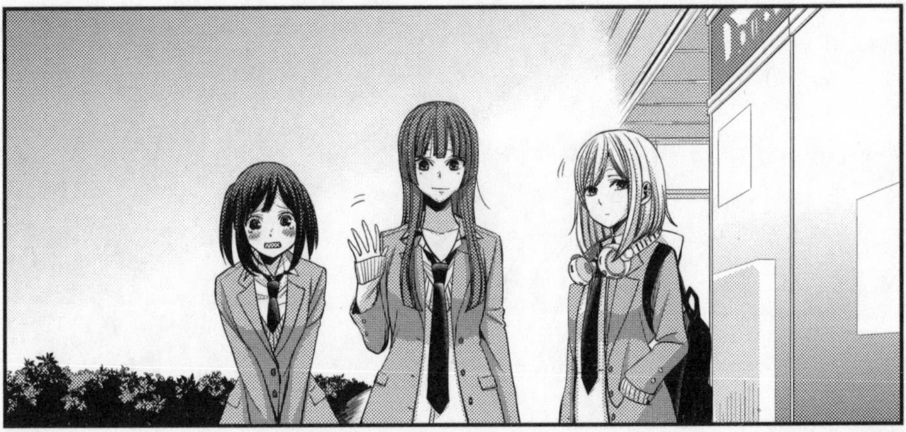

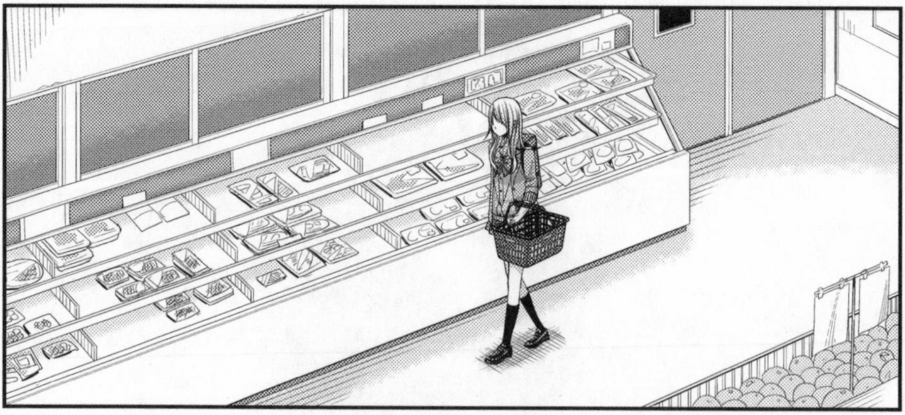

EVERY MINUTE, EVERY SECOND I SPENT WITH YOU WAS INVIGORATING AND FUN.

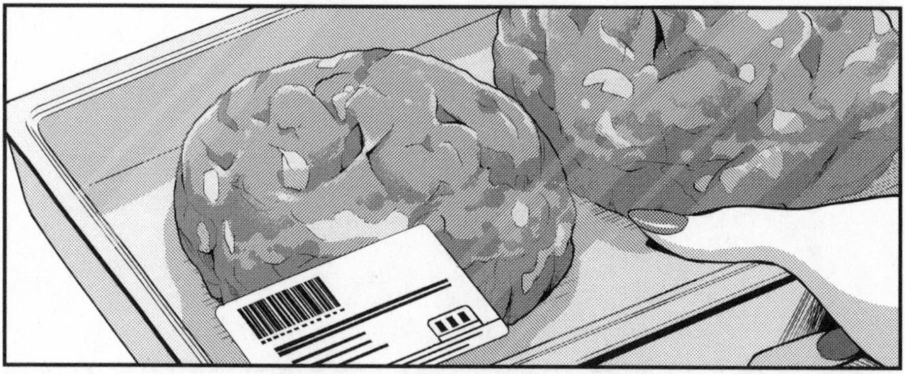

I BECAME SO ENAMORED WITH YOU, I COULDN'T STOP THINKING ABOUT YOU, YUZU.

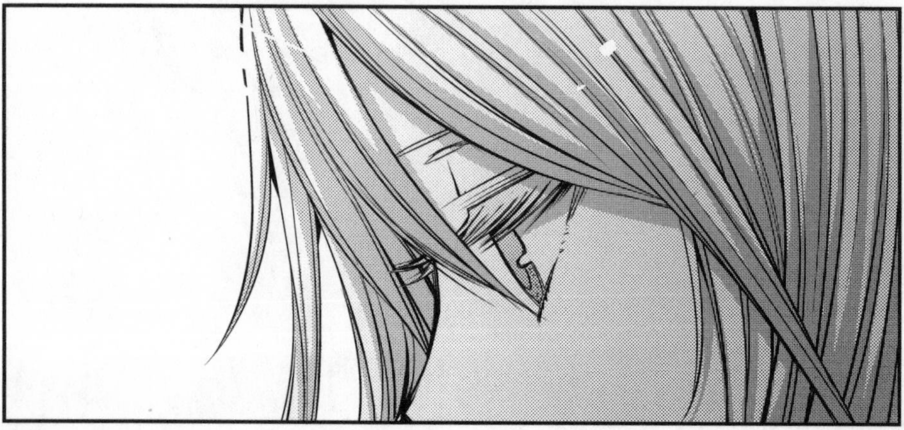

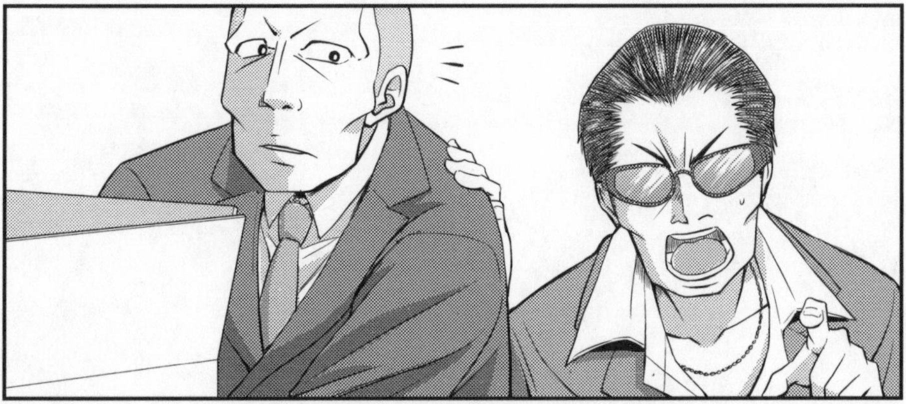

BUT AROUND THAT TIME, I ALSO BECAME AWARE OF A PAINFUL TUGGING AT MY HEART.

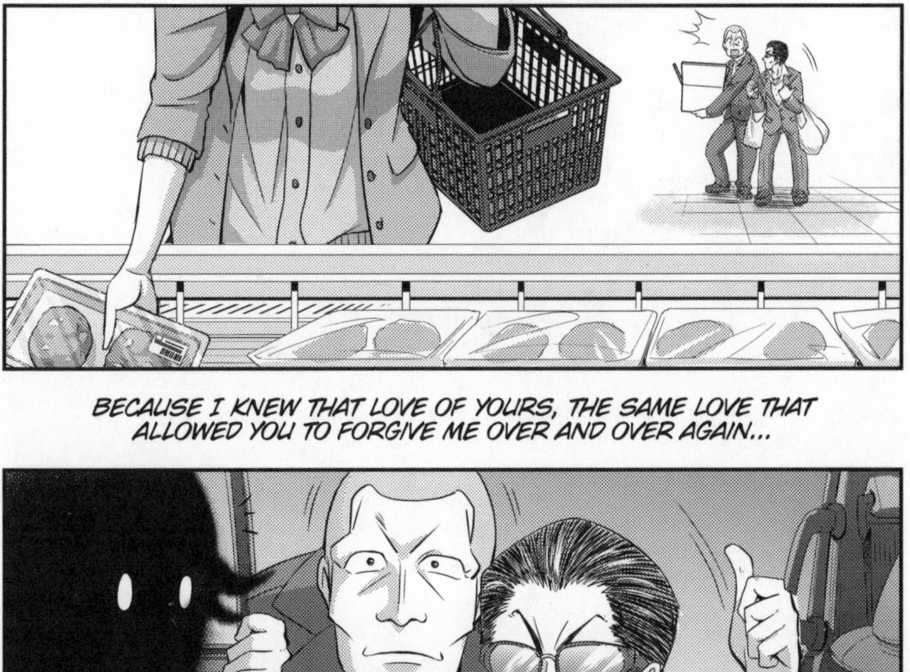

BECAUSE I KNEW THAT LOVE OF YOURS, THE SAME LOVE THAT ALLOWED YOU TO FORGIVE ME OVER AND OVER AGAIN...

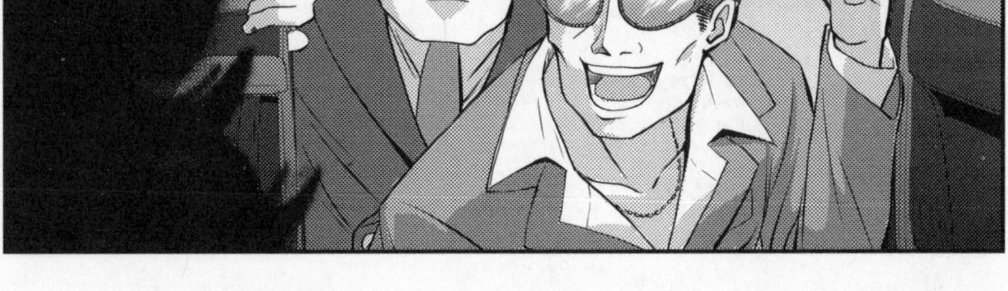

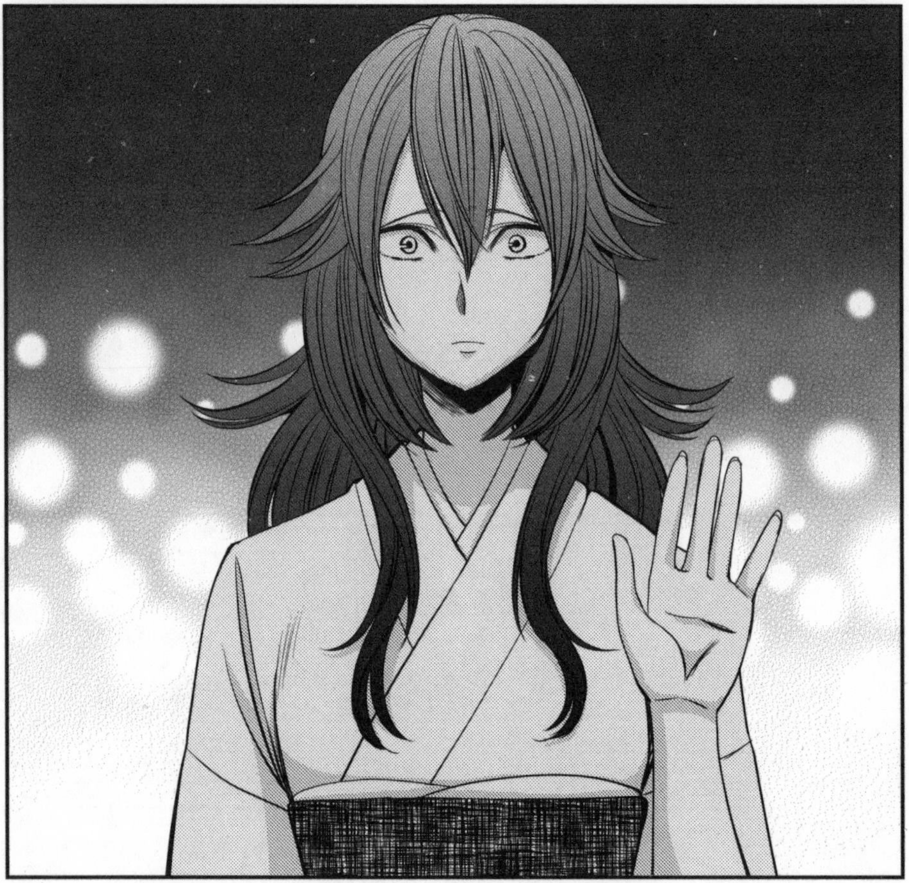

WOULD SOON BRING YOU THE WORST BETRAYAL YET.

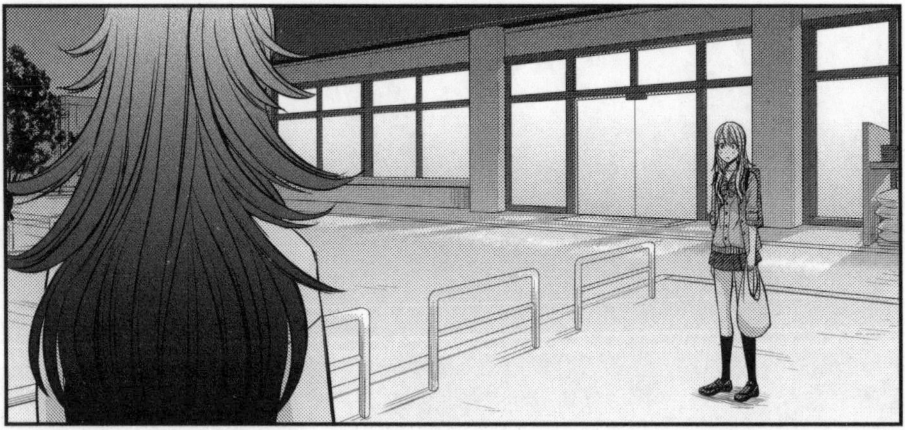

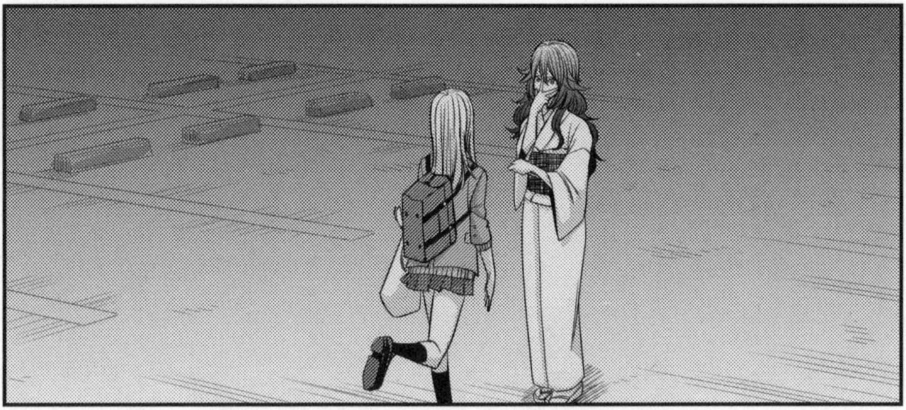

MY INCREASING AWARENESS OF HOW I'VE
REPAID YOUR LOVE WITH CRUELTY...

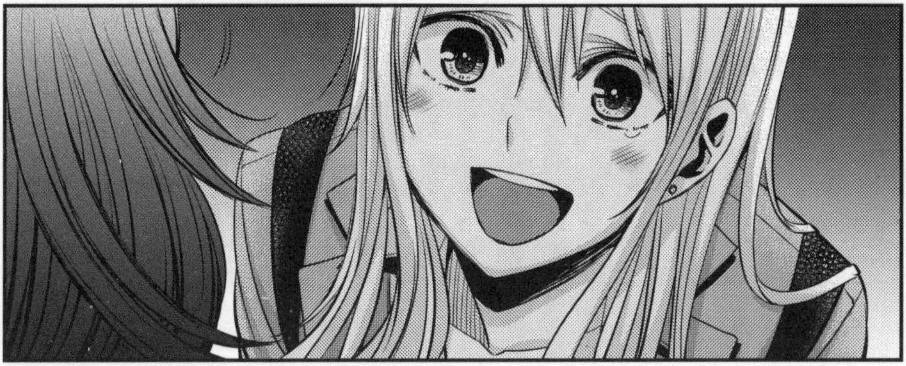

HAS BECOME ALMOST UNBEARABLE.

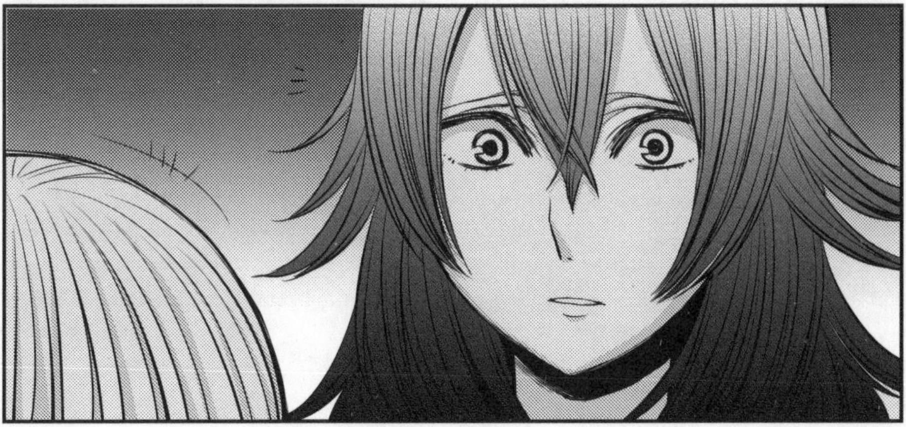

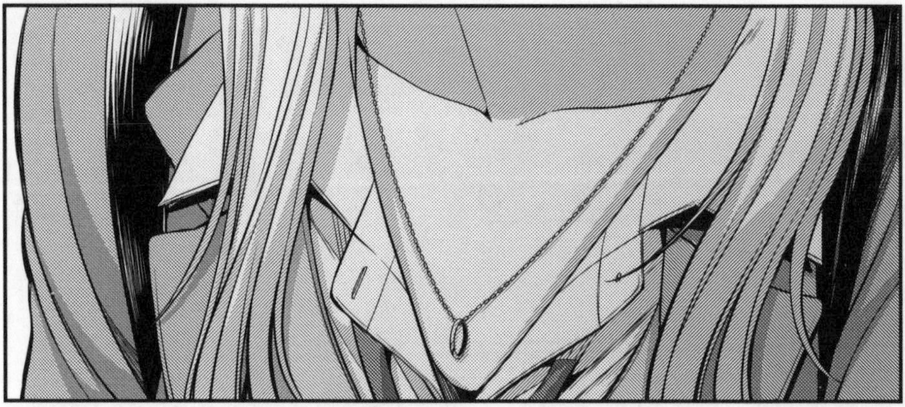

NOT LONG FROM NOW...

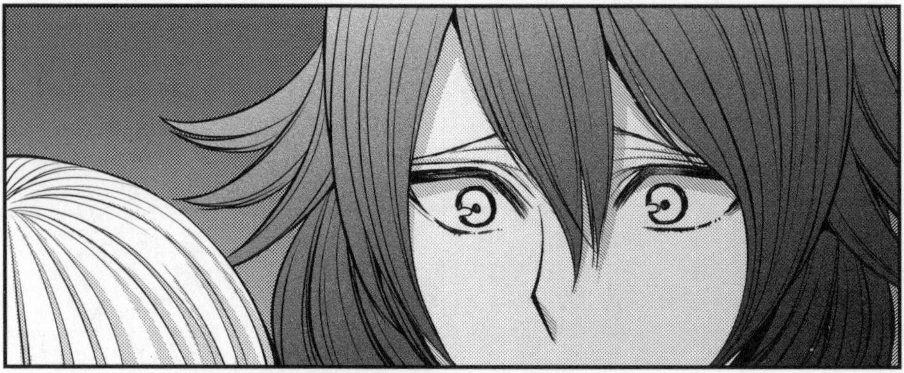

I WILL BE MARRYING MY FIANCÉ AND ASSUMING MY RESPONSIBILITIES AS A MEMBER OF THE AIHARA FAMILY.

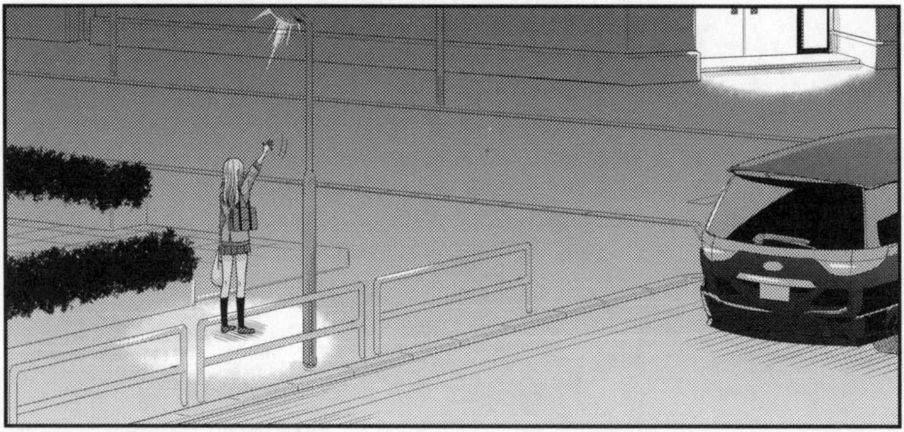

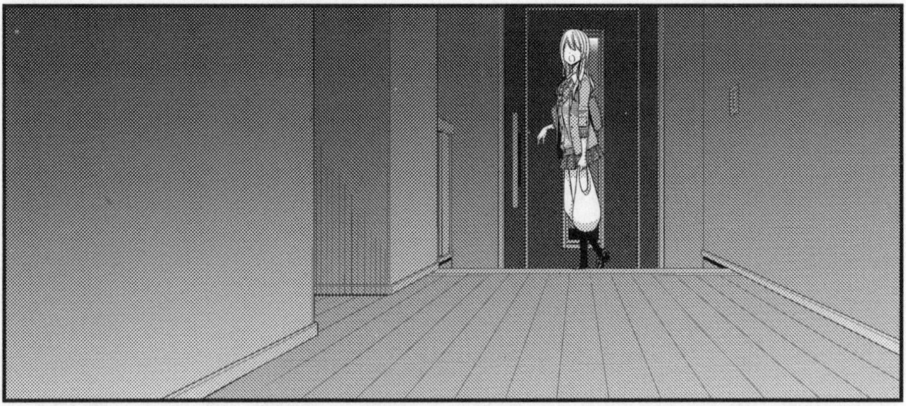

I'VE SPOKEN WITH MOTHER REGARDING THE WEDDING PREPARATIONS.

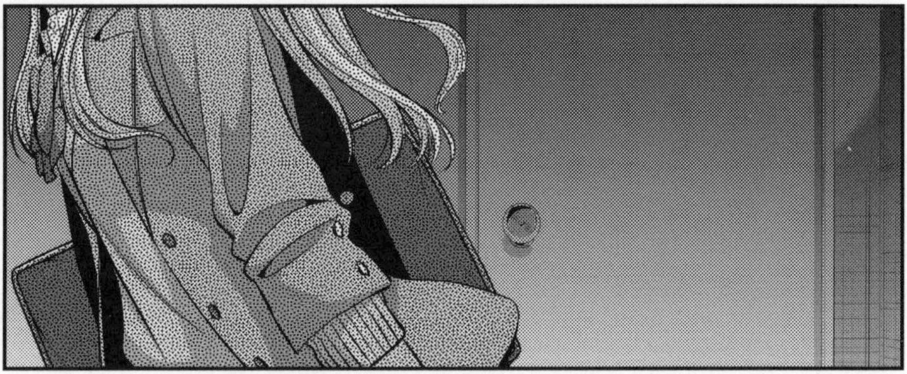

I HAVE ASKED HER NOT TO SAY ANYTHING TO YOU UNTIL AFTER YOU'VE READ THIS.

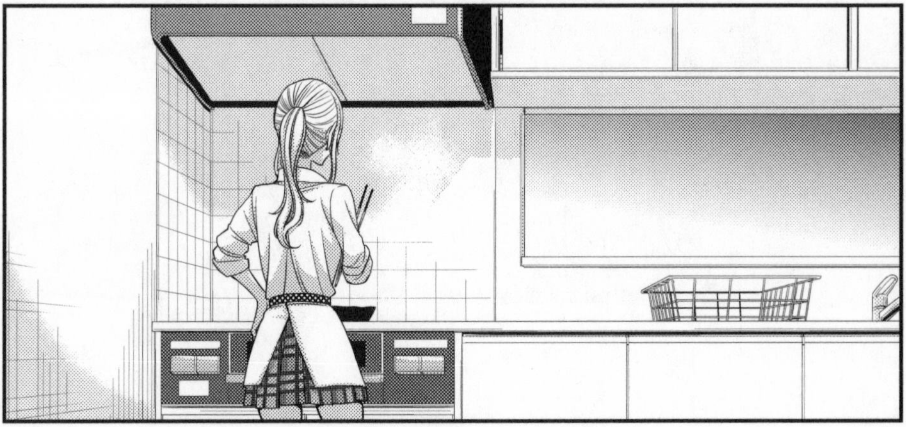

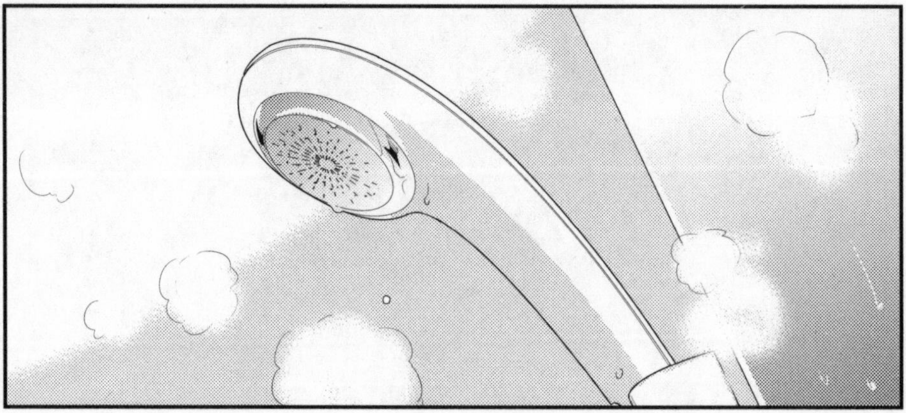

I ASKED HER TO DO THIS FOR YOUR SAKE.

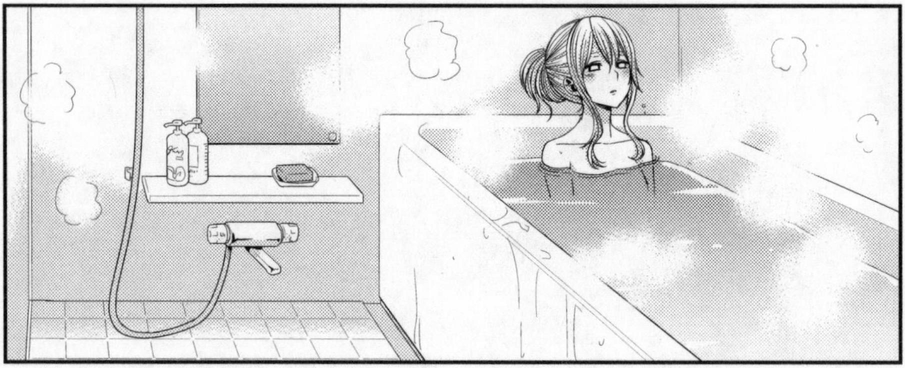

IN ORDER TO MOVE DOWN THE PATH I'VE CHOSEN...

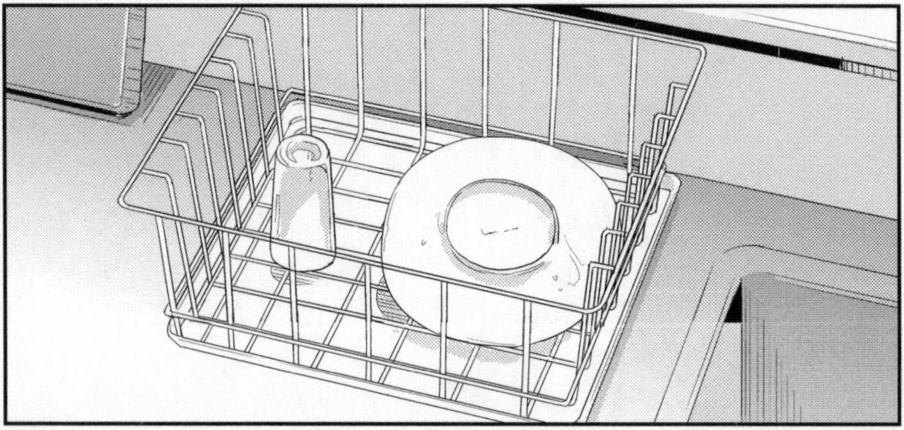

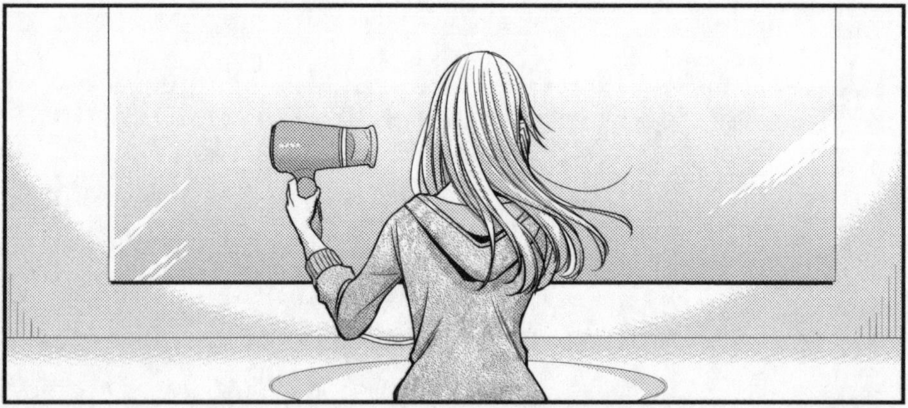

AT BOTH SCHOOL AND FAMILY EVENTS...

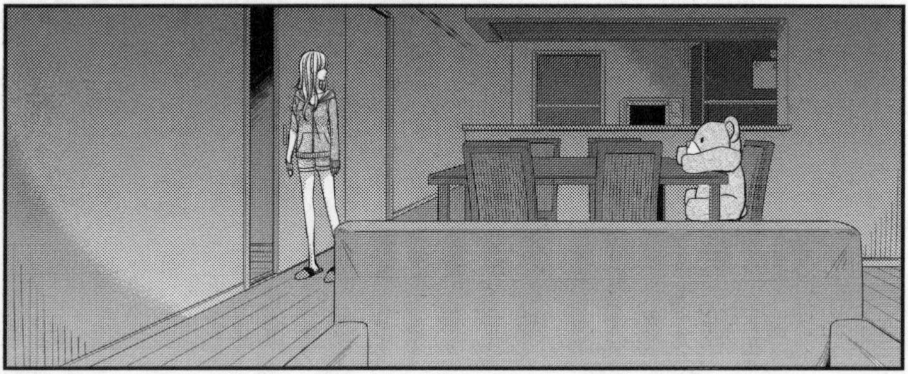

WE SHALL HAVE TO KEEP OUR CONTACT TO THE BARE MINIMUM.

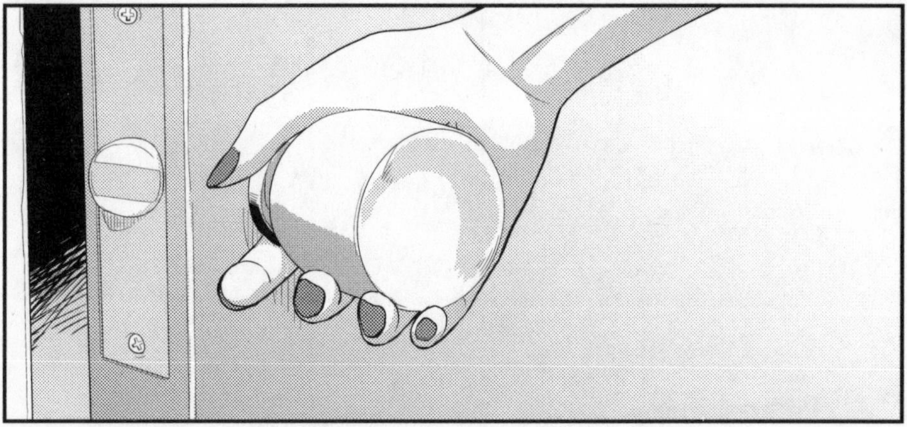

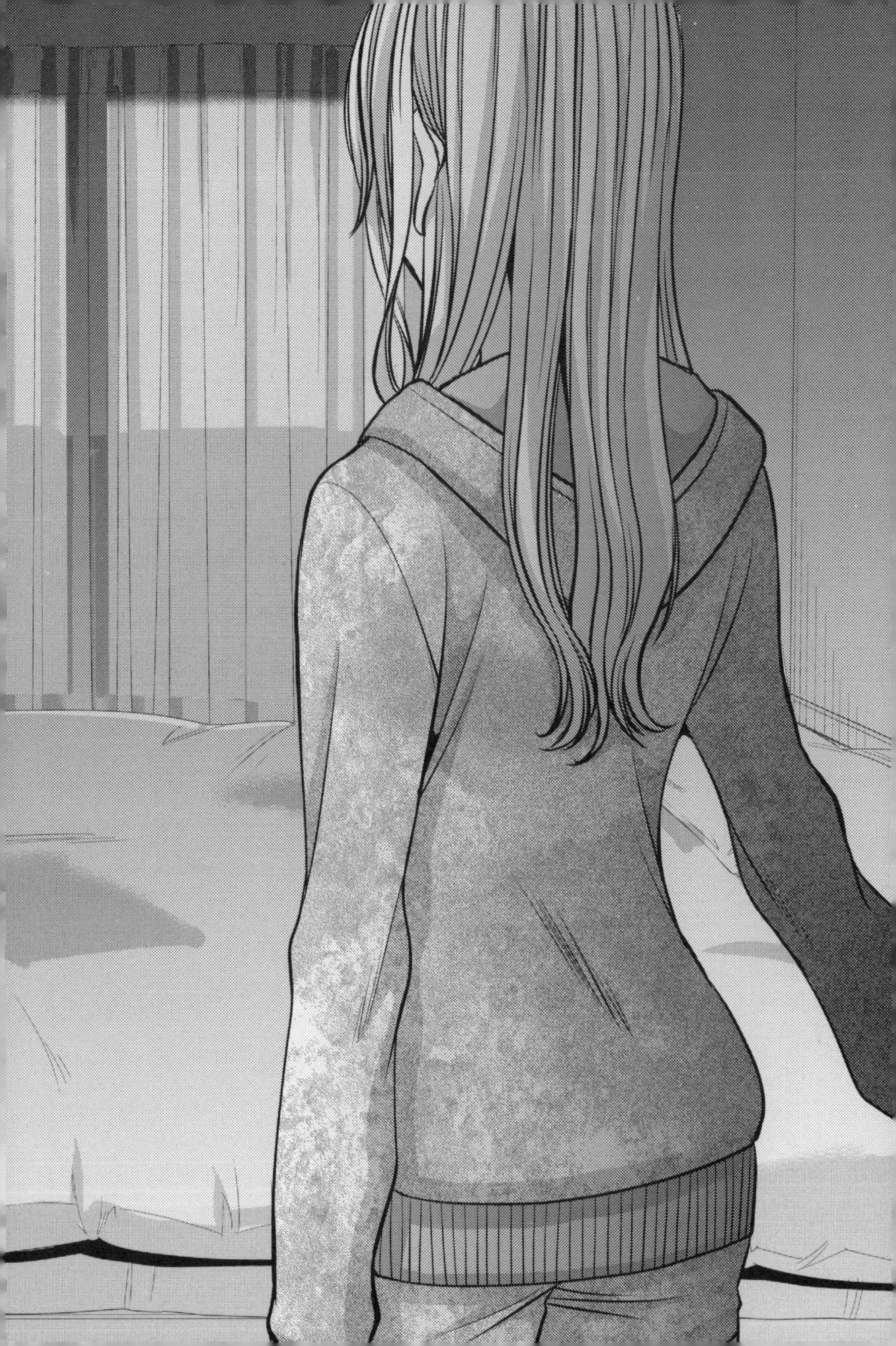

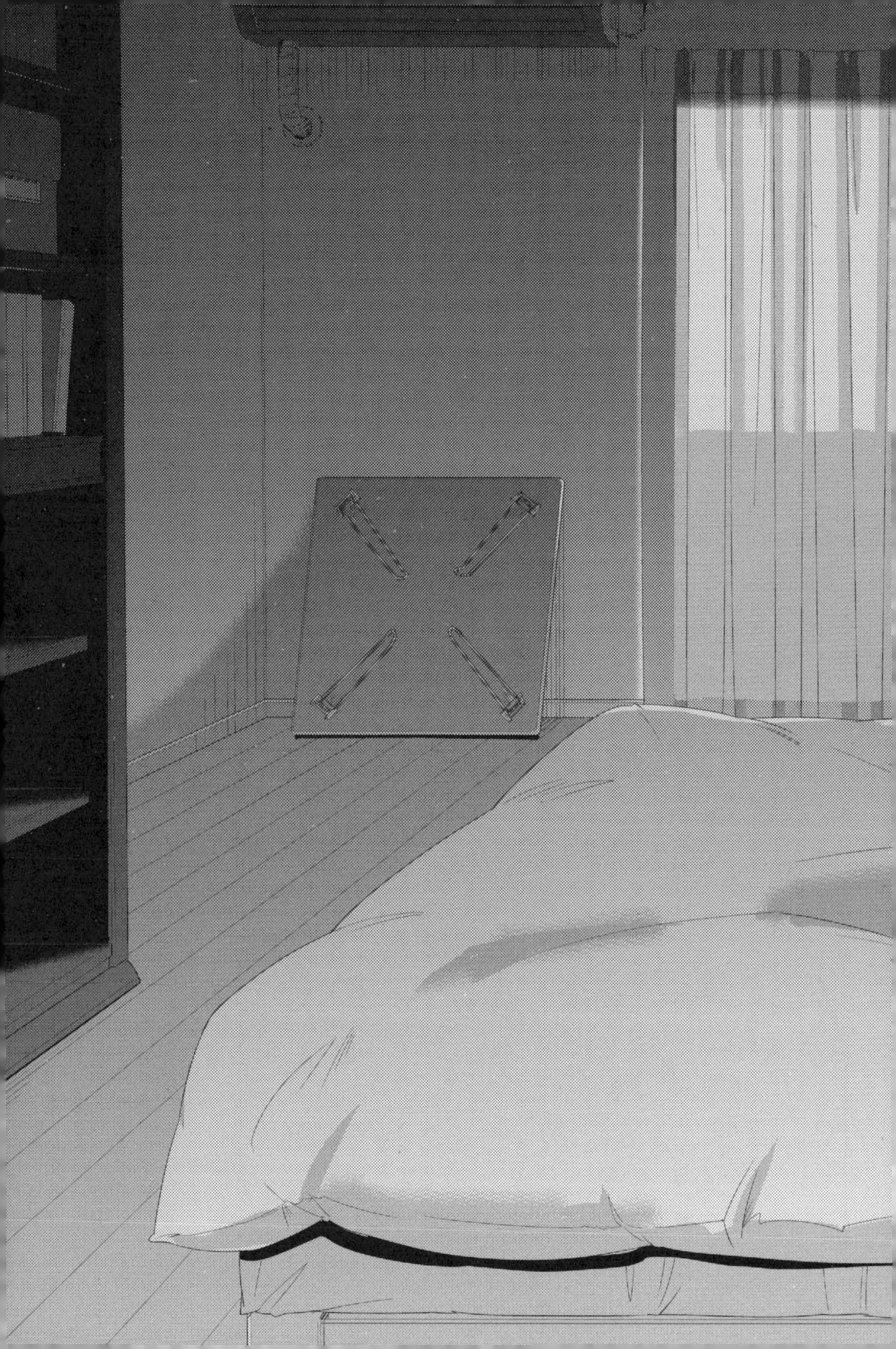

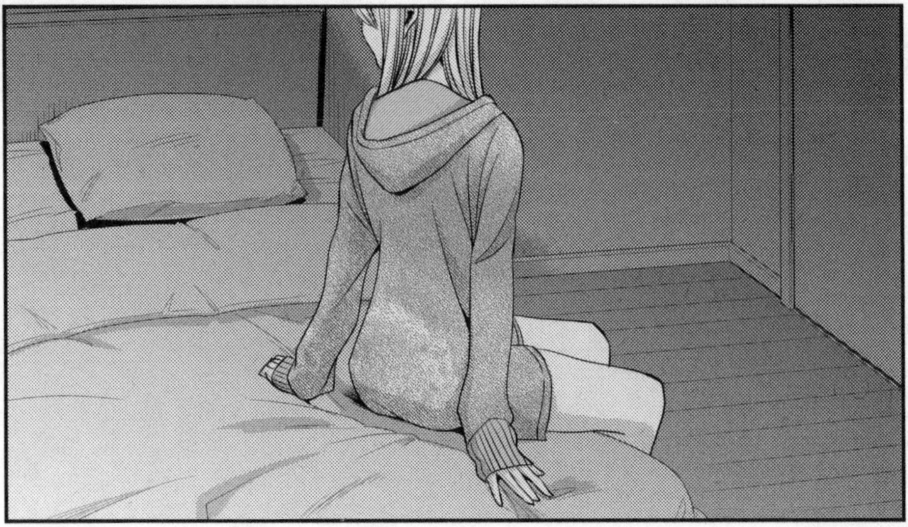

I CANNOT BEAR TO SEE YOU RIGHT NOW.
I'M AFRAID IT WILL CAUSE MY RESOLVE TO WAVER.

THAT'S WHY I'VE DECIDED TO WRITE DOWN ALL THE THINGS I WANTED TO TELL YOU IN THIS NOTEBOOK.

PLEASE FIND IT IN YOUR HEART TO FORGIVE YOUR WEAK AND SELFISH LITTLE SISTER.

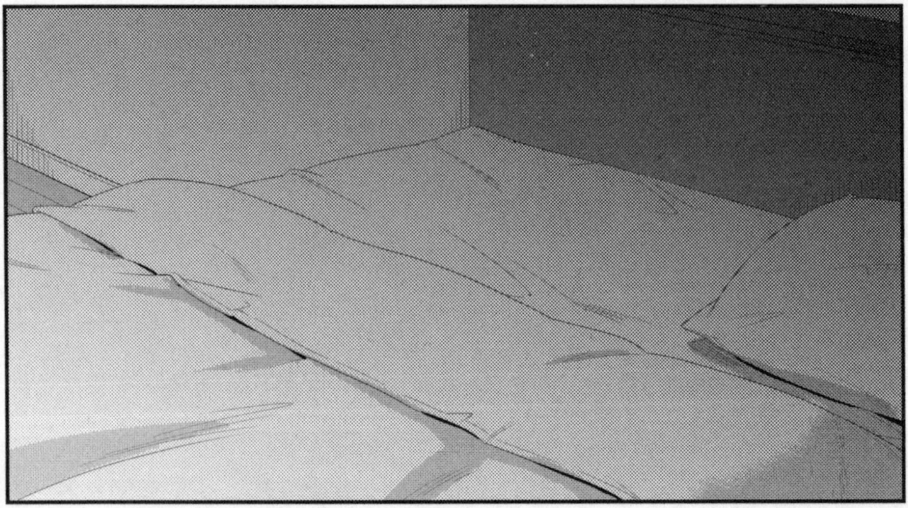

THIS MIGHT BE MY LAST CHANCE TO SAY THIS, BUT...

EVEN AS I TRY TO DISTANCE MYSELF, I WILL ALWAYS THINK BACK ON THE BOND WE HAVE SHARED AS SISTERS WITH FONDNESS.

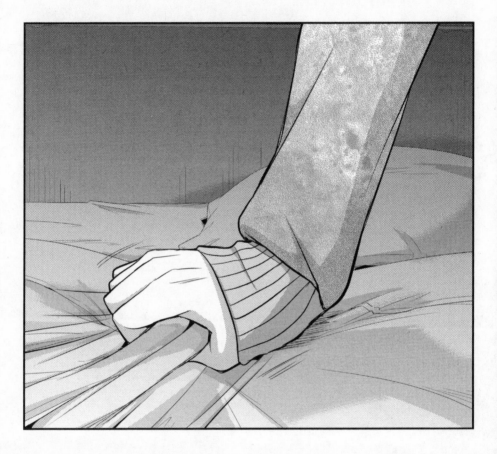

I PRAY YOU FIND HAPPINESS WITH THOSE WHO LOVE YOU.

THANK YOU, YUZU.

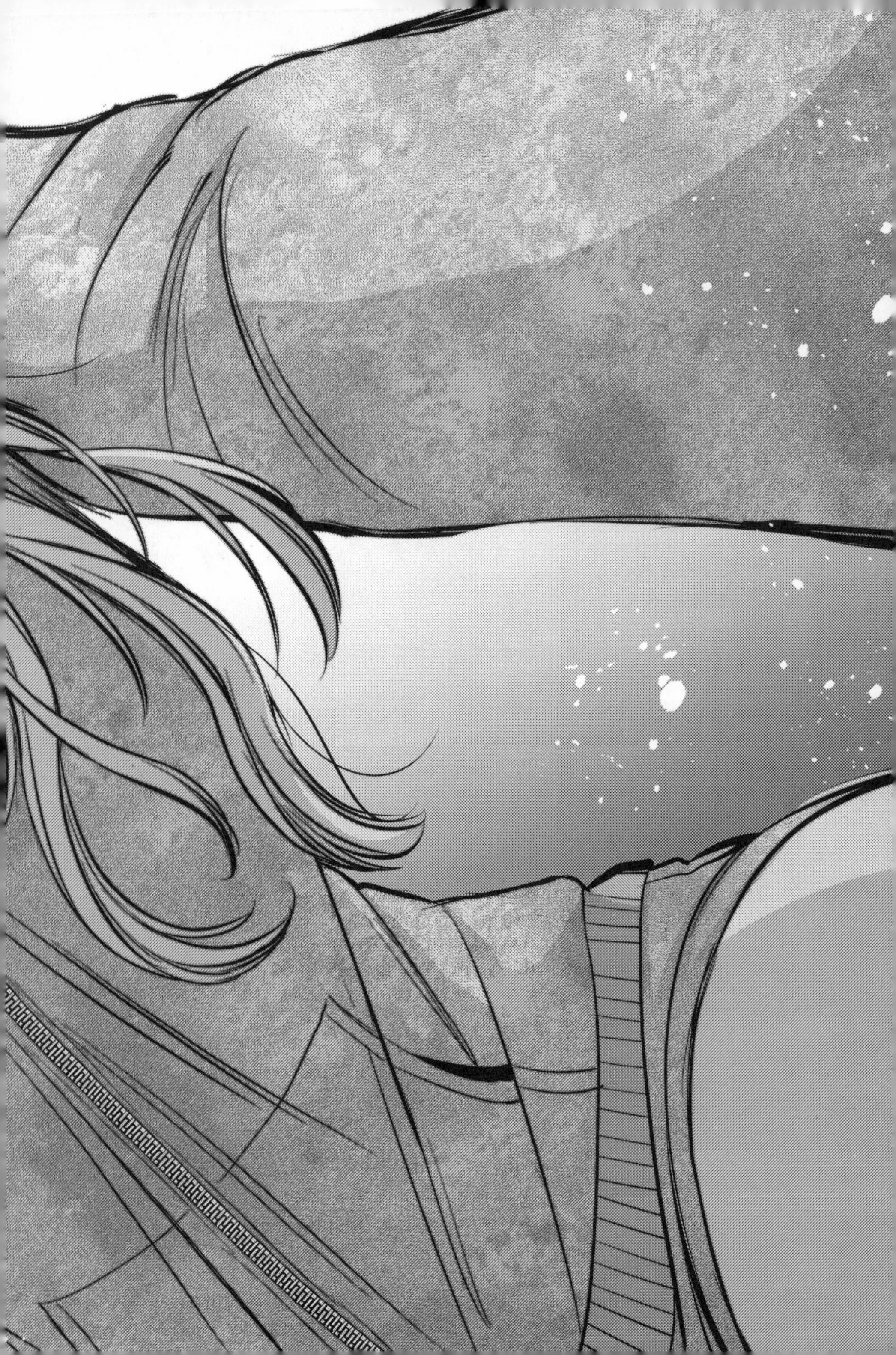

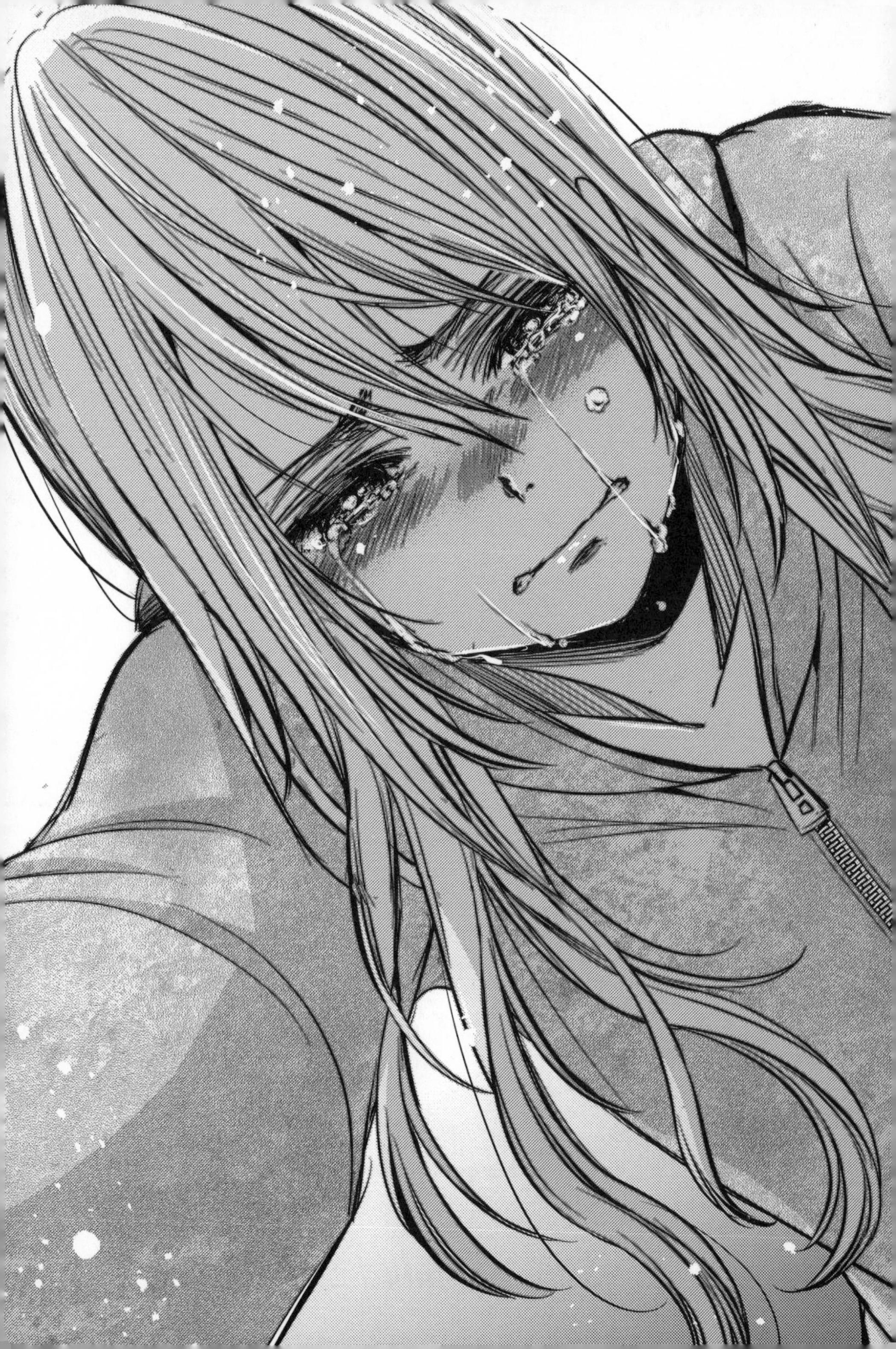

FAREWELL.

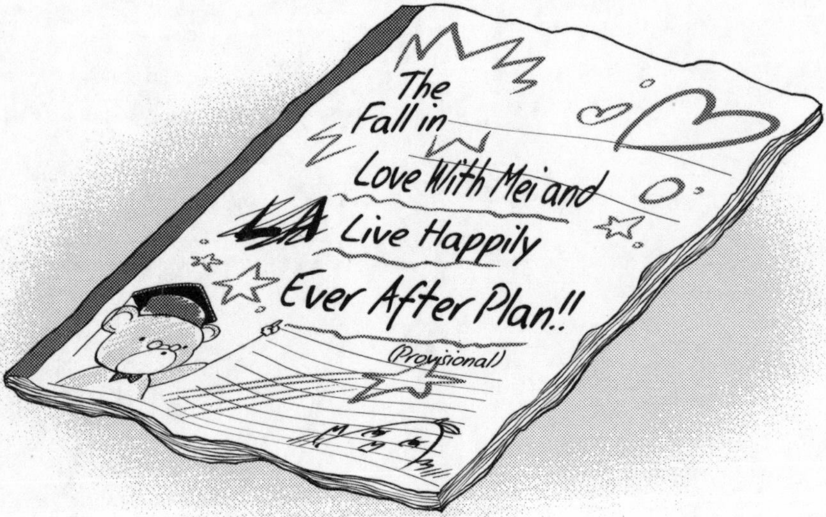
The Fall in Love With Mei and Live Happily Ever After Plan!!
(Provisional)

To be continued...

9

特装版

SABUROUTA
PRESENTS
SECRET LOVE AFFAIR
WITH SISTER

VOLUME NINE

citrus

citrus

SABUROUTA PRESENTS SECRET LOVE AFFAIR WITH SISTER

9

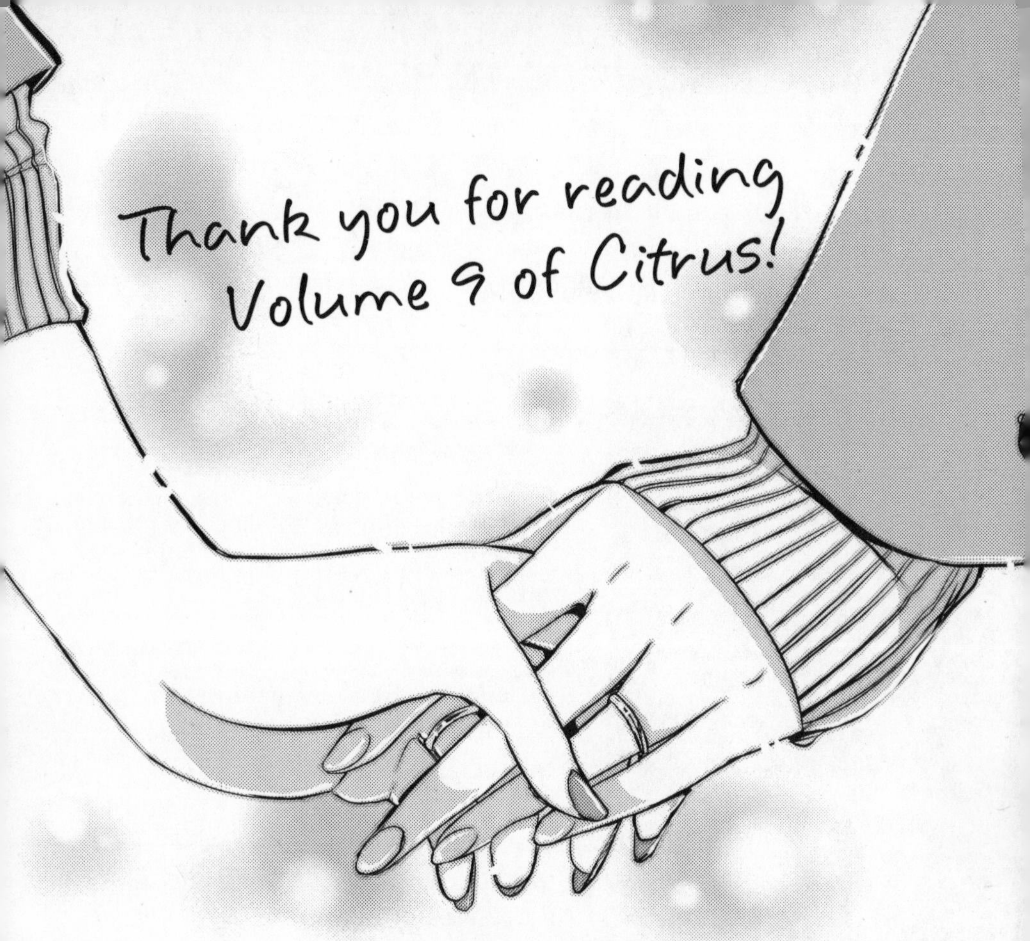
Thank you for reading Volume 9 of Citrus!

"MY FIRST REAL LOVE."♡
THOSE WERE THE WORDS ATTACHED TO CITRUS WHEN IT BEGAN SERIALIZATION.
I'VE SPENT THE PAST FIVE YEARS TRYING TO MAKE A SERIES THAT LIVED UP TO THOSE WORDS...
YUZU AND MEI'S LOVE HAS GROWN SO MUCH THANKS TO THE SUPPORT IT HAS RECEIVED FROM SO MANY PEOPLE.
THOSE TWO ARE SUCH A MESS, BUT I HOPE YOU'LL CONTINUE TO WATCH OVER THEM!

WELL THEN, I'LL SEE YOU IN THEIR HAPPY FUTURE!!

2018.3.23 SABUROUTA

SEVEN SEAS ENTERTAINMENT PRESENTS

citrus

story & art by **SABUROUTA** **VOLUME 9**

TRANSLATION
Amber Tamosaitis

ADAPTATION
Shannon Fay

LETTERING AND RETOUCH
Roland Amago
Bambi Eloriaga-Amago

COVER DESIGN
Nicky Lim

PROOFREADER
Shanti Whitesides
Stephanie Cohen

EDITOR
Jenn Grunigen

PRODUCTION ASSISTANT
CK Russell

PRODUCTION MANAGER
Lissa Pattillo

EDITOR-IN-CHIEF
Adam Arnold

PUBLISHER
Jason DeAngelis

CITRUS VOLUME 9

First published in Japan in 2018 by ICHIJINSHA Inc., Tokyo.
English translation rights arranged with ICHIJINSHA Inc., Tokyo, Japan.

ISBN: 978-1-642750-11-9

Printed in Canada

First Printing: March 2019

10 9 8 7 6 5 4 3 2 1

FOLLOW US ONLINE: ***www.sevenseasentertainment.com***

READING DIRECTIONS

This book reads from ***right to left***, Japanese style. If this is your first time reading manga, you start reading from the top right panel on each page and take it from there. If you get lost, just follow the numbered diagram here. It may seem backwards at first, but you'll get the hang of it! Have fun!!

1
2
3
4
5
6
7
8
9

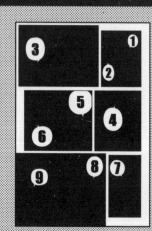